War Songs

Letter from the General Editor

The Library of Arabic Literature makes available Arabic editions and English translations of significant works of Arabic literature, with an emphasis on the seventh to nineteenth centuries. The Library of Arabic Literature thus includes texts from the pre-Islamic era to the cusp of the modern period, and encompasses a wide range of genres, including poetry, poetics, fiction, religion, philosophy, law, science, travel writing, history, and historiography.

Books in the series are edited and translated by internationally recognized scholars. They are published as hardcovers in parallel-text format with Arabic and English on facing pages, as English-only paperbacks, and as downloadable Arabic editions. For some texts, the series also publishes separate scholarly editions with full critical apparatus.

The Library encourages scholars to produce authoritative Arabic editions, accompanied by modern, lucid English translations, with the ultimate goal of introducing Arabic's rich literary heritage to a general audience of readers as well as to scholars and students.

The Library of Arabic Literature is supported by a grant from the New York University Abu Dhabi Institute and is published by NYU Press.

Philip F. Kennedy
General Editor, Library of Arabic Literature

شعر

عنترة بن شدّاد

LIBRARY OF
المكتبة
ARABIC
العربية
LITERATURE

War Songs

'Antarah ibn Shaddād

Edited by
James E. Montgomery

Translated by
James E. Montgomery
with
Richard Sieburth

Foreword by
Peter Cole

Volume editor
Tahera Qutbuddin

NEW YORK UNIVERSITY PRESS
New York

NEW YORK UNIVERSITY PRESS
New York

Library of Congress Cataloging-in-Publication Data

Names: Antarah ibn Shaddad, active 6th century author. | Montgomery, James E. (James Edward), 1962- translator. | Sieburth, Richard, translator. | Qutbuddin, Tahera, editor. | Cole, Peter, 1957- author of foreword.
Title: War songs / Antarah ibn Shaddad ; translated by James E. Montgomery with Richard Sieburth ; foreword by Peter Cole ; volume editor, Tahera Qutbuddin.
Description: New York : New York University Press, 2018. | Includes bibliographical references and index.
Identifiers: LCCN 2018011651 (print) | LCCN 2018013927 (ebook) | ISBN 9781479806553 (e-book) | ISBN 9781479829651 (e-book) | ISBN 9781479858798 (pbk. : alk. paper) | ISBN 9781479880904 (hardcover : alk. paper)
Classification: LCC PJ7696.A53 (ebook) | LCC PJ7696.A53 A2 2018 (print) | DDC 892.7/11--dc23
LC record available at https://lccn.loc.gov/2018011651

New York University Press books are printed on acid-free paper, and their binding materials are chosen for strength and durability.

Series design by Titus Nemeth.

Typeset in Tasmeem, using DecoType Naskh and Emiri.

Typesetting and digitization by Stuart Brown.

Manufactured in the United States of America
c10 9 8 7 6 5 4 3 2 1

Table of Contents

In memoriam Peter Heath (1949–2014)

What is the difference between free and strict, literal translation? between free translation and outright adaptation?

Very often, readability. Strict translation usually makes for stiff English, or forced and un-english rhythms. Outright adaptation is perfectly valid if it makes a good, modern poem. Occasionally, an adaptation will translate the spirit of the original to better use than any other method: at other times, it will falsify the original beyond measure. Much depends upon the translator (also upon the reader).

Paul Blackburn, "Translation (Replies to a *New York Quarterly* Questionnaire)" (1970)

Foreword

On ʿAntarah's *War Songs*

Translation begins in a listening. Its art starts in the ear that takes us in, with all the craftiness that entails. When it's working, translation transports and en*trance*s. It tricks us into suspending disbelief and moves our imagination from where it had been to another place (often distant) and another time (which is somehow now). That mysterious shift through hearing leads to cadence and timbre and balance, to a surface tension that images ride, to currents of feeling swirling beneath them.

Improbably, much of translation takes place in the reception of the original creation, before a single syllable is mouthed or jotted down in the translator's language. The quality of this initial absorption is, in fact, so vital to the transfer of energy translation involves that it's tempting to say it matters even more than what happens next, on the expressive side of the ledger—since without it, *nothing* of worth will happen there. So that when James Montgomery declares, in the name of ʿAntarah ibn Shaddād—

> Fools may mock my blackness
>   but without night there's no day!
> Black as night, so be it!
>   But what a night
> generous and bright!
>   All the paltry ʿAmrs and Zayds
> my name has eclipsed.
>   I am the Lord of War!

he isn't rehearsing hand-me-down gestures, or giving us static English equivalents for words attributed to a valiant poet of pre-Islamic lore; he is writing out of an embodied reading of the Arabic text and tradition, through his deepest instinctive and critical response to it. He is doing all he prosodically can to bear and lay bare a charged aesthetic matrix that mattered centrally to medieval listeners, and might mean something potent for readers in English today. In short, he is, with Richard Sieburth's assistance, performing an early Arabian drama and presenting it to us as a present—a gift of time. Historical time and the time that is rhythm. Existential time and the pulse of a person. Of two people. An entire people. Of peoples.

"All language is vehicular," says Emerson, and none more so than strong translation, which can move across centuries and seas, and then through the difficult inner terrain of every reader, including the translator. What James Montgomery understands, what he conveys within that understanding and hears in his hosting of 'Antarah's verse, is the resonant, layered nature of the "war" that the poet proclaims himself "Lord of," which is to say, the poetry within the violence. And he sees, as plainly, that 'Antarah's fight isn't simply for the honor of the tribe, or for specific values his community prizes: fortitude and bravery; or belonging and fighting to belong, and guarding the weak as part of belonging. Montgomery knows, and his Glaswegian English helps him know, that these lines refer as well to the struggle of a social and literary outsider who both does and doesn't want in—a black man who's proud of his difference, and angry at the difference it makes. He realizes, too, that the fight lives on only in the agon of a poet battling for his poem. And that all these wars are to the death.

Our squadrons stand
  arrayed for battle
banners flapping
  like vultures' shadows.

Motion in stillness, quiet through noise, the chiaroscuro of premonition. Each is deftly deployed, syllable by syllable, in this quatrain and its haunting chiasms. And that—the spirit, and the darkening sap of 'Antarah's combat—is what courses through the turns of these renderings, which channel the translator's own "mental fight" for the poem.

*

"Did poetry die in its war with the poets?"

Montgomery's opening of ʿAntarah's "Golden Ode," one of the best-known poems in the history of Arabic, jolts this volume into high gear. It's a radical reading, pulled off with panache. Instead of the (also powerful if more wistful) musing that inflects the usual construal of the verse—"Have the poets left any place unpatched?"—Montgomery's ʿAntarah bolts out of the gate with a signature defiance, stakes raised high, for himself and for poets to come. For translation too. And that because this isn't "only art" for ʿAntarah, it's life. It's love and loyalty, an idea of the good and magnanimity, a sense of self-worth and *others'* honor, compounded by a vivid if obsessive inwardness,

> evenings when water flows unchecked
> and the lone hopper, look,
> screeches its drunken song
> scraping out a tune
> leg on leg like a one-arm man
> bent over a fire stick.

Will the translator, as poet and scholar, survive the journey into the desert and emerge with the prize of a poetry that gives us "ʿAntarah," an ʿAntarah that's his, and ours, and ancient at once?

> The years passed
> and the East Wind blew.
> Even the ruins
> fell into ruin—
> tired playthings
> of Time
> and the thunder
> and rain.
> Clan Hind lived here once.
> You can't visit them now—
> Fate has spun
> their thread.

When Montgomery sings with such elegiac litheness, translating with fine-tuned attention to pitch and footfall, to the distribution of weight along a line, to the deployment of texture and effects of sound, we have our answer, as his poem, ʿAntarah's poem, reaches us on a visceral level with unmistakable force through its suppleness. Or maybe we're lifted and taken back to it. Or both: ancient poet and modern reader meet through the magical agency of the translation, in a space between that exists as fiction, or myth.

More miraculous still in this mix is that the translation can follow the currents of the sixth-century verse through further modulations, in the same poem, from tenderness into ferocity, from a gentle resignation to fierce plasticity:

> I am Death.
>   I've felled many
>   a foe, their chests
> dyed in rivers of red jiryāl,
>   their bodies unburied
>   on the open plain,
> their limbs torn
>   to shreds
>   by dusky wolves,
>   aortas pierced
> by the pliant spear
>   gripped tight
>   as I closed in.

Then back again:

> I've served wine
>   to high-born and brave
>   at dawn,
> bewitched
>   pert-breasted girls
>   with a flicker of shyness
> in their eyes,
>   white as the marble
>   effigies of goddesses.

War Songs is full of such terror and grace. As Montgomery notes in his panoramic introduction, the warriors of this pre-Islamic desert world "cherished their vehicles of war . . . their weaponry and armaments" ("we skewered their loins / with Rudaynah spears / that screamed as if / squeezed in a vise"), and he grasps that just as horse and camel, sword and spear complete the warrior, making him what he is, freeing him to do what he's meant to do—in a word, ornamenting him in the etymological sense (*ornamentum* > L. to equip)—so too the poets of this warrior culture took up the tropes of the poem, the equipment and weapons of sensibility, to intensify our sense of experience, to let us dwell *on* it and *in* it, to make it memorable and pass it on.

Among the many marvels of Montgomery's inspired assembly of ʿAntarah's songs—easily the finest and boldest translation we have of a single pre-Islamic poet in English—the sheer nerve of it bounds off the page. The verve. Montgomery doesn't shy away from convention's challenge: to focus consciousness around a moment and bring it suddenly to larger life. He doesn't apologize, doesn't expurgate. He translates form and ornament through function. Understanding their purpose in the Arabic poem, he finds ways to get like work done in English, breaking down the Arabic line, for instance, into a variably staggered measure, one that allows him to magnify images within their off-kilter metrical frames, to bring out the directional tugs of rhetoric, the animating sonorities and their odd valences, in a way that the Arabic quantity does. All of which yields the rush and thrusts of the verse, the sharp swerves of perspective and tone. Call it modern, or the Arabic's musical spell, kinesthesis or analepsis. It doesn't matter. Picking his spots, Montgomery heads into the fray—sacrificing wisely, but preserving the heart of the poetry's concretion, and making even place and proper names earn their keep, as a kind of percussion section in this orchestra:

Ask Khathʿam and ʿAkk
  about our feats.
    Ask the kings.
      Ask Ṭayyiʾ of the Mountains.
Ask Ḍabbah's folk about Shibāk
  when in the fray
    the Bakr yielded
      their wives and ʿIqāl's kin.
Ask Clan Ṣabāḥ
  how we butchered them
    at Dhāt al-Rimth
      above Uthāl.

Ask Zayd and Sūd.
Ask al-Muqaṭṭaʿ
and Mujāshiʿ ibn Hilāl
how our spears
sought them out
how our horses
filled them with fear . . .

One reads this and wants to applaud. The enumeration of tribes and sites, like Homer's list of ships or the Old Testament's genealogies, are tests of investment through technique. And if, for all that, it seems the poetry doth protest just a little too much for contemporary comfort, if the self-vaunting (*fakhr*, literally "pride") comes across as a bardic wee bit out of control, this, it soon becomes clear, is part of its action-hero or rapper-like over-the-topness, the artfully hyperbolic presentation of a fabled, contest-crazed figure, one who's endowed with super- or at least superior powers, which he wields against the tallest odds. It's a figure who, in the weave of Montgomery's lines, calls to mind the dragon-stalking Beowulf and Pound's wyrd-weary Seafarer, as it also invokes the Achilles of Logue's cinematic *War Music*, or Prudentius' *Psychomachia*, with its allegorical war for the soul.

Throughout, Montgomery gives us what Pound said a translator must: "Trace of that power which implies the man"—here, a figure of elemental vitality, a magnetic literary character who, in the fullest sense, is a product of translation's sustained audition. And palpably within that hearing, inside the poetry's winning belligerence, and its half-hallucinatory boasts and assault, ʿAntarah's reiteration of prowess betrays an anxiety that belongs to us all. There is, again, the pathos of the not-quite-member of the tribe (excluded, in this case, by virtue of his race). But evident too are other aspects of exile's anxiousness echoing across these lines. For ʿAntarah is always on the cusp, always at the precarious edge, or stranded in the slippery middle. He is inside the fight but beyond it (composing); within the present, but before and past it; together with his beloved (ʿAblah in memory), but forever far-off and denied her love. As daunting warrior and defender of repute, he serves as spokesman for his clan. But as poet whose ultimate weapons are words, as solitary soldier of extreme exposure—vulnerable in the face of Fate and Time—he wars at the margins to defend the center, the heart of the human matrix that made him.

It's in that trial, played out against the desert's starkness, that we discover the poet's resolute spirit, which James Montgomery takes up in these versions and releases to you now.

Peter Cole
Yale University

Introduction

Belligerent, defiant, brutal, uncompromising, unsettling—the voice of ʿAntarah ibn Shaddād, legendary warrior and poet of clan ʿAbs, rings loud and clear today, some fifteen hundred years after he lived, loved, and fought.

ʿAntarah's life and exploits are legendary. Many are the tales of his valor, of how he single-handedly held the line against marauders and saved the day. But in fact we know next to nothing about him, and what we do know seems at best amplified and larger than life, if not fantastical. As with Arthur of Camelot, we encounter ʿAntarah the legend, not ʿAntarah the man.

From the moment in the third/ninth century that ʿAntarah appears, charging full tilt against the record of history, he is cloaked in uncertainty, having already become the stuff of legend.[1] There are, however, points where all versions of the legend converge: that ʿAntarah was black and born a slave to a black mother, herself a slave; that he belonged to the tribe of ʿAbs; that he lived in the second half of the sixth century; that he was the most ferocious and accomplished warrior of his age; that he won his freedom in battle; and that he excelled as a poet.

ʿAntarah is an elemental force of nature. The name "ʿAntarah" (also "ʿAntar") is variously explained.[2] One suggestion is that it is onomatopoeic and means "the blowfly, bluebottle" (*Calliphora vomitoria*) because the word replicates the sound the blowfly makes. Another that it means "valorous, valiant." There is also a verbal form (*ʿantara*) that means to "thrust," i.e., with a spear or a lance. The name "ʿAntarah" is thus polyvalent. It conveys an adeptness with the lance and valor in battle as well as skin color: the blowfly, with its loud buzz, red eyes, transparent wings, and black body, is often found around carrion and dead meat.

ʿAntarah was one of the three "Arab ravens" of the pre-Islamic era (a time known in Arabic as the *Jāhiliyyah*), that is, black poet-warriors born to black women. The mother of this raven (or was he a blowfly?) ʿAntarah was an Ethiopian woman called Zabībah, whose name means "black raisin."[3] According to one source, he was given the nickname "Cleftlip," an epithet that denotes a deformity of the lip.[4] And one version of the story of his death has him killed not by human hand, but by a rainstorm.[5] After all, how could a human hand kill someone who identified so closely with death that he could claim, "Death I know—it looks like me, grim as battle"?[6]

Even ʿAntarah's lineage, a topic of such importance to both pre-Islamic Arabs and the scholars who recorded and studied pre-Islamic lore, is enveloped in uncertainty. Was he ʿAntarah son of Shaddād, or son of ʿAmr son of Shaddād, or son of Muʿāwiyah son of Shaddād? If his father's name was ʿAmr or Muʿāwiyah, why had this name been eclipsed in ʿAntarah's lineage by that of Shaddād? And was Shaddād his grandfather or paternal uncle?[7] Whatever solution they offer to this conundrum, the sources agree that Shaddād was a famous knight and that he was known as "the Rider of Jirwah." In other words, Shaddād is a paragon of the northern Arab elite cavalryman. While we may not know for sure who ʿAntarah's father was, all our sources agree that it was his father who gave ʿAntarah his freedom after ʿAntarah had distinguished himself in battle.

Some of ʿAntarah's poems mention his love for a woman named ʿAblah.[8] Legend has it that she was his cousin, and that he asked for her hand in marriage but was refused. As "ʿAntar and ʿAblah," this story of unrequited and doomed love enchanted and captivated subsequent centuries and continues to weave its spell today.

ʿAntarah's poetry breathes a spirit of indomitability, pride, and loyalty to kith and kin. It can seem inward-looking, solipsistic even, consumed by its own world and isolated from events beyond the pasture lands of ʿAbs, caught up in the hurly-burly of the squabbles, battles, and power politics of his clan. There are, however, indications that ʿAntarah and ʿAbs were not completely cut off from the wider world: he charges into battle with bamboo lances from India, wields curved Indian blades, brandishes broadswords from Yemen and sabers from Mashārif in Syria, shoots arrows as thin as strips of leather from Ḥimyar, and rides Mahrah camels from South Arabia.

ʿAntarah may have lived in an isolated region, the highlands of Arabia, but his poetry is the poetry of a society in turmoil. The myriad clan conflicts that his verses so fiercely evoke were not isolated phenomena, but were a part of wider unrest among the tribes of the peninsula. And the unrest among the tribes of Arabia was not isolated from the turbulence in the world that surrounded Arabia, as the superpowers of Rome and Iran continued to wage war on one another, and the kingdoms of Axum and Ḥimyar spiraled into decline.

The Arabian peninsula

The Arabian peninsula (or Arabia) extends today from the deserts of modern Syria and Jordan in the north to Yemen in the south, from the Red Sea coast of Saudi Arabia in the west to the Gulf states and Oman in the east. It is the largest peninsula in the world, occupying a landmass about as big as the Indian subcontinent. Its terrain slopes from west to east, and is characterized by two great ergs, or sand-dune deserts: the Empty Quarter (al-Rubʿ al-Khālī) in the south, stretching from Yemen to the Gulf states, and the ʿĀlij (or al-Nafūd) in the north. These ergs are connected by a long strip of sand known as the Dahnāʾ (see Maps, pp. lix–lx). The heights of Yemen and Dhofar in Oman are blessed in summer with monsoon rains, but the rest of the peninsula receives little rain. Settlement patterns are therefore largely dictated by access to groundwater in the form of oases and wells, and by the need to travel to such sources of water or in search of areas of rainfall. In the pre-Islamic era, survival often depended on a group's skill in gaining access to water.

Thus, the Arabian peninsula of the sixth century was geographically hemmed in, caught between the landmass of Iran to the east, Rome (Byzantium) to the northwest, and Africa to the west. It survived on the periphery of the two world superpowers of Late Antiquity: Sasanian Iran and Rome. And as a peninsula, an "almost-island," it was both connected to and somewhat separated from this world on its three sides (by sea and desert). Culture and society were also peninsular, they mimicked geography—prior to the advent of Islam, Arabia both formed part of, and was independent of, the world of Late Antiquity, characterized by a curious combination of belonging to, and differing from, this world.

Rome and Iran

The Roman Empire and Sasanian Iran were not friends: at best their relations comprised an uneasy stasis characterized by mutual mistrust. Both shared a conception of universal empire and their sovereigns presumed a claim to universal authority, which was often expressed in the form of religion.

For the Romans, who had become Christian under the emperor Constantine (r. AD 305–37), this conception of empire was the universal establishment of Christian rule, including forced conversion and the eradication of paganism—in other words, the establishment of a God-guided kingdom. For the Zoroastrian Sasanians, universal authority was expressed through a social structure that amounted to a caste system of four social estates: priests (a class that included judges), landed gentry (the warrior class), cultivators, and artisans (a class that included merchants). As long as the four estates were kept discrete, the Sasanians did not ordinarily persecute members of other religious communities, because the communities of Jews, Buddhists, Manicheans, and Christians simply had no place in the stratified hierarchy. The Romans and Iranians, then, cherished two imperial visions that were never really going to get along with one another.

The roots of the animosity between Rome and Iran stretched back to Rome's encounter with the Parthians (248 BC–AD 224), the predecessors of the Sasanians, as the Romans expanded into the eastern Mediterranean. The Sasanians (ca. AD 224–ca. AD 650), originally a landholder family from the highlands of southwest Iran, inherited this animosity and pursued it with zest. At their greatest extent, Sasanian rule extended from the Oxus River in the northeast to the Euphrates in the Fertile Crescent, giving them effective control of the silk trade with the Mediterranean.

The sixth century witnessed an increase in hostilities. In AD 531, Khusro I Anusheruwan (known as Kisrā Anushīrwān in Arabic sources) (r. AD 531–79) wrested control of Sasanian Iran from his father. Between AD 540 and 562, during the reign of Emperor Justinian (r. AD 527–65), Khusro's Sasanians invaded Syria, formally a province of the Roman Empire. A peace treaty was negotiated in AD 562. In the last years of his rule, between AD 570 and 578, Khusro I conquered the kingdom of Ḥimyar in the Yemen and expelled its Axumite overlords. But by the end of the century, the Sasanian emperor Khusro II Aparviz (r. AD 591–628) had to depend upon troops provided by the Roman emperor Maurice in order to recapture his throne, yet when Maurice was assassinated in AD 602, Khusro II was quick to invade Roman Syria.

The Romans were not idle during the sixth century. Their involvement in Arabia was largely through the manipulation of proxies, including the Axumite kingdom, the Hujrids of Kindah, or the Jafnids of Syria. In part, this was a natural consequence of established Roman policy in the region implemented through the province of Roman Arabia, but it was more immediately a consequence of geography: the Syrian desert, devoid of food and water, was not the place for an army to cross, whether Roman or Sasanian. With the terrain so inimical to conventional warfare, both sides resorted to the cultivation of alliances and diplomacy.

The Romans and the Iranians developed links with two powerful Arabic-speaking clans at either end of the northernmost points of Arabia: the Jafnids of Ghassan in the west and the Nasrids of Lakhm in al-Ḥīrah near the Euphrates in the east. The Romans made the Jafnids into imperial foederati, confederates, bestowing a kingship upon them and recognizing them as phylarchs (tribal leaders). The Jafnids were charged with restraining the Arabic-speaking tribes and preventing them from interfering with trade routes and the collection of tax tribute. They supplied the Roman army with troops and waged war against the Nasrids of Lakhm, who acted on behalf of the Sasanians. Nasrid influence stretched along the eastern Arabian littoral and even into Oman. Their influence has been detected in Yathrib (the settlement that under Islam was to become Medina), to the extent that in the sixth century the Nasrids may have appointed a governor there. Roman and Iranian interest in the Arabian peninsula did not stop with the recruitment of elite warrior-rulers from the north to do their dirty work for them. Their activities extended as far as Yemen and Ethiopia, or the kingdoms of Ḥimyar and Axum.

Axum and Ḥimyar

We do not know much about the kingdom of Axum.[9] Its ruler was known as the negus and his territory included modern Eritrea and the northern part of Ethiopia. It may even have stretched farther west into Sudan. Christianity took hold in Axum in the fourth century. From the fourth to sixth centuries, Axum grew astonishingly rich in African products such as gold, ivory, rhinoceros horn, and tortoiseshell.

The fate of Axum is closely tied up with the history of South Arabia. In about 110 BC the South Arabian tribe of Ḥimyar formed itself into a kingdom and brought South Arabia under its control. By the third century AD, under the rule of Shammar Yuharʿish, Ḥimyar had conquered the southern Arabian region of Ḥaḍramawt and expelled the Axumites from the Yemeni coast. In the following centuries, the Ḥimyarites sought to extend their influence over the tribes of the interior, venturing deep into the Yamāmah and maybe even as far as Ḥajr (modern-day Riyadh) (see Maps). During the fourth century they converted to Judaism, and in the fifth century they exerted their dominion over Maʿadd, the main tribal confederation of the northern Arabs of Najd, by installing the Hujrids as their proxies under a chieftain of the powerful tribe of Kindah.

With Roman help, Kaleb Ella Asbeha, negus of Axum (r. ca. AD 520–40), invaded Ḥimyar, placing a Christian king on the throne. This led to a reprisal from the Jewish royal family, and the new Himyarite ruler, Yūsuf, slaughtered the Axumite garrison and in AD 523 executed several hundred Christians, who became known as the Martyrs of Najrān. This event led to an Axumite invasion in AD 525, the death of Yūsuf, the eventual replacement of the Himyarite kingdom with an Axumite protectorate, and enforced conversion to Christianity.

One of the Axumites who had remained in Ḥimyar after the return of the negus Kaleb to Ethiopia was a man named Abraha (in Arabic sources: Abrahah), who assumed control of the protectorate. In AD 547, he received ambassadors from Rome, Iran, and Ethiopia, and from the Nasrids and Jafnids. In ca. AD 550, he constructed the Christian cathedral of Sanaa, and five years later mounted a major expedition into central Arabia, but that expedition resulted in his defeat and retreat.

Perhaps the most notable construction project undertaken by the kingdom of Ḥimyar was the Ma'rib Dam, which was 650 meters wide and 15 meters high. Ma'rib (presumably the church and not the dam) was where, in AD 552, Abraha chose to receive the delegations of ambassadors, but sometime between AD 575 and 580, during the childhood of Prophet Muḥammad, the dam is reported to have burst and not been repaired. The collapse of the dam signaled the end of the kingdom of Ḥimyar and may have led to a massive influx of mercenaries and professional soldiery maintained by the kingdom into central and northern Arabia.[10]

During the second half of the sixth century, the frontiers between Rome and Iran were destabilized, and the interior of Arabia was thrown into turmoil. On the eve of the advent of Islam—and toward the end of ʿAntarah's life—the Jafnids were overthrown by Rome in AD 573, and the Nasrids by the Sasanians in AD 602. Ḥimyar had been unable to repair the dam that it so crucially depended on. And in AD 604, the Sasanian army was defeated by an army of Arabian tribesmen at the Battle of Dhū Qār.

Arabs in Arabia

The term "Arab" is apparently an old one. Its earliest appearance is thought to occur in Assyrian texts from the seventh century BC, though this has been disputed. But there is no indication in this or any of its subsequent occurrences that it is an ethnonym, i.e., the name of an ethnic group. In fact, it is likely that for many centuries inhabitants of Arabia were not widely or even automatically known as Arabs. Other names, such as the Greek names *homēritai* (i.e., Ḥimyarites) and *sarakēnoi* (Saracens), predominate—presumably they are designations of specific groups of inhabitants of regions of Arabia.

Two basic solutions to the identity of the Arabs has been proposed, one maximalist, the other minimalist. The maximalist solution is to take "Arab" as an atemporal designation of transhumant tribespeople, that is, nomadic pastoralists who herded camels, or other domestic animals such as goats and sheep, in designated winter and summer camping grounds. Yet the probable percentage of the population of the Arabian peninsula that may at any one time have been nomadic was small, even allowing for returns to nomadism after a period of sedentarization. As Donner notes, "Most Arabians . . . are, and have been, settled people."[11] If the "Arabs" were transhumant tribespeople, they would not have been particularly numerous. And if the "Arabs" were nomads, we should not presume that they would necessarily be Bedouins, i.e., people of the desert. Bedouins could, counterintuitively, be settled for much of the year, and could also share some of the features of the nomad's lifestyle, such as camel pastoralism.[12]

The word "Bedouin" represents the hinge point at which the maximalist solution becomes minimalist: its historical frame of reference is specifically the fifth and sixth centuries AD; its geographical frame is North Arabia (specifically Najd), the highlands of modern Saudi Arabia, and the imperial satellites of the Jafnids in the west and the Nasrids of al-Ḥīrah.[13] Thus, Macdonald argues (in the context of North Arabia) for greater discrimination in the use of the label "Bedouin,"[14] and Zwettler would establish "its most restrictive" designation as "the camel-raising and -riding Arab nomads of the late antique Near East."[15] Whittow has advocated replacing the term "Arab" with the term "Bedu," in accordance with contemporary anthropological and ethnographic practice.[16] Dostal, arguing for an Iranian (Parthian) influence for the saddlebow and its associated weaponry and cultural complexes (including tent types, customs, and clothing), distinguishes between nomads, "half-bedouins (breeders of small-cattle)," and "full bedouins (camel-breeders)."[17] Retsö, in a bold argument that has not won many supporters, argues that the Arabs were a "razzia-loving warrior caste" and imagines them forming:

> a socio-religious association of warriors, subject to a divinity or ruler as his slaves . . . separate from ordinary settled farmers and city-dwellers, living in their own lots often outside the border between the desert and the sown.[18]

The notion of a "socio-religious association of warriors" (one that celebrates the desert wastes, wherever their residence may be) is appealing. The lifestyle would have been typified by unsettledness, by the rapid shifts from sedentary to nomad and back again.[19]

Whether or not we accept Retsö's suggestion of a "socio-religious association of warriors," during these centuries the northern Arabian peninsula witnessed the emergence of aristocratic "rider-warriors" (the term is Walter Dostal's), adept at warfare with both horse and camel, implicated, to varying extents, in the Roman and Iranian imperial reliance (in North and Central Arabia) of confederations of rider-warriors as mercenaries or proxies, and characterized by developed military technology such as body armor and the lance.[20] We can perhaps go further and identify these "rider-warriors" as the elites of Maʿadd. In the three centuries before Islam, Maʿadd were:

> predominantly camel-herding . . . bedouins and bedouin tribal groups—irrespective of lineage or place of origin—who ranged, encamped and resided throughout most of the central and northern peninsula . . . and who had come to adopt the *shadād*-saddle and . . . by the third century, to utilize it so effectively as a means of developing and exploiting within a desert environment the superior military advantages offered by horses and horse cavalry.[21]

These elites were organized in their various kin groups, and Zwettler notes that their principles of organization were not exclusively based on blood relationship or kinship; rather, they operated as

> colleagues, associates or cohorts in an amorphous, far-ranging, almost idealized aggregation of like-minded compeers and communities who shared many of the same social, cultural and ecological experiences, aspirations, opinions, and values.

According to Zwettler, this is how, by the middle or the end of the seventh century, "Maʿadd entered the genealogical realm, where it became an eponym for the 'progressive' Northern Arabs."[22] As part of this process, tribalism and genealogy emerged as central defining features of the descendants of Maʿadd. It is, then, the inability of the imperial powers of Rome and Iran to control their buffer zones through the Jafnids and Nasrids, and the various mercenaries they relied on, that created in the second half of the sixth century the state of instability and turmoil that characterized northern Arabia.[23]

The elites of Maʿadd shared another important feature: language. The language of these groups was the *ʿarabiyyah*, the Arabic we encounter today in the poetry of pre-Islamic Arabia. We should not overstate the evidence, but we should bear in mind the observation that the predominance of this *ʿarabiyyah* is an accurate, if not fully representative, account of the linguistic situation during the centuries under discussion. Jenssen reminds us that "very little . . . can be known about Arabic before the dawn of Islam." He notes that of all the varieties of Arabic similar to the Arabic of pre-Islamic poetry, it was only this latter variety that was in fact preserved "in the form of a corpus of text and a systematic description."[24] The survival of the *ʿarabiyyah*, preserved in a specific corpus of poetry, the qasida poem, suggests that at some stage this "classical" Arabic emerged as a dominant form of expression of a dominant group. The users of this *ʿarabiyyah* were the masters of qasida poetry: they controlled both language and society, as renowned warriors and chieftains or as figures closely connected to these chieftains.

ʿAbs of Ghaṭafān

The inhabitants of the Arabian peninsula were caught up in this turbulence that engulfed the world on their borders during the sixth century. Often they were the agents of turmoil. ʿAntarah belonged to a kin group known as ʿAbs, transhumant pastoralists who lived in Najd and belonged to the larger kin group of Ghaṭafān, itself claiming descent from the super-lineage group Qays ʿAylān. Ghaṭafān contained other conglomerated kin groups, including Sulaym and Dhubyān (see Map 1), and Dhubyān in turn comprised three distinct kin groups: Fazārah, Murrah, and Thaʿlabah.

By the middle of the sixth century, Ghaṭafān was a conglomeration in a state of upheaval. ʿAbs, under the leadership of Zuhayr ibn Jadhīmah, had gained hegemony of Ghaṭafān and over the Hawāzin (see Map 1), who also claimed descent from Qays ʿAylān. Ghaṭafān had to contend with some powerful neighbors, chief among whom was ʿĀmir ibn Ṣaʿṣaʿah. The killing of Zuhayr, chieftain of ʿAbs, by a member of ʿĀmir signaled the decline in ʿAbs's hegemony. Before long, as a result of a power struggle between ʿAbs and Fazārah of Dhubyān, hostilities broke out and quickly escalated into the forty-year War of Dāḥis and al-Ghabrāʾ. This power struggle is expressed in the sources as a quarrel between two chieftain protagonists: Qays ibn Zuhayr (of ʿAbs) and Ḥudhayfah ibn Badr (of Fazārah). A pretext for conflict was afforded by a horse race between the protagonists. Each chief agreed to race two horses, a stallion and a mare. Qays chose to run Dāḥis and his mare al-Ghabrāʾ, but Ḥudhayfah's men cheated and slowed Qays's racehorses down, so Qays lost the wager.

In the war that ensued, ʿAbs initially enjoyed notable successes, but eventually the combined forces of Dhubyān proved too strong and ʿAbs were expelled from their ancestral pasturelands. It was in this crucible of exile and wandering that ʿAntarah's warrior spirit was tested and found true. We encounter him participating in the battles of ʿUrāʿir and al-Farūq, and repeatedly saving his people from calamity. ʿAbs and Dhubyān were eventually reconciled by the end of the sixth century. In the siege of Medina known as the War of the Trench (5/627), Ghaṭafān, under the leadership of ʿUyaynah ibn Ḥisn of Fazārah, fought on the side of the Meccans against the Muslims.[25]

Whatever the historicity of the narrative of the War of Dāḥis and al-Ghabrāʾ, the turbulent relationship between kin groups within the same lineage group over a prolonged period is typical of the kind of turmoil that dominated much of Arabia during the sixth century.

The Poets and Their Cosmos

The elite warriors of sixth-century Maʿadd chose to express their views of the world, their war culture, and their ethos in qasida poetry, which is poetry composed in a prestige language (classical Arabic) in works of varying length and complexity, from simple poems to complex odes.

Like the society the warrior-poets lived in, qasida poetry was in a state of turmoil. This oral poetry emerged abruptly in the second half of the sixth century, was subject to an astonishing variety of experimentations, manipulations, conceptualizations, and imaginings in the seven or eight decades before the advent of Islam, and continued to thrive well into the Umayyad era (41–132/661–750).

The poetry of ʿAntarah is one of the many examples of the emergence in the course of the sixth century of the warrior-poet as spokesperson of a war culture, a complex of ideals celebrated in qasida poetry. These ideals were informed by a universal vision of manly virtue (*muruwwah*),[26] at the very heart of which lay a passionate and uncompromising adherence to honor (*ʿirḍ*), set within "a universal perspective where the paradigm for how one must live and die is founded on the principle of chance."[27]

These warriors were united, yet kept distinct by their scrupulous adherence to an ever-changing and flexible social dynamic of alliance and protection, as well as by their expression of ties, kinship, and loyalties through genealogy, both acquired (*ḥasab*) and inherited (*nasab*).[28] They cherished their vehicles of war, the she-camel and the horse, as well as their weaponry and armaments, and perfected the raid and the hunt. War was often retributive, driven by the need for vengeance, although it was also hazarded to win spoils: women, camels, livestock, and slaves. War was how a man preserved, acquired, and displayed honor and glory. It was the ultimate realization of risk and chance. For these warriors, war was effectively a religion.[29]

The cosmos of the pre-Islamic qasida poets is stark. Everything is governed by Time (or Fate) and its avatar, Death. At the heart of the cosmos stands man, either alone, or with his family and/or his kin group. The cosmos was unpredictable: a man knew that it could and would inevitably infect him, his honor, and his society with a most terrifying disease: disunity and disintegration. What he did not know was when this would happen. The events of this cosmos play out in the desert, the landscape where a man on camelback pits himself against Time and risks his all, in a series of actions whose outcomes are determined solely by chance.

The poet-warriors were unanimous in their celebration of and devotion to the majesty of the qasida and the *ʿarabiyyah*. Poetry as memorialization offered man a victory over Time: if his feats were immortalized in verse, and his descendants and kin group perpetuated his memory, man would thus vanquish Time. Therefore, memory and kin group solidarity were central to the perpetuation of an individual's glory, an all too fragile and ephemeral possession unless reinforced by constant and repeated efforts to acquire more glory.

Poetry existed to celebrate the winners in the deadly game of war or to commemorate the valiant losers who died on the battlefield. In their commemoration of glorious ancestors, the masters of qasida poetry sought, through the perpetuation of genealogy and the memorization of poetry, to preserve this glory against the depredations of Time.[30] They did not do this through, say, a cult of heroes, but by positioning the last living member of a line of glorious ancestors as the guarantor of the perpetuation of glory. It was this elite warrior's heroic duty to embody and consolidate former glory, but also to build upon it and surpass the deeds of his forbears.[31]

The Qasida

Pre-Islamic qasida poetry is a public art form and is in a profound way theatrical: it cannot function without an audience. In its orality, it is addressed to, and entirely dependent upon, a group of listeners; it appeals to others and voices challenges to them; it cries defiance against Time; it trumpets the triumph of man; it memorializes his afterlife. It is the poetry of performance, and its soundscapes are performed on the stage of the cosmos.[32]

Out of this simple set of elements (Time, man, and the sweltering heat of the desert), a profound and imaginative poetic tradition was fashioned. Its themes were as simple as its elements: ruins and abandoned encampments, lost loves, arduous desert crossings, honor and glory, battles and raids.

Thus, many qasidas explore variations on the following narrative pattern: while on a desert journey, a poet comes across some ruins. His discovery forces him to stop and determine whether this is the site where he once enjoyed happiness with a woman who was subsequently either lost or denied to him. He explores his memories of their time together, but then resumes his journey on camelback, possibly comparing his camel to some other animal of the desert, such as an oryx, a wild ass, or an ostrich. His journey brings him to a destination: this destination can be physical, such as a patron or chieftain, or metaphysical, such as a celebration of honor, nobility, and glory, perhaps through acts of communal generosity by feeding the needy in times of famine and drought, perhaps through the provision of wine for others, perhaps through military exploits in the battlefield, or through the righting of a wrong.

Not all qasida poems fit this simplistic and generalized characterization: there are many variations on the pattern, across time, region, lineage, and kin group. But what is typical of all of this poetry is its economy—it fashions complex and profound works of art out of a simple set of components.

ʿAntarah's "Golden Ode" and the Undoing of the Qasida

The poems ascribed to ʿAntarah belong to a number of distinct genres: there are personal and tribal vaunts, war chants, full-blown qasidas, threats, and vituperation. His fame and reputation as a poet, however, are entirely dependent upon his most important composition, known both as his *Muʿallaqah*, "Suspended Ode," and as his "Golden Ode" (Poem 1). This is a difficult poem, one dominated by grotesquery, where meaning and established order are in flux. It is a poem that pushes the qasida as art form to the very edge of signification and derives its meaning from the obliteration of existence in death.

The occasion of its composition is roughly the last decade of the sixth century, a time before the first truce in the War of Dāḥis and al-Ghabrā'. The concluding verses refer to both sons of Ḍamḍam as alive: Harim ibn Ḍamḍam died after the first truce of the war, at the hands of Ward ibn Ḥābis, a kinsman of ʿAntarah. The poem begins with a desolation so extreme that it defies recognition. The poet is on a journey, on camelback. He comes across an area that he thinks was once inhabited by ʿAblah, the woman he loves. But so much time has passed, so much has happened to the poet, that he cannot at first be sure. The despair and sadness that overcome him, and his inability to move on, gradually convince him that this is in fact the place. He pleads with the ruins, trying to conjure up the time when they were full of life, in an attempt to revivify not only the ruins but poetry itself, slaughtered by earlier poets and left unburied on the battlefield (lines 1–8).

The poet's identification of the desolate site brings home to him the emptiness of the present: ʿAblah is beyond the poet's reach, physically (i.e., geographically) and temporally (because the past is irrecoverable). It awakens memories of the epiphany of the beloved on the night of the departure of her tribe, memories that now engulf the poem, in a comparison between the strong perfumed scent that accompanies the vision of the beloved and a musk pouch, a heady wine, and flowers growing in a lush meadow, a remote and sacred enclosure rarely visited even by the animals of the desert. But in this terrestrial paradise, beauty is sullied—the screeching insect is intoxicated and out of control, its actions like a one-armed amputee trying to light a fire with two fire sticks. Under the surface of this apparent plenty, then, lurk pain and grotesquery. Such memories accentuate the desolation of lines 1–8 and intensify the poet's sense of his loss, for he is denied the luxuries his beloved enjoys: she sleeps in comfort, while he, true to his bellicosity, passes the night on his horse, poised to launch a dawn raid, which as poet he will soon turn to (lines 9–26).

In a good number of pre-Islamic odes, the poet effects a transition (known in Arabic criticism as *takhalluṣ*, literally "setting oneself free" or "being rid of") from the first movements of the ode (frequently referred to in Arabic poetic criticism as *dhikr al-aṭlāl*, evocation of ruins, and *nasīb*, the amatory episode) to the desert adventure (*raḥīl*) and description of the camel (*waṣf al-nāqah*). Most odes conclude their desert adventures and descriptive scenes with an incantation of the exploits of poet or tribe (*mufākharah*). In some odes, such as the *Muʿallaqah* of Zuhayr, the destination of the desert adventure is a warlord or a regent (this is typical of panegyric poems, known as *madīḥ*), and the poem's conclusion marks a return to civilization from the desolation of the ruins and the desert.

In ʿAntarah's poem, the destination is ʿAblah, the beloved, and not a patron. The shape of the qasida is thus temporarily destabilized, because the transition does not mark a progression but rather signals a return to the beginning, to the *nasīb*. This destabilization is conveyed syntactically through the fact that the question posed at line 27 concludes with the final verse of the movement, line 39 (lines 27–39).

Shape-shifting dominates the description: the camel resembles an ostrich that in turns resembles a funeral bier, an incomprehensible foreigner, and a slave wearing a fur cloak; the ostrich's flock resembles Yemeni camels; when the poet's camel runs she seems to be attacked by a cat tied to her side; the journey converts her into a brick fortress, supported on tentpoles. Her legs are like fifes, and she sweats tar. After her metamorphosis from ostrich to human-made structure, her final act of shape-shifting is the abandonment of her gender altogether as she becomes a stallion, the consummation of the denial to allow her to produce milk at the onset of the passage. Once more, pain and grotesquery abound: the camel is physically maimed (her teats are snipped); the slave has had his ears docked; the foreign camel herder is incomprehensible; the cat is ferocious in its attacks on the poet's she-camel.

With the camel now transmogrified almost beyond recognition, the poet addresses ʿAblah, his destination. It is as yet unclear whether ʿAntarah has reached her—he entertains the possibility that she may refuse to lower her veil before him. The words he addresses to her epitomize the pre-Islamic warrior ethos: the fulfillment of the warrior's identity through excess, whether as implacable vengeance or unbounded generosity. And the poet's demand that ʿAblah recognize his merits with praise reminds us that this ethos is ineffectual and empty without its celebration in verse (lines 40–46). The force of this apostrophe and its significance for the shape of the qasida should not be underestimated. It means that, somewhat uncommonly in the pre-Islamic poetic corpus, the boasting intoned in the remainder of the ode (i.e., the *mufākharah*) is addressed directly to the poet's beloved, and not to his tribe or opponents. So, once again, the shape of the qasida is destabilized and the shape-shifting of the desert adventure continues in line 42, in metaphor and simile: the harm the poet inflicts on his enemies is a snarling lion (*bāsil*, in Arabic); in the mouth of his enemies his actions taste as bitter as colocynth.

Now it becomes clear that the dawn raid, alluded to in line 25 and line 26, is about to begin. The raid is launched (line 47): three champions are felled in rapid succession. The sequence is structured as a priamel,[33] with the most significant kill coming last—at the end of the ode. Again, grotesquery abounds: the severed jugular of the first victim hisses like breath whistling through a harelip; the poet feeds savage hyenas and other predators with butchered flesh, the thud of his spear sounding a clarion call that dinner is ready; spilled blood (as red as resin) and rotting flesh (dark as indigo) frame the three vivid close-ups that zoom in on the killing and pulsate with battle lust, as the poet delights in slaughtering his highborn opponents (lines 47–63).

ʿAblah, the poet's target, is now easy prey: she is an exposed and vulnerable gazelle that beckons and invites him to pounce. But do these verses depict the aftermath of the raid or are they a memory of the time when the poet and his beloved were together? Why is the poet accompanied by a slave girl on the raid? The scene is perhaps more appropriate for the period when ʿAntarah pursued ʿAblah before her tribe struck camp. Once again, meaning is destabilized and uncertainty flits over the chronography, shape, and direction of the poem (lines 64–67).

With the poet's prey apparently captured, the poem launches into an exultant boast (*mufākharah*), as the poet reiterates his exploits on the battlefield. In a panoramic battle description, ʿAntarah holds the line and leads his tribe to victory in a hard-won contest—the combatants lose the power of language; the poet's horse almost acquires it. The only words to be heard are the chants, "ʿAntar!" and, "Ho ʿAntar, Onward!" (lines 73 and 78), which frame the poet's charge into the fray and his rout of the enemy (lines 68–78).

Many pre-Islamic qasidas end on this note of unbridled exultation, but not so this Golden Ode, for the poet addresses a further bout of self-justification to ʿAblah. The extent of the poem's instability becomes clear, for ʿAntarah has not yet been able to reach her, seize his prize, and fulfill his desire—ʿAblah remains unattainable, physically and figuratively beyond his reach. The poet is now at war with both kinfolk and foe: the clan that bars his way to ʿAblah traces its descent from Baghīḍ, an ancestor of both the ʿAbs, the poet's own tribe, and the Dhubyān, its inveterate opponents in the War of Dāḥis and al-Ghabrāʾ (lines 79–81). The poet launches into the final (and in a sense the only real) expression of self-glorification (*mufākharah*) in the qasida as he challenges his opponents to combat (lines 82–85).

The poem concludes with a disturbing, intensified image of the desolation it began with: a corpse left unburied on the field of battle, carrion for hyenas and vultures. In this way, we are led by this shimmering mirage of a qasida to ponder the one true reality. It is the conclusion the ode has been straining to reach: Death, the obliteration of existence, is the only true reality; it is the real subject of the ode.

The Abbasid Discovery of ʿAntarah

The story of the discovery of ʿAntarah is the story of the recovery of the *Jāhiliyyah* in the second/eighth and third/ninth centuries, when this body of oral verse came to be salvaged, recorded, and studied by Abbasid language experts, scholars, enthusiasts, and intellectuals. Ibn Qutaybah (d. 276/889), one of the architects of high Arabic culture, and part of the second wave of scholars who devoted their lives and energies to this corpus of poetry and the Qurʾan, summed up pre-Islamic poetry thus:

> Poetry is the source of the Arabs' learning, the basis of their wisdom, the archive of their history, the repository of their battle lore. It is the wall built to protect the memory of their glories, the moat that safeguards their laurels. It is the truthful witness on the day of crisis, the irrefutable proof in disputes. He who has no decisive proof to support his claims of nobility, or his claims about his ancestors' glory and praiseworthy deeds, will find that his efforts are in vain, even if his glorious deeds are famous. Their memory will be effaced over time even if they are momentous. But he who has his merits committed to rhyming verse and bound in meter, and gives them renown through a choice verse, a memorable maxim, or a subtle notion, will immortalize them for all time. He will secure them against disavowal, and protect them from the plots of enemies. He will repel the jealous eye. Even if his glories are modest, they will forever be evident for all to see and recollect.[34]

By the middle of the third/ninth century, discussion of pre-Islamic hero warriors had become so widespread that al-Jāḥiẓ (d. 255/868–69), theologian, author, and prominent intellectual, could write in a discussion of lexicography:

> There are warrior-knights who, with their steeds, attain the pinnacle of fame and yet still fail to enjoy the same reputation as those who are much less deserving. Consider how our uneducated colleagues think that Ibn al-Qirriyyah is a more famous orator than Saḥbān Wāʾil, and that ʿUbayd ibn al-Ḥurr is a greater paragon of knighthood than Zuhayr ibn Dhuʾayb. The same is true of their treatment of ʿAntarah ibn Shaddād and ʿUtaybah ibn al-Ḥārith ibn Shihāb, and they love to quote ʿAmr ibn Maʿdī Karib but have never even heard of Bisṭām ibn Qays.[35]

Al-Jāḥiẓ is annoyed that a lack of specialized knowledge means that for many of his contemporaries ʿAntarah ibn Shaddād is a warrior of greater renown than ʿUtaybah ibn al-Ḥārith, the chieftain of the Tamīm kin group.[36]

The genesis of the legend of ʿAntarah and the story of the collection of his poetry are accordingly unclear, but the cultural currents that led to it being written down gather around a series of narratives known as "The Battle Lore of the Arabs" (*Ayyām al-ʿArab*), i.e., the stories of the wars, conflicts, and skirmishes that were fought by the North Arabian tribes a century or so before the advent of Islam. Any form of fighting, from the slinging of stones to full-scale military engagement, qualified as worthy of record and justified the label of "battle day."[37]

A typical battle narrative is told in an unadorned prose style and is usually identified by the name of the place where the incident occurred. Accuracy of geographic and genealogical detail is paramount, with scant regard paid to chronological accuracy. The main protagonists, the tribal context, and the bone of contention that led to the dispute are introduced, and then the narrative is typically focused on the actions of individuals, as a composite picture of the events of the battle is drawn. Sometimes tribal champions exchange poetic taunts before engaging in combat. Often dialogues proliferate. The narrative culminates in a rehearsal of the poetry, usually boasts and vaunts, composed to celebrate the victory or commemorate the memory of the glorious dead. Poems relating to the event are quoted, often as fragments. Poetry is central. It corroborates and ensures the veracity of the narrative, while the narrative contextualizes, justifies, and explains the poetry. In this way, the powerful and enduring concept that poetry is "the (historical and genealogical) register of the Arabs" (*al-shiʿr dīwān al-ʿarab*) took root and became widespread.

These tales of tribal conflict began life as the collective memory of an oral society; as one of the means whereby, unsystematically but consistently, the pre-Islamic kin groups of North Arabia communicated and imagined their visions of themselves, and commemorated their histories. Under the rule of the Umayyad dynasty that followed the first half century of early Islam, tribal allegiance dominated political conflict:

> The reevaluation and transformation of tribalism fostered the interest in preserving *tribal* lore as an object of tribal pride and as argumentative basis in the ongoing struggles for political power.[38]

Thus, battle lore emerged as tribal apologetics, a contested and disputed lore of immense political clout and relevance.

As the Abbasid dynasty (132–656/750–1258) court in Baghdad and elite society began to be shaped by new social, cultural, and political structures, genealogy and tribal battle narratives gradually lost much of the political immediacy they had enjoyed during the Umayyad era (41–132/661–750), when tribes in Syria and Arabia jockeyed for preeminence and politics were largely expressed through tribal loyalties. This was when genealogy and battle narratives emerged as subjects to be studied and codified.

By the end of the second/eighth century, a large-scale, major collection of poetry with a commentary incorporating battle narratives was composed in the garrison town of Kufa by al-Mufaḍḍal al-Ḍabbī (d. 90/784). In this monumental collection, known as *al-Mufaḍḍaliyyāt*, the battle narratives are used as context for and commentary on the poems. Al-Mufaḍḍal's approach to narrative as context for and commentary on poetry set the standard to be followed in subsequent centuries. Thus, when we encounter ʿAntarah's poetry in the two collections of the fifth/eleventh century, it is presented predominantly in this form, with narrative as preface to the poem, and the poem with commentary interspersed after every two, sometimes three, verses.

Genealogy and battle narratives were of central concern for two antiquarian enthusiasts and expert philologists: Abū ʿUbaydah Maʿmar ibn al-Muthannā of Basra (ca. 210/825) and Hishām ibn al-Kalbī of Kufa (d. 204/819 or 206/821). Ibn al-Kalbī was the undisputed master of Arabian genealogy: his masterpiece was known as *The Roll Call of Genealogy* (*Jamharat al-nasab*).[39] He also composed a work on the battle days of the Arabs that has not survived. The two key works on battle days composed by Abū ʿUbaydah have also been lost. The shorter of Abū ʿUbaydah's two monographs is thought to have covered either 75 or 150 battle days, whereas his major work, *Deaths of the Knights* (*Maqātil al-fursān*), is thought to have contained narratives of either 1,200 or 1,600 battle days. Abū ʿUbaydah also composed a monumental collection of poetry, *The Flytings of Jarīr and al-Farazdaq* (*Naqāʾiḍ Jarīr wa-l-Farazdaq*), a series of high-profile public slanging matches expressed in poetry by two major Umayyad poets. In this work, Abū ʿUbaydah's expertise on pre-Islamic battle days is evident: it is our primary source for the War of Dāḥis and al-Ghabrāʾ waged between the ʿAbs and Fazārah.[40] The principles of organization of Abū ʿUbaydah's battle-lore books is not known, but evidently he created a corpus of battle lore that became canonical.

The works of Abū ʿUbaydah and Ibn al-Kalbī were informed by, and helped shape, a wider intellectual, cultural, and religious process that developed over the course of the third/ninth century. In their quest for a pure, original Arabic to set the pristine (divine) Arabic of the Qurʾan against, the philologists of third/ninth century Iraq sought to imagine a correspondingly pure, original Arabia inhabited by noble warrior nomads. It is hard to think of a figure that could have met their requirements more completely than ʿAntarah ibn Shaddād, legendary warrior, chivalrous Arab, tragic lover, and composer of one of the poetic masterpieces of the *Jāhiliyyah*, "the Suspended Odes" (*al-Muʿallaqāt*).[41] Yet we know almost nothing of how ʿAntarah's poetry and its associated battle lore was collected. Glimpses of this process of discovery are afforded by four types of textual evidence:

1. The comments of al-Jāḥiẓ (d. 255/858–59), and the entries on ʿAntarah provided by Ibn Qutaybah (d. 276/889) and Abū l-Faraj al-Iṣbahānī (d. 356/967).
2. The redactions and commentaries of the poetry of six pre-Islamic poets by two scholars from al-Andalus: Abū l-Ḥajjāj Yūsuf ibn Sulayman the Grammarian, known as al-Aʿlam al-Shantamarī (the man from Faro with the harelip) (d. 476/1083); and Abū Bakr ʿĀṣim ibn Ayyūb al-Baṭalyawsī (d. 494/1101), from Badajoz. Both philologists include ʿAntarah ibn Shaddād as one of the six pre-Islamic poets. Al-Shantamarī's redaction includes twenty-seven poems, and he notes that the philologist al-Aṣmaʿī (d. 213/828 or 216/831), whom he identifies as the ultimate source for his own redaction, accepted without question the attribution of twenty-three of these.[42] The redaction of al-Baṭalyawsī includes thirteen more

poems than those commented upon by al-Shantamarī, i.e., forty poems in total. Al-Baṭalyawsī does not indicate the provenance of his collection, though he provides more variant readings in his commentary than does al-Shantamarī, and Abū ʿUbaydah looms largest among those scholars whose variant readings al-Baṭalyawsī does quote. Both scholars include, as prefaces to the poems and commentary, a number of poetry narratives (*akhbār al-shiʿr*) that seem to be descendants or retellings of apposite narratives from the battle-lore tradition.

3. The anthology of Abū Ghālib ibn Maymūn (d. 597/1201), *The Ultimate Arab Poetry Collection* (*Muntahā l-ṭalab min ashʿār al-ʿArab*), compiled in ten parts between 588/1192 and 589/1193. Ibn Maymūn offers versions of five poems by ʿAntarah, including the "Suspended Ode" (*Muʿallaqah*). One of these five poems (Poem 28) is only attested in *The Epic of ʿAntar*, and another (Poem 29) is a considerably enlarged version of a poem that we encounter in the other collections (i.e., Poem 5).[43]
4. The origins of *The Epic of ʿAntar* date from the fifth/eleventh and sixth/twelfth centuries. The two extant traditions of the *Epic* (Cairene and Levantine) contain a great deal of poetry. The Levantine tradition contains a version of Poem 28 in the current volume, one of the five poems by ʿAntarah included by Ibn Maymūn for inclusion in his anthology, thereby attesting to the emergence and development of the ʿAntar legend in the fifth/eleventh century.

Of by far the greatest relevance for the story of the discovery of ʿAntarah in the third/ninth century are text groups one and two, and I will confine my discussion to them. It is hard to know what to make of the passage from al-Jāḥiẓ, for his interest is not in ʿAntarah as such, but rather in the shortcomings of the assessments of those who prefer ʿAntarah ibn Shaddād over ʿUtaybah ibn al-Ḥārith ibn Shihāb. It would be foolhardy to extrapolate from this passage more than a passing indication that by the middle of the third/ninth century interest was being taken in the deeds of ʿAntarah, an inference that is corroborated by the entry on the poet included a decade or so later by Ibn Qutaybah in his *Book of Poetry and Poets* (*Kitāb al-Shiʿr wa-l-shuʿarāʾ*). That entry comes in two sections: biography and appreciation. The second section (Appendix §§1.8–13) concerns ʿAntarah's originality (§§1.8–10) and provides several examples of some choice verses, one example of a verse in which ʿAntarah is criticized for going too far (§1.12), and one citation of some verses in which he boasts of his blackness (§1.13). The first section (§§1.1–7) initially discusses the uncertainty hovering over ʿAntarah's lineage and proceeds to structure its points according to ʿAntarah's life, from birth to death: his manumission and recognition by his father, his mother and color, his involvement in the War of Dāḥis and al-Ghabrāʾ, his emergence as a major poet with his "Golden Ode," and his death.

In §1.2 Ibn Qutaybah quotes a sample of the verses of Poem 43 in the present volume that ʿAntarah declaims as he charges into battle on the day he wins his freedom. This quotation by Ibn Qutaybah is significant because these verses are not included in al-Shantamarī's redaction of (al-Sijistānī's? version of) al-Aṣmaʿī's recension, though they are included as the final poem in al-Baṭalyawsī's recension. This meager piece of evidence is an indication that al-Baṭalyawsī's recension of poems not included in al-Aṣmaʿī's redaction may in fact include materials that predate Ibn Qutaybah. Noteworthy are similarities between comments in Ibn Qutaybah and remarks provided by al-Shantamarī and al-Baṭalyawsī, suggesting that these poetry narratives may in fact be quoted from material that also predates Ibn Qutaybah.[44] We may even be tempted to discern in Ibn Qutaybah's entry a core of the ʿAntar legend in the stress placed on slavery and birth, and in the story of ʿAntarah's solitary death, when his elemental life force is reclaimed by nature.

The entry on ʿAntarah in al-Iṣbahānī's *Great Book of Songs* (*Kitāb al-Aghānī al-kabīr*) (Appendix 2), a sweeping panorama of Arabic court culture, musical history, and poetic creativity across the ages, may be longer and somewhat more involved than that of Ibn Qutaybah, but it shares the same basic structure, with the addition of recapitulations and alternative versions of key incidents, as well as notes on musical performances of ʿAntarah's verses and sections explaining difficult, obsolete, and obscure vocabulary. Interestingly, al-Iṣbahānī's version of the seduction of ʿAntarah by his father's wife, so reminiscent of Zulaykhah's attempted seduction of Joseph in the Qurʾan (Q 12 (Yūsuf)), is quoted by al-Baṭalyawsī.[45]

More significant, however, is a narrative given by both al-Iṣbahānī and al-Baṭalyawsī: the incident in which ʿAntarah's valor incurs the animosity of Qays ibn Zuhayr.[46] Al-Iṣbahānī's source is Abū ʿAmr al-Shaybānī; al-Baṭalyawsī's is Ibn al-Sikkīt, from whom he also derives the obscure tale of ʿAntarah's brothers and their colt, which according to al-Iṣbahānī originates with both Ibn al-Aʿrābī and Abū ʿUbaydah (via al-Sukkarī and Ibn Ḥabīb).[47] The tale of ʿAntarah's death is also shared by both sources.[48] Al-Baṭalyawsī gets his version from the Egyptian grammarian Ibn al-Naḥḥās (d. 338/950), al-Iṣbahānī his version from Abū ʿUbaydah and Ibn al-Kalbī.[49] This brief comparison suggests that al-Baṭalyawsī may have had access to sources that included a range of material possibly originating from the first century of the discovery of ʿAntarah.

ʿAntarah's poetry survived because of the amazing fifth/eleventh century efflorescence in Arabic philology that characterized al-Andalus, the Muslim-controlled regions of the Iberian peninsula. Al-Shantamarī was born in Shantamariyyat al-Gharb (modern-day Faro in Portugal) in 410/1019 and died in Seville in 476/1083. He studied Arabic language, lexicography, grammar, and classical poetry in Cordoba, and wrote extensively on grammar and lexicography. He so excelled in these subjects that he was given the honorific "the Grammarian." He notes in the introduction to his magnum opus, his recension of and commentary on the six pre-Islamic poets, that his transmission of this text goes back through the scholars of his native al-Andalus to al-Sijistānī (d. 255/869) and ultimately to al-Aṣmaʿī. It is, however, not clear whether al-Aṣmaʿī, at the beginning of the chain, or al-Shantamarī, at the end, or any of the seven links in the chain, was responsible for the actual collection in one book of the recensions of the work of these six poets.[50] Al-Shantamarī's commentary is largely confined to lexical and grammatical problems and only rarely offers any variant readings or mentions his sources.

In all likelihood, the bringing together in one collection of al-Aṣmaʿī's disparate recensions of these six poets is the work of his pupil Abū Ḥātim al-Sijistānī, an assumption we are encouraged to make by the inclusion of compositions by ʿAntarah not sanctioned by al-Aṣmaʿī. Al-Sijistānī, an expert on Arabic poetry and its lore, prosody, and vocabulary, was a pupil of both Abū ʿUbaydah and al-Aṣmaʿī and the teacher of Ibn Durayd (the third link in al-Shantamarī's chain). While it is not clear whether this collection contained any commentary, be it by al-Aṣmaʿī or al-Sijistānī, what is clear is that al-Aṣmaʿī was a rigorist when it came to assessing the attributions of poems to poets, prone to err on the side of caution and with a distinct preference (in the case of ʿAntarah) for poems composed in the classical meters, and a tendency to exclude pieces composed in the more popular, improvisatory meter of *rajaz*.

Al-Baṭalyawsī (d. 494/1101) was an official from Baṭalyaws (Badajoz) working in the law courts of the Berber dynasty of the Aftasids (r. 413–87/1022–95). While his collection of the six poets contains the poetry of the same six poets to whom al-Shantamarī devoted his commentary, in the case of ʿAntarah the range of poems is more extensive than those of his predecessor, for it includes many of the more occasional, shorter, improvisatory pieces composed in *rajaz*. Perhaps al-Baṭalyawsī intended his version of the six poets to supplement the version made famous by al-Shantamarī. This would imply that al-Baṭalyawsī himself compiled the collection out of various redactions of the poetry of the six poets, a supposition that might be corroborated by the diligence with which he indicates his authorities, but this is outright conjecture.

The order of the poems in al-Baṭalyawsī's recension is completely different from the order in al-Shantamarī. Al-Baṭalyawsī is careful to note variant readings, and wherever possible identifies his authority for an item of information or a reading. His favorite source for variants is Abū ʿUbaydah, but he also mentions Abū ʿUbayd al-Qāsim ibn Sallām (d. 224/838), al-Mufaḍḍal (d. 90/784), Ibn al-Sikkīt (d. 244/858), and Ibn Qutaybah.

Al-Baṭalyawsī's redaction contains an excerpt quoted by Ibn Qutaybah in his entry on ʿAntarah but not included by al-Aṣmaʿī/al-Sijistānī–al-Shantamarī. My hypothesis (a large claim based on scanty evidence) is that the forty poems recorded by al-Baṭalyawsī represent the range of poems that were available to al-Aṣmaʿī, who omitted those poems that his rigorism found problematic or deemed suspect. I also think it is possible that this range of poems preserved by al-Baṭalyawsī was derived ultimately from one of the works of Abū ʿUbaydah via Ibn al-Sikkīt.[51]

In sum, we owe what we know of ʿAntarah's poetry to two scholars who lived some five centuries after he did, and who wrote their commentaries on the Iberian peninsula, thousands of miles away from the highlands of Arabia where ʿAntarah achieved fame. It is a remarkable story of the literate continuities of Islamic civilization and Arabic scholarship during its classical era, and of the imaginative hold that pre-Islamic Arabia exerted over successive generations of readers and scholars.

The Epic of ʿAntar

The Epic of ʿAntar represents the last stage of the discovery of ʿAntarah in the premodern Arabic-speaking world. It is an enormously popular epic, and one of ten or so similar epics that have survived.[52] In its printed versions, it can run to some five thousand pages and mixes things real and imagined, pseudo-historical and phantasmagoric, in a universe of moral consistency offered by the resolute chivalry and bravery of its eponym, as 'Antar overcomes the disadvantages of his slave birth and color, and emerges as the most celebrated warrior of the age, vanquisher of emperors and kings, winning the hand of his beloved 'Ablah.[53]

The origins of the *Epic* date to the fifth/eleventh and sixth/twelfth centuries: the earliest written copy dates from 872/1466, and was at one stage in its long history kept in the Ottoman imperial library. It survives today in two main versions: Cairene and Levantine.[54] While its written tradition was relatively stable, the *Epic* was principally the prerogative of semiprofessional storytellers who recounted the exploits of 'Antar in the marketplace, coffeehouse, or village square.

The action takes place on a global setting, in some arenas that are real, such as Arabia, Africa, Byzantium, and Persia, and in others that are patently unreal, and where enchantment looms large, such as the Kingdom of al-Wāḥāt, a realm protected by a Greek statue that 'Antar must first overcome before he can gain entry. Nevertheless, the *Epic*'s claim on historical veracity is strong. It is ostensibly narrated by al-Aṣma'ī, but this is a long-lived al-Aṣma'ī who knew 'Antar personally, and who is four hundred years of age when the *Jāhiliyyah* comes to an end. The characters of the *Epic*, be they Sasanian emperors or Crusader knights, are mostly historical personages, and 'Antar has a son by a Frankish princess: this son is called Jufrān, an echo of Godfrey of Bouillon (d. AD 1100), one of the leaders of the First Crusade.

The Epic of 'Antar is basically a quest narrative in which a hero is given a series of challenges. 'Antar, the son of Shaddād and Zabībah (an Ethiopian slave who turns out to be the daughter of a Sudanese king), falls in love with 'Ablah, the daughter of his paternal uncle Mālik, who promises, and then breaks his promise, to marry her to 'Antar, demanding a dowry of one thousand camels bred only by al-Mundhir, the Nasrid king of al-Ḥīrah. Before he can set off on his quest, however, 'Antar must first become a knight. By guile and trickery, he gains possession of the fabulous black stallion al-Abjar. And as a reward, he is given an equally fabulous black sword, known by the epithet "Thirsty," a weapon fashioned from a rare black stone.

In this way, the request of a dowry becomes the pretext for 'Antar fighting, both for and against the masters of the civilized world. The rambling narrative, with its regular climaxes and stereotyped battle scenes, is ultimately given coherence and stability by its protagonist, who time and again demonstrates that chivalry and devotion to justice are what help make sense of life.

Poetry is one of the *Epic*'s principal vehicles for exploring the psychology of chivalry and the nobility of sentiment of its hero. According to Peter Heath, the *Epic* contains some ten thousand verses. We do not know who the composer or composers of this cornucopia of poems were, or when they were composed. This raises a number of questions that we are unable at present to answer with any confidence. Are the poems the work of the semiprofessional narrators of the *Epic*? Or were they the product of a higher social class, men of culture adept at formal Arabic? Can we hear different "authorial" or compositional voices in the poems? Can we glean any clues or answers from the Arabic of the poems? Did these compositions somehow find their way into the corpus when it was collected, existing perhaps in disparate anthologies or popular works? Or did they constitute an integral part of the *Epic* from its earliest beginnings? What is the exact relationship between those poems found in the redaction of al-Aṣmaʿī (such as Poems 5 and 27), and the expanded and extended versions of them preserved in later collections (i.e., Poems 29 and 50 respectively in the present translation). And, perhaps most obviously, how should we refer to the "author" of these poems, what name should we use: ʿAntar, or the ʿAntar poet/s, or the Sīrah poet/s?

The few examples of this poetry that we have included in our translation and edition were part of the original selection of poems made for the Library of Arabic Literature by Peter Heath. Peter's knowledge of and love for the *Epic* shone through his selection. However, my own rather "purist" (or perhaps puritanical?) tendencies as a scholar of pre-Islamic poetry were initially challenged when we were called on to work with the selection. I found it difficult to engage with these poems as "poems," as compositions of aesthetic worth and appeal in and of themselves. But at one point in my work, I realized that the poems of the *Epic* are in fact themselves acts of translation, part of a complex poetic and cultural process in which later poets invoked and sought to inhabit, through the vehicle of imagination, what Peter Cole refers to as that other "time which is always past, yet somehow now." It was how these poets heard and experienced the *Jāhiliyyah*. So in order to be true to them as poems I could not think of them simply as pastiches, but rather had to listen for the voice of ʿAntarah that these poets were hearing and invoking and to which they sought to be true.

My own quest to find a voice for ʿAntarah across all the poems and my act of listening were a turning point that led me to a nuanced appreciation of these poems as poems. In a certain way, I started to hear them as kinsfolk of, say,

Catullus's Latin versions of Sappho's Greek lyrics, and of how generally Roman poets inhabited Greek models. So, without wishing to dismiss the plethora of questions that the poems in *The Epic of ʿAntar* raise (about authorship, provenance, history, context), the significance of this poetic corpus lies for me not in the conundrum of authorship but in the presence of imagination, voice, and translation.

The centuries-long "discovery" of ʿAntarah is far from over. His popularity in the Arabic-speaking world has never waned, and movies, TV shows, comics, and cartoons in Arabic abound. He is also on the cusp of reaching an English-speaking audience in a new comic-book series titled *Antar the Black Knight*, with scripts by the prize-winning Nigerian-American novelist Nnedi Okorafor and artwork by Eric Battle.[55]

Acknowledgments

You would not be reading this book had I not received the help of many people. Gratitude first and foremost goes to the late Peter Heath, for his selection of texts and encouragement. Were it not for the guidance of two inspirational teachers and gifted translators, Peter Cole and Richard Sieburth, the project would have taken a very different direction. Richard made such contributions to the translations that in the end he became joint translator of the volume, though I claim responsibility for the mistakes in the book. Peter Cole encouraged me to listen for the poems—only my wrongheadedness and tin ear got in the way.

My collaborators at the Library of Arabic Literature (LAL), fellow editors, colleagues, and friends responded to my requests promptly and placed a great deal of trust in me: the meaning of true collaboration is yielding your words entirely to another's discretion. Robyn Creswell and Jeannie Miller, the guest translators who popped in from time to time to help us out, made key interventions and provided an objective correlative to many of our exuberant notions.

My volume editor, Tahera Qutbuddin, has been as generous with her time as with her erudition. Her deep intimacy with classical Arabic poetry has saved me many a blush. LAL's general editor, Philip Kennedy, and my fellow executive editor, Shawkat Toorawa, have been unflagging in their support and enthusiasm.

LAL is fortunate to have such a capable (and patient) editorial director in Dr. John Joseph Henry (Chip) Rossetti (how he manages to answer so many emails in the course of a day is a mystery to me), and our assistant editor Lucie Taylor is the epitome of intelligent efficiency. My copyeditor, Keith Miller, my proofreader, Wiam El-Tamami, LAL's amazing digital production manager, Stuart Brown, and our paperback designer, Nicole Hayward, have done a splendid job in producing such handsome books.

On behalf of LAL I would like to thank Gila, Manal, Antoine, Amani, and the team at the NYU Abu Dhabi Institute, who make our visits there so memorable, enjoyable, and productive. We are indebted to the audiences who turned up in Abu Dhabi and Dubai during December 2013 to hear a trial run of some of our translations. Their words of engagement came at just the right time.

Nnedi Okorafor, the writer of *Antar the Black Knight*, kindly let me see the scripts for the first two issues of the comic-book series.

Over the course of the project, I amassed electronic copies of over twenty-five manuscripts. Anyone familiar with the labyrinths of manuscript collections will know that I have had to rely on the kindness of many experts—in the Bibliothèque Nationale de France in Paris, the British Library in London, the Bodleian Library at Oxford, the Universitäts- und Forschungsbibliothek Erfurt/Gotha, the Austrian National Library in Vienna, and Dār al-Kutub in Cairo. I would like to thank Sumayya Ahmed for skillful help in liaising with the Bibliothèque Nationale du Maroc in Rabat; Dr. Mohamad Al Idreesi for providing me with such wonderful images of the manuscripts from al-Khizānah al-Ḥasaniyyah in Rabat; Khaleel Hasan Abdel Wahab for his help; and Dr. Ferruh Ozpilavci, associate director of the Manuscript Division of the Ministry of Culture, Turkey, and Prof. Hayrettin Yücesoy for advice on the collections of the Süleymaniye Library, Istanbul. Emily Selove and Geert Jan van Gelder graciously assisted by consulting volumes of *The Epic of ʿAntar* held at Exeter University Library. Geert Jan also provided advice on a few tricky verses. Elizabeth Key Fowden commented on the introduction and was liberal with her infectious enthusiasm.

Thanks are also due to my PhD student Robert Gard, who told me about camel burials and provided me with a reading list. Steven Bustos and his team at the Soho Grand Hotel, New York, helped the project in so many ways. I am grateful to them for providing a home away from home.

For the last three years, I have been fortunate to train two hours a week with Jonas Zimnickas, one of the most naturally gifted instructors I have ever met. Under his patient insistence I have developed a deep respect for ʿAntarah's feats of strength.

I have looked after this project for more than six years. The last four years have been very difficult for my family, yet never once did my wife, Yvonne, and children, Natasha, Sam, and Josh, waver in their dedication to making it possible for me to see the volume through to publication. I am humbled by their love and devotion.

A Note on the Text

The Edition

ʿAntarah's poetry exists today in two distinct traditions: a tradition consisting of twenty-seven poems (associated with al-Aṣmaʿī and the commentary of al-Shantamarī) and a forty-poem tradition (associated with al-Baṭalyawsī's commentary). The Arabic text presented in the current volume is based upon the oldest extant manuscripts for each of the three main recensions that we have: the redaction of al-Aṣmaʿī that formed the basis for al-Shantamarī's commentary, the selection by Ibn Maymūn, and the recension and commentary by al-Baṭalyawsī. The edition of the poems taken from *The Epic of ʿAntar* is based entirely upon the texts as edited by Shalabī, *Sharḥ dīwān ʿAntarah ibn Shaddād.*[56]

In my presentation of these materials, I took three principal decisions, the first concerning the order in which to present the poems, the second concerning the critical apparatus, and the third concerning the manuscript tradition of those prized pre-Islamic poems known as the *Muʿallaqāt.*

I present first the most authoritative, and best known, collection of the poetry of ʿAntarah: the text of the earliest surviving manuscript (Paris BNF Arabe 3273) containing al-Aṣmaʿī's redaction, preserved presumably in al-Sijistānī's version, which is similar, though not identical to, that of al-Shantamarī's recension and commentary.[57] The manuscript has been collated and corrected by a later hand on the basis of a recension very similar to, if not identical with, the recension used by al-Shantamarī. For this reason, my edition presents the readings preserved in the manuscript prior to its subsequent collation and correction.[58] I next present two poems recorded by Ibn Maymūn, whose selection provides a useful glimpse into how the ʿAntarah corpus was developing just under one hundred years after the death of al-Baṭalyawsī. The poems in al-Baṭalyawsī's recension but not included in al-Aṣmaʿī/al-Sijistānī–al-Shantamarī come next, and finally the poems selected by Peter Heath from *The Epic of ʿAntar.*

In order to prepare my edition of ʿAntarah's poetry, I collated twenty-one manuscripts. I consulted my volume editor and LAL's senior editorial team and we decided *not* to include the full critical apparatus of the poems in this hardcover version of the book, but to make it available on the website of the Library of Arabic Literature (www.libraryofarabicliterature.org), because of the complexity of annotation and the challenges posed by alignment of the facing-page Arabic and English texts.[59]

I list here the manuscripts I used in preparing my edition; a fuller discussion of each manuscript, with an indication of the sigla used, is included in the online edition. Because a number of these manuscripts cannot be dated with certainty, the list is arranged according to the current location of the manuscript:

Al-Aṣmaʿī/al-Sijistānī–al-Shantamarī:

Paris: 1. BNF Arabe 3273 (the oldest extant manuscript, in Maghribī script, and without full commentary); 2. BNF Arabe 3274 (with full commentary); 3. BNF 5322 (without commentary) ; 4. BNF Arabe 5620 (with full commentary).

Istanbul: 5. Nuruosmaniye 3849 (in *naskh*, without full commentary); 6. Laleli 1748 (without commentary).

Rabat: 7. al-Khizānah al-Ḥasaniyyah 2126 (with full commentary); 8. al-Khizānah al-Ḥasaniyyah 1065 (with full commentary); 9. BNM Q223 (with full commentary).

Cairo: 10. Dār al-Kutub Shiʿr Taymūr 450 (with full commentary); 11. Dār al-Kutub 11626 zāʾ (without commentary); 12. Dār al-Kutub 7727 Adab (without commentary); 13. Dār al-Kutub Adab 81 shīn (without commentary).

London: 14. BL Or 3155 (commentary on Zuhayr, Ṭarafah, and ʿAntarah).

Gotha: 15. Gotha MS 2191 (without commentary).

Ibn Maymūn:

Istanbul: 16. Laleli 1941.

Al-Baṭalyawsī:

Istanbul: 17. Feyzullah Efendi 1640 (with full commentary); 18. Beyazit 5385 (with full commentary).

Vienna: 19. Codex Mixtus 781 (with full commentary).

Cairo: 20. Dār al-Kutub 1837 Adab (contains an independent supralinear commentary on al-Baṭalyawsī's recension of ʿAntarah by the renowned Mauritanian scholar al-Shinqīṭī).

The following manuscript seems to be a hybrid of the recensions of both al-Shantamarī and al-Baṭalyawsī:

Paris: 21. BNF Arabe 5702.

In the case of the poems taken from *The Epic of ʿAntar*, I collated two available editions, that of Shalabī and al-Bustānī, and reproduced the text of Shalabī.

Poem 44	*Sharḥ dīwān ʿAntarah*, ed. Shalabī, 31–38; *Dīwān ʿAntarah*, ed. al-Bustānī, 108–12.
Poem 45	*Sharḥ dīwān ʿAntarah*, ed. Shalabī, 64–65; *Dīwān ʿAntarah*, ed. al-Bustānī, 131–32.
Poem 46	*Sharḥ dīwān ʿAntarah*, ed. Shalabī, 74; *Dīwān ʿAntarah*, ed. al-Bustānī, 142.
Poem 47	*Sharḥ dīwān ʿAntarah*, ed. Shalabī, 84; *Dīwān ʿAntarah*, ed. al-Bustānī, 151–52.
Poem 48	*Sharḥ dīwān ʿAntarah*, ed. Shalabī, 88–89; *Dīwān ʿAntarah*, ed. al-Bustānī, 155.
Poem 49	*Sharḥ dīwān ʿAntarah*, ed. Shalabī, 91–92; *Dīwān ʿAntarah*, ed. al-Bustānī, 159.
Poem 50	*Sharḥ dīwān ʿAntarah*, ed. Shalabī, 176–78; *Dīwān ʿAntarah*, ed. al-Bustānī, 69–70.
Poem 51	*Sharḥ dīwān ʿAntarah*, ed. Shalabī, 178–80; *Dīwān ʿAntarah*, ed. al-Bustānī, 70–71.

The edition published in *Dīwān ʿAntarah ibn Shaddād: A Literary-Historical Study* and made available on the website comprises an edition with a full critical apparatus of all the poems edited in the current volume (apart from Poems 44–51, taken from *The Epic of ʿAntar*), and four further editions of the extant recensions, based in every case on all the manuscripts available to me. The reader is referred to the website for a full discussion.

I have not yet been able to track down or gain access to several manuscripts referred to in library catalogues or reference works.[60] Codicologists will be interested (and may not be surprised) to learn that I have so far been unable to compile a family tree, a *stemma codicorum*, of the family of the al-Shantamarī manuscripts. I suspect that, in spite of a plethora of materials, I do not yet have enough material to fill in the gaps.

My edition of Poem 1, ʿAntarah's *Muʿallaqah,* concentrates exclusively on the poem as it is extant in the manuscripts of the three main recensions (al-Aṣmaʿī/al-Shantamarī, Ibn Maymūn, and al-Baṭalyawsī). I decided not to compare these traditions with the versions of the poem extant in the commentaries of scholars such as the third/ninth century scholar Abū Zayd al-Qurashī, al-Zawzanī (d. 486/1093), and al-Tibrīzī (d. 502/1109). This is an independent tradition that would require a separate study.

Of course, this is not the first edition of the poetry of ʿAntarah ibn Shaddād. In London in 1870, in his seminal *The Divans of the Six Ancient Arabic Poets,* Wilhelm Ahlwardt published his influential edition of the poems in al-Shantamarī's recension (without the commentary).[61] ʿAntarah was included as the second of the six poets. Ahlwardt was blessed with great good fortune. Not only was he a philologist of the highest caliber; he also had access to the oldest extant manuscript (Paris BNF Arabe 3273). I have relied heavily on his edition in the preparation of my text, and have like him based my edition upon this Paris manuscript. I have also benefited greatly from the excellent edition by Luṭfī l-Tūmī of al-Baṭalyawsī's commentary: *Sharḥ al-ashʿār al-sittah al-jāhiliyyah.* Al-Tūmī's edition is based on two of the four extant manuscripts of the recension.

The first editions of the poetry of ʿAntarah as an individual corpus, and not as part of the collection of the six poets, appeared in the last quarter of the nineteenth century, and there have been many subsequent editions.[62] I have found especially useful the work of Muḥammad Saʿīd Mawlawī, *Dīwān ʿAntarah* (1964). Mawlawī's edition is an exemplary piece of philology, and his introduction to the volume is erudite, thorough, and authoritative. Mawlawī's edition is based upon six manuscripts, one of which was a manuscript of al-Baṭalyawsī's recension and commentary, and he is scrupulous in his annotations.

The Translation

This is the first translation of a classical Arabic poet to be published as part of the Library of Arabic Literature. It is fitting that it be the result of a collaborative enterprise undertaken over the past six years by the editors of LAL. Poetry is by far the hardest form of writing in any language to translate, so it is unusual (if not absurd) for the translation of a poet's oeuvre to be attempted as a team effort. And yet this is just what we found ourselves trying to achieve. After intense scrutiny, we decided that the versions produced collaboratively should be reimagined and refashioned. But that in no way diminishes the original achievement of our collective endeavor.

An outline of the genesis of the project will serve to clarify our decisions. From the moment Philip Kennedy (LAL's general editor), Shawkat Toorawa, and I (LAL's executive editors) began to work on LAL, we were in no doubt that translating classical Arabic poetry into English would be the hardest part of the project. It is not that no one prior to LAL had tried to translate classical Arabic poetry into European languages. Indeed, there have been numerous successes, many of them truly impressive. But the task LAL sets its translators—to render Arabic into modern, lucid English—seemed to us from the outset of the project to be a skill that was certainly beyond *our* abilities. Our early efforts were marked, for example, by a fixation on inclusiveness, by a determination not to lose any part of what we could hear in the source texts, and by a refusal to acknowledge that a lucid translation will often require less, not more. The editorial board of LAL (with a few demurrals) agreed with our assessment of the situation, and during a panel session devoted to LAL as part of an international conference on World Literature and Translation convened in December 2011 at New York University Abu Dhabi, the board discussed with the conference participants its hesitations about translating classical Arabic poetry into English. This led to a number of fruitful conversations, for which the editors would like to thank the participants.

Scholarship and serendipity often go hand in hand. In early 2012, Philip Kennedy received an invitation from a production company that was looking to make an English-language movie of the adventures of ʿAntarah, possibly to star Dwayne "The Rock" Johnson in the title role. The outcome of this encounter was a proposal that LAL produce a book of translations of poems by ʿAntarah, perhaps to accompany the movie.

Philip contacted the late Peter Heath, the world expert on ʿAntarah and then chancellor of the American University of Sharjah, and invited him to participate by selecting poems he deemed appropriate for such a publication. Peter chose ten, two from al-Aṣmaʿī's redaction, Poems 4 and 6 in the current edition, and all eight poems from *The Epic of ʿAntar* translated in this book.

The first challenge was to determine the feasibility of a translation, and so we decided to convene a workshop at the end of our board's editorial meeting in May 2012 in New York. We knew that if we were going to have any success in translating ʿAntarah (and classical Arabic poetry in general), we had to go back to the classroom and learn how to do it. Accordingly, an invitation was sent out to two inspirational translators who had been supporters of LAL from the outset: Richard Sieburth of New York University and poet and translator Peter Cole (Yale University).

A workaday translation of one poem had been prepared by me and circulated in advance of the meeting. On the first day of the workshop, this poem was projected onto a screen and, under the tutelage of Peter and Richard, all present were encouraged to produce a critique of the strengths and weaknesses of this version. It soon became evident that there were many more weaknesses than strengths! Peter and Richard then talked the group through what it might mean to undertake a modern, lucid English translation of a poem from an era and culture (with attendant aesthetic and formal assumptions) that would be radically unfamiliar to a reader who had no knowledge of classical Arabic poetry.

During the second day of the workshop, each participant was invited to prepare a translation of the poem that had been critiqued the previous day. These translations were projected line by line on a screen and discussed in depth. Ten versions of the poem were produced. Thanks to the wonderful pedagogical skills of Peter and Richard and the confidence that their guidance had inspired in us, the editors of LAL decided to tackle the ʿAntarah project head-on and a second group session was scheduled to take place at our editorial meeting in Abu Dhabi in December 2012.

Though the ʿAntarah movie project had in the meantime come to naught, the LAL editors were keen to persist with the translation. The emphasis placed by LAL on translating integral texts would not support the kind of selection made by Peter Heath that we were then working with, so we decided to translate the corpus of ʿAntarah's poetry in Wilhelm Ahlwardt's 1870 edition of al-Aṣmaʿī's redaction.

During four workshops over the next two years, Ahlwardt's edition of al-Aṣmaʿī's redaction was translated by a series of small teams of LAL editors, occasionally augmented with invited guests. While the composition of these small teams changed from workshop to workshop, the method remained the same. Each team's translations were projected onto a screen and subjected to a detailed line-by-line, word-by-word critique.

Discussions, always genial, returned time and again to the question of voice—did the translation capture and do justice to ʿAntarah's voice? As one might expect, there was at this stage considerable disparity and variation in the modulations of this voice, but we made the conscious decision to allow the project to grow organically and for the time being merely to assemble our translations as we progressed.

In the summer of 2014, the project was handed over to me and I was asked to prepare the book for publication. I worked on the translations over the course of the following year, sending my reworkings of our versions to the members of the teams for approbation, rejection, or contestation. At this stage, my efforts revolved around trying to find a consistent voice for ʿAntarah, translation being, after all, a consistent set of decisions applied to the text or texts to be translated.

In the summer of 2015 I sent these versions to Richard Sieburth for his feedback and input. Richard's reworkings were brilliant, incisive, and, for me, transformative. As I read through Richard's skillful recastings, I became vexed by one of the biggest challenges to any translation of a classical Arabic poem into a lucid, modern English version—the fact that in Arabic poetry, a line of verse will almost always be a self-contained entity, in that it functions as both a metrical unit of verse and a unit of syntax. There are very few instances in which this unity of one line of verse is syntactically incomplete in such a way that the line requires enjambment, i.e., a further verse is required to complete its syntax, and thus provide its meaning. Classical Arabic poetry may regularly assemble its meaning paratactically through a sequence of lines, but it prefers to keep the lines in this paratactic sequence discrete. In modern English poetry, on the other hand, an individual line can be either a unit of verse or of sense, but is not ordinarily a unit of syntax. It seemed to me that an English translation of an Arabic poem that preserves the molecular harmony of syntax and verse in the source text would run the risk of seeming awkward in modern English. It would not, by definition, be lucid.

The translations assembled in 2015 represented my attempts to explore what I thought was an intractable challenge. Encouraged by the example set by Michael Sells in his 1989 volume *Desert Tracings*, I decided to experiment with form. It was for this reason that I opted not to have a single format for the poems; their appearance on the page was not to be uniform throughout the volume. I employed a number of formats, including, for example, labile and hard caesuras, and dividing one line of Arabic into two or three lines of English. The formatting of each poem in translation represented both the results of my engagement with the format initially chosen by the team that translated it, and my thoughts on the poem after many repeated readings of it in the course of finalizing the project.

I submitted the manuscript to LAL for its blind peer-review process in July 2017. I also sent it to Richard Sieburth. The executive editors invited Peter Cole to write the foreword to the volume, sending him the manuscript as an indication of the contents and style of the book. As ever, I received extremely helpful feedback from the reviewers, and the book was much improved by them. Then, on September 16, Richard forwarded an email from Peter that would change everything. Peter pointed out that the one thing he had missed when reading the translations was the very thing we had set out to achieve—a consistent voice. He very kindly gave a few examples of the sorts of things he meant. And then he encouraged me, with Richard's help, to reimagine the whole corpus of translations afresh.

I realized straightaway that my vexation with the formal incongruities of Arabic and English poetry had made me miss the basic point about any literary translation—that its success depends on the words you choose and on how you use those words. It sounds so simple and obvious, yet it is so difficult to achieve. In the course of the most exhilarating (and possibly the most taxing) fortnight I have ever experienced as an academic, the whole project was overhauled and recast.

I produced a new version of each poem and sent it to Richard for comment. (I have a folder containing seventy-six documents of versions, retractions, corrections, cajolings, exhortations, and tracked changes.) Every line and word was discussed and analyzed, and sometimes disputed. I learned that I needed to pay particular attention to how I chose to organize words on the page, where the line breaks would fall, and where the stress would reside. I also learned that uniformity of format across all poems (and sometimes even within a single poem) would not help; quite the opposite: it could work to the detriment of the poem. The first intractable poem was Poem 28. The challenge lay in capturing the arc of this long poem—my principal solution was to use either a three- or a four-break line, to allow me the leeway required to maintain the drive of the poem. But by far the hardest poem in the volume to translate was ʿAntarah's best poem: the *Muʿallaqah*. I have counted fourteen versions to date, and as I write Richard and I are still debating the translation of the final line.

And so, six years on, the volume is finished. It demonstrates a pleasing harmony. LAL could not have attempted it without the initial instruction and guidance of Peter and Richard; I could not have finished it without Richard's brilliant lyricism and Peter's patient encouragement. To have had the chance to work with such fabulous scholars on this volume has been one of the highlights of my career.

I have introduced my translation of each poem with a few words intended both to help readers unfamiliar with this poetic tradition by providing them with some orientation, and to inform readers interested in the practical matters of translation of some of the decisions that underlie the versions of the poems offered in this volume. The poems have been given English titles.

In order to document my account of the genesis and the process of this translation, I provide the following list that identifies the teams of translators who worked on each poem and the years in which the versions were produced.

Poem 1	JEM (2015)/JEM–RS (2017)
Poem 2	GJ–MP–JEM (2014)/JEM–RS (2017)
Poem 3	JEM (2014)/JEM–RS (2017)
Poem 4	JL–ST (2013)/JEM–RS (2017)
Poem 5	CR–DS (2013)/JEM–RS (2017)
Poem 6	MC–TQ (2015)/JEM–RS (2017)
Poem 7	JB–JM–JEM (2013)/JEM–RS (2017)
Poem 8	CR–DS (2013)/JEM–RS (2017)
Poem 9	JB–DS (2014)/JEM–RS (2017)
Poem 10	JL–ST (2013)/JEM–RS (2017)
Poem 11	MC–TQ (2013)/JEM–RS (2017)
Poem 12	CR–ST (2014)/JEM–RS (2017)
Poem 13	RC–PK–RS (2013)/JEM–RS (2017)
Poem 14	JL–ST (2013)/JEM–RS (2017)
Poem 15	JL–ST (2013)/JEM–RS (2017)
Poem 16	CR–DS (2013)/JEM–RS (2017)
Poem 17	JB–DS (2014)/JEM–RS (2017)
Poem 18	JL–ST (2013)/JEM–RS (2017)
Poem 19	RC–PK–RS (2013)/JEM–RS (2017)
Poem 20	MC–TQ (2013)/JEM–RS (2017)
Poem 21	JB–DS (2014)/JEM–RS (2017)
Poem 22	RC–PK–RS (2013)/JEM–RS (2017)

Poem 23	JB–JEM (2012)/JEM–RS (2017)
Poem 24	MC–TQ (2013)/JEM–RS (2017)
Poem 25	RC–PK–RS (2013)/JEM–RS (2017)
Poem 26	CR–DS (2013)/JEM–RS (2017)
Poem 27	JB–JM–JEM (2013)/JEM–RS (2017)
Poem 28	JEM (2016)/JEM–RS (2017)
Poem 29	CR–DS (2013) + JEM (2016)/JEM–RS (2017)
Poem 30	JEM (2016)/JEM–RS (2017)
Poem 31	JEM (2016)/JEM–RS (2017)
Poem 32	CR–DS (2013) + JEM (2016)/JEM–RS (2017)
Poem 33	JEM (2016)/JEM–RS (2017)
Poem 34	JEM (2016)/JEM–RS (2017)
Poem 35	JEM (2016)/JEM–RS (2017)
Poem 36	JEM (2016)/JEM–RS (2017)
Poem 37	JEM (2016)/JEM–RS (2017)
Poem 38	JEM (2016)/JEM–RS (2017)
Poem 39	JEM (2016)/JEM–RS (2017)
Poem 40	JEM (2016)/JEM–RS (2017)
Poem 41	JEM (2016)/JEM–RS (2017)
Poem 42	JEM (2016)/JEM–RS (2017)
Poem 43	JEM (2016) JEM–RS (2017)
Poem 44	SA–JL (2014)/JEM–RS (2017)
Poem 45	JL–ST (2012)/JEM–RS (2017)
Poem 46	PK–RS (2012)/JEM–RS (2017)
Poem 47	CR–DS (2012)/JEM–RS (2017)
Poem 48	JL–ST (2012)/JEM–RS (2017)
Poem 49	JEM (2012)/JEM–RS (2017)
Poem 50	JB–JM–JEM (2013) + JEM (2016)/JEM–RS (2017)
Poem 51	JB–JEM (2012) + JEM (2016)/JEM–RS (2017)

Key: SA: Sean Antony; JB: Julia Bray; MC: Michael Cooperson; RC: Robyn Creswell; GJ: Gemma Juan-Simó; PK: Philip Kennedy; JL: Joseph Lowry; JEM: James Montgomery; JM: Jeannie Miller; MP: Maurice Pomerantz; TQ: Tahera Qutbuddin; CR: Chip Rossetti; DS: Devin Stewart; RS: Richard Sieburth; ST: Shawkat Toorawa.

Maps

I have prepared two maps for this volume, the first designed to display the distribution of tribes (loosely conceived) in pre-Islamic Arabia ca. AD 600, the second to illustrate the topography of the poetry of ʿAntarah. Both maps are admittedly dense and replete with information. I hope that the maps will repay the reader's attention.

The first map is principally based on the one furnished by Régis Blachère in his magisterial *Histoire de la littérature arabe des origines à la fin du XVᵉ siècle de J.-C.*, volume two, page 248. With the aid of cartographer Martin Grosch, I adapted Blachère's map to show settled tribes, as well as natural features. The one alteration we were forced to make to Blachère's original was to shift northward the location of the lands of ʿAbs, who by the end of the century had been driven north, expelled from their traditional pasture grounds during the War of Dāḥis and al-Ghabrāʾ. I also chose the unusual term "transhumant" to describe the non-sedentary groups, in order to stress that the nomadism and pastoralism of these groups were controlled and were principally determined by the seasons.

In order to produce the second map, I relied on the seminal work by Ulrich Thilo on the place names of pre-Islamic poetry (*Die Ortsnamen in der altarabischen Poesie*) and the amazing topographical lexicon of al-Bakrī (d. 487/1094), *The Comprehensive Lexicon of Names of Cities and Places* (*Mustaʿjam mā staʿjama min asmāʾ al-bilād wa-l-mawāḍiʿ*). Martin Grosch then checked my identifications and conjectures against his databases, GeoSearch among them. We agreed that we should look for modern names that we could identify with some confidence (however modest) and match them with the names provided in the poetry. Much of the work remains conjectural, and we have indicated such conjectural sites with gray symbols, using bold type for all the toponyms found in ʿAntarah's poetry. The result is, I think, a fairly remarkable visual attestation of just how prominent the highlands of Najd and Yamāmah are in ʿAntarah's poems.

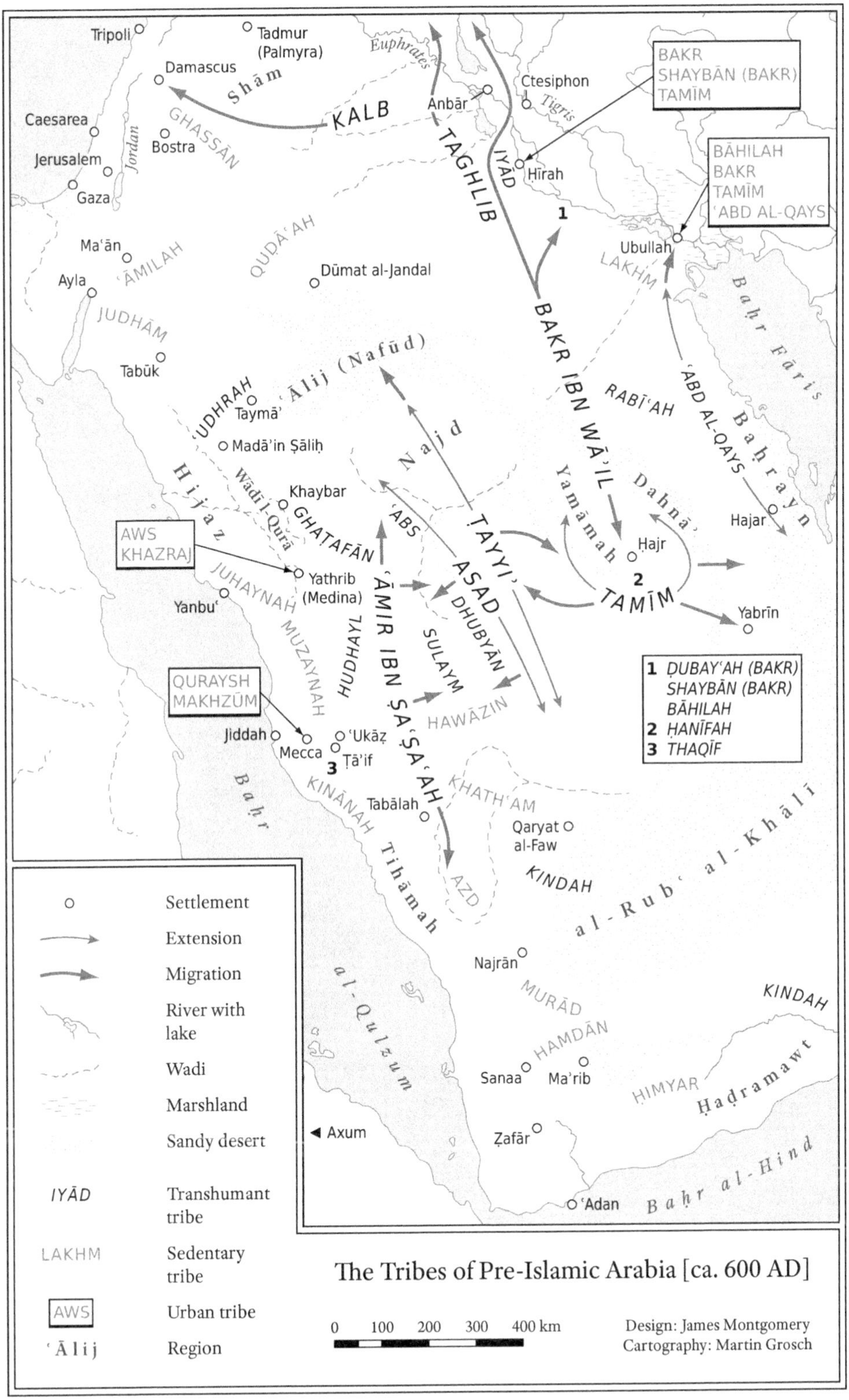
Tripoli
Tadmur (Palmyra)
Euphrates
Damascus
Shām
KALB
Anbār
Ctesiphon
Tigris
BAKR
SHAYBĀN (BAKR)
TAMĪM
Caesarea
GHASSĀN
Bostra
Jordan
TAGHLIB
IYĀD
Ḥīrah
BĀHILAH
BAKR
TAMĪM
ʿABD AL-QAYS
Jerusalem
Gaza
1
QUḌĀʿAH
Ubullah
Maʿān
ĀMILAH
LAKHM
Ayla
Dūmat al-Jandal
JUDHĀM
BAKR IBN WĀʾIL
Baḥr Fāris
Tabūk
ʿĀlij (Nafūd)
RABĪʿAH
ʿABD AL-QAYS
ʿUDHRAH
Taymāʾ
Najd
Madāʾin Ṣāliḥ
Baḥrayn
Ḥijāz
Wādī l-Qurā
Yamāmah
Dahnāʾ
Khaybar
ʿABS
ṬAYYIʾ
Hajar
GHAṬAFĀN
Ḥajr
AWS
KHAZRAJ
ASAD
2
Yathrib (Medina)
TAMĪM
JUHAYNAH
Yanbuʿ
ʿĀMIR IBN ṢAʿṢAʿAH
DHUBYĀN
Yabrīn
MUZAYNAH
SULAYM
HUDHAYL
1 ḌUBAYʿAH (BAKR)
SHAYBĀN (BAKR)
BĀHILAH
2 ḤANĪFAH
3 THAQĪF
QURAYSH
MAKHZŪM
HAWĀZIN
Jiddah
Mecca
ʿUkāẓ
Ṭāʾif
3
Baḥr
KINĀNAH
Tabālah
KHATHʿAM
Qaryat al-Faw
al-Rubʿ al-Khālī
Tihāmah
AZD
KINDAH
Settlement
Extension
Migration
River with lake
Wadi
Marshland
Sandy desert
IYĀD
Transhumant tribe
LAKHM
Sedentary tribe
AWS
Urban tribe
ʿĀlij
Region
Najrān
al-Qulzum
MURĀD
KINDAH
HAMDĀN
Sanaa
Maʾrib
ḤIMYAR
Ḥaḍramawt
Axum
Ẓafār
ʿAdan
Baḥr al-Hind
The Tribes of Pre-Islamic Arabia [ca. 600 AD]
0 100 200 300 400 km
Design: James Montgomery
Cartography: Martin Grosch

A *Dhū l-'Ushayrah*
B *Dhū Akhtāl* ?
C *Dhāt al-Rimth* ?

Kathīb (□)
Shibāk (□)
Sīf (□)

Nujayrah (□)
Ridā' (◡)

1 Ṭawī
2 *Uthāl*
3 *Qārah*
4 *Ghaylam*
5 *Mutathallam*
6 *Lakīk*
7 *Dhāt al-Ḥarmal*

○ Settlement
□ Place
◡ Well
● Waterhole
▲▲ Mountain range
◯ Cluster of sites

Khaybar Settlement, place
Jifār Well, waterhole
'Ālij Region
Tigris River, wadi

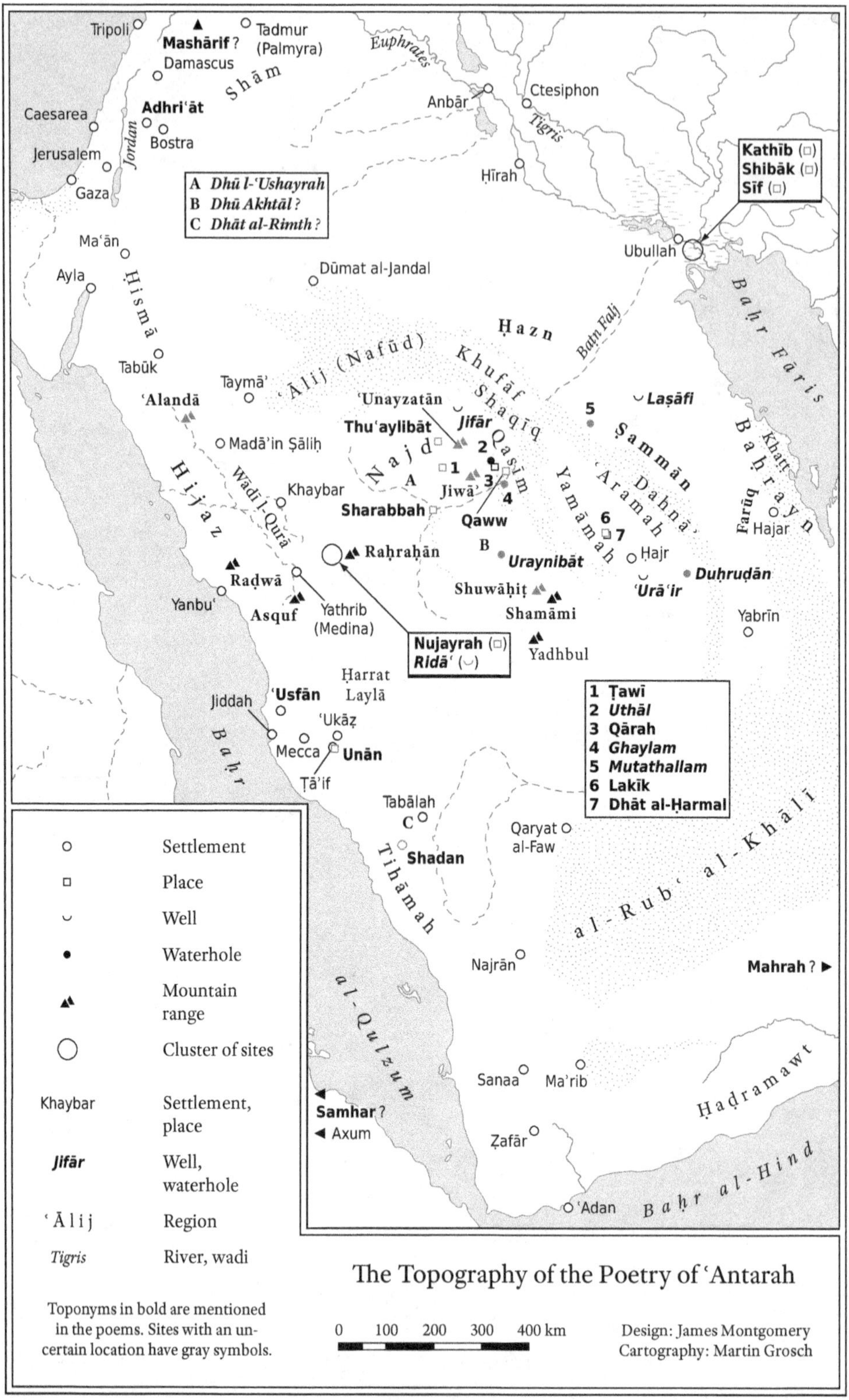

The Topography of the Poetry of 'Antarah

Toponyms in bold are mentioned in the poems. Sites with an uncertain location have gray symbols.

0 100 200 300 400 km

Design: James Montgomery
Cartography: Martin Grosch

Notes to the Introduction

1 The appendices to this book contain translations of the earliest account of ʿAntarah (by Ibn Qutaybah), the entry on him in al-Iṣbahānī's *Book of Songs*, the extensive narratives that accompany almost all the poems in the commentaries by al-Shantamarī and al-Baṭalyawsī, and many of the narrative settings for those poems to be found in *The Epic of ʿAntar*.

2 In the popular tradition, the hero's name is invariably ʿAntar, in the erudite tradition ʿAntarah.

3 See Appendix §2.2, §2.10. Zabībah was presumably an Ethiopian chattel slave (*amah*) and concubine (*jāriyah*), perhaps captured in battle and/or imported from South Arabia. That she bore children to other men (Appendix §2.2) might imply that her ownership changed hands.

4 Appendix §2.1.

5 Appendix §1.6, §2.29.

6 Poem 6, p. 37.

7 See Appendix §1.1, §2.1, §§3.1.1–2.

8 The root *ʿ-b-l* expresses largeness in size and fleshiness of body—in other words, ʿAblah is an instantiation of the abundantly fleshy (steatopygous) female worshiped by many northern Arab poets: see Montgomery, "The Empty Ḥijāz." Neither Ibn Qutaybah nor al-Iṣbahānī (see Appendices 1 and 2) make any mention of the beloved ʿAblah, implying that this aspect of the legend was not yet as developed as it was later to become.

9 In Arabic sources, Axum is referred to as "Ḥabashah."

10 After Robin, "Marib"; Müller, "Mārib," notes that according to inscriptions the dam was still functioning in the early seventh century and so there may have been no cataclysm to which mass migration could have been attributed.

11 Donner, *The Early Islamic Conquests*, 11. On Arabian nomadism: Donner, "The Role of Nomads," 21–33; Hodgson, *The Venture of Islam*, 147–51.

12 See the detailed study of Arabs and Arabness by Webb, *Imagining the Arabs*. One of his key arguments is that the philologists of the third/ninth century fashioned a "canonical" notion of Arabness that has influenced how we think about Arab origins ever since. See his chapter three, "Arabness from the Qur'an to an Ethnos," for a discussion of the Qur'anic use of the terms *aʿrāb* and *bādūn*.

13 See the important work of Miller, *Tribal Poetics in Early Arabic Culture* and "Seasonal Poetics." His basic point is that we must distinguish between Najdī and Ḥijāzī tribal customs and poetic traditions. We should further distinguish distinct traditions (be it by family, kin group, lineage, or poetic association) within the wider tradition of Najd; on this, see Montgomery, "The Deserted Encampment."

14 Macdonald, "Was the Nabataean Kingdom a 'Bedouin State'?," 102, n. 2.

15 Zwettler, "Maʿadd," 268, n. 78.

16 Whittow, "Rome and the Jafnids," 219 and n. 33.

17 Dostal, "The Evolution of Bedouin Life," 12 and 29.

18 Retsö, *The Arabs in Antiquity*, 583 and 587.

19 See Millar, *The Roman Near East*, 221–22 and 511–15.

20 Dostal, "The Development of Bedouin Life," 129; see also Zwettler, "Maʿadd," 280–84, for a judicious assessment of Dostal's theories, and subsequent critiques and modifications that stress the importance of the cavalry and consider the pack camel to be ancillary to the horse in military and logistical terms. On the elitism of the camel "nomads," see Hodgson, *The Venture of Islam*, 150. See also Donner, "The Bakr b. Wā'il Tribes," 22, who notes: "The great majority of the groups within the B. Shaybān were nomadic or partly nomadic, and it was on this warrior aristocracy of powerful nomadic groups that the Shaybān's claims to leadership or noble status among the Bakr tribes rested."

21 Zwettler, "Maʿadd," 285.

22 Zwettler, "Maʿadd," 285–86.

23 Whittow, "Rome and the Jafnids," 222–23, argues that "great power competition from the third century onwards had led to a phase of political development among the Bedu which transformed the previously unthreatening Bedu pastoralists into groupings capable of forcing the settled powers to take note."

24 Jenssen, "Arabic Language."

25 I have relied on Bellamy, "Dāḥis" and Fück, "Ghaṭafān."

26 See Montgomery, "Dichotomy in *Jāhilī* Poetry."

27 Jamil, "Playing for Time," 67.

28 See Miller, "Warrior Elites on the Verge of Islam."

29 Jamil, "Playing for Time," 68.

30 My understanding of pre-Islamic poetry has been greatly enhanced by the study of Nadia Jamil, *Ethics and Poetry*, whose reconstruction of the pre-Islamic cosmos I find exciting and inspiring.

31 The prevalent view of the desert as the landscape domesticated and tamed by the heroism of the desert traveler originates in English with the writings of the Blunts: see

Melman, "The Middle East/Arabia," 113–15. It is not clear, however, whether the pre-Islamic warriors viewed the desert in such terms, or indeed whether they viewed themselves as heroes, however heroic they may have considered their actions to have been. It is also not clear whether they developed specific hero cults, along the lines of how the ancient Greeks made heroes of dead contemporaries, and how Pindar made heroes of the kings and athletes he composed for: see Currie, *Pindar and the Cult of Heroes*. Pre-Islamic laments for dead warriors do tend to suggest that deceased contemporaries may have been assimilated into a cult of heroic ancestors, and although there do not appear to have been any physical cultic centers for the heroic dead, perhaps the memorization and recitation of poetry replaced any specific cultic locus. Recent discoveries of ancient human and horse or camel burials in the Gulf states suggest that there may have been a physical aspect to the memorialization of the heroic dead (see the articles listed in the further reading, under "camel burials"). The sparseness of this evidence and the temporal and geographical distance between these protohistoric sites and the qasida poetry of the sixth century notwithstanding, I do wonder whether the desert journey on camelback, so often read as simply a heroic vaunt, may not actually be a defiance of Time, an evocation of the quest for postmortem memorialization.

32 Montgomery, "Listening for the Poem."

33 The priamel is a technique of eulogy common in ancient Greek poetry, in which three things are praised, usually in an ascending order and couched in similar terms, with the fourth expressed as an exception to the preceding three. See Carson, *If Not, Winter*, 362.

34 Ibn Qutaybah, *The Excellence of the Arabs*, 2:151 (§2.8.1).

35 Al-Jāḥiẓ, *Bayān*, 1:20.19–21.4. Tahera Qutbuddin informs me that ʿAntarah's poetry was used to incite warriors in Umayyad times, and referred me to Ṣafwat, *Jamharat khuṭab al-ʿArab*, 2:464: "Who will recite the poetry of ʿAntarah to rouse the troops?"

36 See further Appendix §2.31.

37 The battle lore recorded by al-Shantamarī and al-Baṭalyawsī for the poetry of ʿAntarah has been translated as part of Appendix 3. I have relied on the excellent article by Isabel Toral-Niehoff, "Talking about Arab Origins." See also Webb, *Imagining the Arabs*.

38 Toral-Niehoff, "Talking about Arab Origins," 51.

39 See Ibn al-Kalbī, *Ǧamharat an-Nasab*.

40 Abū ʿUbaydah, *Naqāʾiḍ*, 1:83–108.

41 Legend has it that these poems were so called because they were inscribed on fabric and "suspended" from the walls of the Kaaba. The original meaning of the word was probably "the Choice or Precious Odes." The *Muʿallaqāt* were a fluid corpus: the number

of poems included varied from seven to ten, and in total fourteen such poems are so designated. See Lecomte, "al-Muʿallaḳāt."

42 The poems the attribution of which was questioned, though al-Aṣmāʿī is not mentioned by name, are Poems 24, 26, and 27. Al-Aṣmāʿī rejected the attribution to ʿAntarah of Poem 23, ascribing it to Kuthayyir ibn ʿUrwah al-Nahshalī, a pre-Islamic poet about whom almost nothing is known.

43 Ibn Maymūn's versions are edited in full in the online edition of the Arabic text at www.libraryofarabicliterature.org.

44 See Appendix §1.2 and §1.4 (Ibn Qutaybah) and Appendix §§3.1.1–2 (al-Shantamarī and al-Baṭalyawsī).

45 See Appendix §2.5, §§3.10.1–2.

46 See Appendix §2.14, §§3.6.1–2.

47 See Appendix §§2.19–20, §3.30.1.

48 See Appendix §2.26, §3.33.1.

49 See the relevant entries in the Glossary for more information about these scholars.

50 The *isnād* (chain) for the *riwāyah* (transmission) is: al-Aṣmaʿī → al-Sijistānī → Ibn Durayd → Abū ʿAlī l-Qālī → Ibn Abī l-Ḥabbāb → Ibn Faḍālah → al-Ṭuṭāliqī → Abū Sahl al-Ḥarrānī → al-Shantamarī. See ʿAwwād and al-Tūmī, in al-Baṭalyawsī, *Sharḥ al-ashʿār*, 1:10 (introduction).

51 Consider the following comment, made by al-Baṭalyawsī as part of his commentary on the seventh poem in his recension (i.e., Poem 3): "This is a verse that Abū ʿUbaydah included, but not quoted by Yaʿqūb" (i.e., Ibn al-Sikkīt): al-Baṭalyawsī, *Sharḥ al-ashʿār*, 2:272.

52 For a full discussion, see Lyons, *The Arabian Epic.*

53 I have relied on Heller, "Sīrat ʿAntar," Heath, "Sīrat ʿAntar," and Cherkaoui, "ʿAntarah."

54 For these two print versions (Cairene and Levantine), see Heath, "Sīrat ʿAntar." I have only had access to the Levantine version of *The Epic of ʿAntar*, but have relied on the editions of the poetry as provided by both al-Bustānī and Shalabī. See Appendix 3 for translations of a few of the narrative settings for this poetry.

55 It will be published by IDW Publishing. A trailer produced for Comic-Con San Diego 2017 was posted on You Tube: https://www.youtube.com/watch?v=evUoMj1VjWc. See also the website: https://antartheblackknight.com. Arberry, *The Seven Odes*, 153–70, tells the story of how the romance of ʿAntar and ʿAblah captivated the European world in the eighteenth and nineteenth centuries.

56 As outlined above, there is a possibility that the material underlying the recension preserved by al-Baṭalyawsī predates the selection of al-Aṣmaʿī (as it survives in al-Shantamarī's recension of al-Sijistānī's(?) version).

57 I make an entirely artificial distinction between the process and stage of redaction, whereby al-Aṣmaʿī or Abū ʿUbaydah gathered the poetry of ʿAntarah for dissemination among pupils, and the processes and stages of version and recension, whereby these pupils and subsequent scholars prepared the redactions of their teachers or predecessors for dissemination. It is unclear whether the collection of *six* pre-Islamic poets is to be attributed to al-Aṣmaʿī or al-Sijistānī, or even to al-Shantamarī. It is also unclear what, if anything, the choice of the number *six* has to do with other collections, such as the *seven Muʿallaqāt*, though in fact the actual number of poems included among the *Muʿallaqāt* varies from seven to eight to ten, and the poems and poets included in the various collections also display considerable variation.

58 Ahlwardt's edition of the manuscript in *The Divans of the Six Ancient Arab Poets* is based on the corrected readings.

59 The full critical apparatus can be found on the Library of Arabic Literature's website at www.libraryofarabicliterature.org/extra-2/. It is also available in print format: see Montgomery, *The Dīwān of ʿAntarah ibn Shaddād: A Literary-Historical Study.*

60 The manuscript of the commentary of Muḥammad ibn Ibrāhīm ibn Muḥammad al-Ḥaḍramī (d. 609/1212) does not quote the poetry it was intended to explicate: see al-Ḥaḍramī, *Mushkil iʿrāb al-ashʿār al-sittah al-jāhiliyyah.* I would like to thank Dr S. Nasser of Harvard University for giving me access to a copy of the text.

61 See also two further editions: *Sharḥ dawāwīn al-shuʿarāʾ al-sittah al-jāhiliyyīn*, edited by Muḥammad ʿAbd al-Munʿim Khafājī; *Six Early Arab Poets*, edited by Albert Arazi and Salman Masalha.

62 I have consulted *Sharḥ dīwān ʿAntarah ibn Shaddād*, edited by ʿAbd al-Munʿim ʿAbd al-Raʾūf Shalabī, and *Dīwān ʿAntarah*, edited by Karam al-Bustānī; unfortunately, the commentary attributed to al-Khaṭīb al-Tibrīzī in *Sharḥ dīwān ʿAntarah*, edited by Majīd Ṭarād, is in fact an amalgam of the commentaries of al-Shantamarī and al-Baṭalyawsī (though, according to Sezgin, *Geschichte*, 2:112, al-Tibrīzī did indeed write a commentary on ʿAntarah). Other editions include those of Amīn Saʿīd (n.d.), Fawzī ʿAṭawī (1968), Sayf al-Dīn al-Kātib and Aḥmad ʿIṣām al-Kātib (1981), ʿUmar Fārūq al-Ṭabbāʿ (1995?), and Muḥammad Ḥammūd (1996).

Al-Aṣmaʿī's Redaction

~ 1 ~

Did poetry die?

This ode is a complex work of art characterized by an impulse to destabilize meaning and confound expectation, and by a relish for the grotesque. Nothing is quite what it seems, and the poem's descriptions and utterances are labile, slippery, and unstable—its reality is a shimmer of confusion. The exultant savagery to which the ode gives voice wreaks havoc on all but its own stridency, as ultimately meaning is found only in battle and death, and possibly in the poetry that sings of them. Many pre-Islamic odes engage in a conversation, whether with the poet's beloved, his patron, his tribe, or his opponents. ʿAntarah's ode is not in conversation with ʿAblah, as we might first suspect, but with Death, who, with its avatars (the hyenas and vultures), arrives at the end of the poem like a god in response to a prayer. Through its presence in the world and in the poem, Death, the ultimate absence, sanctifies the poet's worshipful act of killing and the soundscape in which he piously chants its majesty.

هَلْ غَادَرَ ٱلشُّعَرَاءُ مِنْ مُتَرَدَّمِ   أَمْ هَلْ عَرَفْتَ ٱلدَّارَ بَعْدَ تَوَهُّمِ
أَعْيَاكَ رَسْمُ ٱلدَّارِ لَمْ يَتَكَلَّمِ   حَتَّى تَكَلَّمَ كَٱلْأَصَمِّ ٱلْأَعْجَمِ
وَلَقَدْ حَبَسْتُ بِهَا طَوِيلًا نَاقَتِي   أَشْكُو إِلَى سُفْعٍ رَوَاكِدَ جُثَّمِ
يَا دَارَ عَبْلَةَ بِٱلْجِوَاءِ تَكَلَّمِي   وَعِمِي صَبَاحًا دَارَ عَبْلَةَ وَٱسْلَمِي
دَارٌ لِآنِسَةٍ غَضِيضٍ طَرْفُهَا   طَوْعِ ٱلْعِنَاقِ لَذِيذَةِ ٱلْمُتَبَسَّمِ
فَوَقَفْتُ فِيهَا نَاقَتِي وَكَأَنَّهَا   فَدَنٌ لِأَقْضِيَ حَاجَةَ ٱلْمُتَلَوِّمِ
وَتَحُلُّ عَبْلَةُ بِٱلْجِوَاءِ وَأَهْلُنَا   بِٱلْحَزْنِ فَٱلصَّمَّانِ فَٱلْمُتَثَلَّمِ
حُيِّيتَ مِنْ طَلَلٍ تَقَادَمَ عَهْدُهُ   أَقْوَى وَأَقْفَرَ بَعْدَ أُمِّ ٱلْهَيْثَمِ
شَطَّتْ مَزَارَ ٱلْعَاشِقِينَ فَأَصْبَحَتْ   عَسِرًا عَلَيَّ طِلَابُكِ ٱبْنَةَ مَخْرَمِ
عُلِّقْتُهَا عَرَضًا وَأَقْتُلُ قَوْمَهَا   زَعْمًا وَرَبِّ ٱلْبَيْتِ لَيْسَ بِمَزْعَمِ
وَلَقَدْ نَزَلْتِ فَلَا تَظُنِّي غَيْرَهُ   مِنِّي بِمَنْزِلَةِ ٱلْمُحَبِّ ٱلْمُكْرَمِ
كَيْفَ ٱلْمَزَارُ وَقَدْ تَرَبَّعَ أَهْلُهَا   بِعُنَيْزَتَيْنِ وَأَهْلُنَا بِٱلْغَيْلَمِ
إِنْ كُنْتِ أَزْمَعْتِ ٱلْفِرَاقَ فَإِنَّمَا   شُدَّتْ رِكَابُكُمُ بِلَيْلٍ مُظْلِمِ
مَا رَاعَنِي إِلَّا حَمُولَةُ أَهْلِهَا   وَسْطَ ٱلدِّيَارِ تَسَفُّ حَبَّ ٱلْخِمْخِمِ
فِيهَا ٱثْنَتَانِ وَأَرْبَعُونَ حَلُوبَةً   سُودًا كَخَافِيَةِ ٱلْغُرَابِ ٱلْأَسْحَمِ
إِذْ تَسْتَبِيكَ بِأَصْلَتِيٍّ نَاعِمٍ   عَذْبٍ مُقَبَّلُهُ لَذِيذِ ٱلْمَطْعَمِ
وَكَأَنَّمَا نَظَرَتْ بِعَيْنَيْ شَادِنٍ   رَشَأٍ مِنَ ٱلْغِزْلَانِ لَيْسَ بِتَوْأَمِ

البحر: الكامل.

Did poetry die in its war with the poets?
Is this where ʿAblah walked? Think![1]
The ruins were deaf—refused to reply,
then shouted out in a foreign tongue.[2]
My camel tried to withdraw—
I couldn't move,
ranting at the charred stones.
"Speak. Live. Prosper.
Here in Jiwāʾ ʿAblah dwelled,
a timid gazelle, doe eyes,
sweet smile, soft neck."
I reined in my camel, big as a fort—
I needed to weep, needed the shame.
ʿAblah lived in Jiwāʾ,
our people in Ḥazn, Ṣammān, and Mutathallam.[3]
Rise, desolate traces, from dust
now that ʿAblah's gone
too far for a lover's visit.
The pursuit's too hard, Bint Makhram.[4]
By chance we came together
as I battled your tribe.
By God, this is no idle boast.[5]
You seized my heart
make no mistake
about my love—
with your people in ʿUnayzatān,
ours in Ghaylam, how can I visit?
Did you decide to leave?
The night was black, your camels
readied. I shuddered at the sight
of pack camels by the tents,
chewing khimkhim, and forty-two
dark milch camels,
their coats' sheen like a raven's wing.

وَكَأَنَّ فَارَةَ تَاجِرٍ بِقَسِيمَةٍ   سَبَقَتْ عَوَارِضَهَا إِلَيْكَ مِنَ ٱلْفَمِ

أَوْ رَوْضَةً أُنُفًا تَضَمَّنَ نَبْتَهَا   غَيْثٌ قَلِيلُ ٱلدِّمْنِ لَيْسَ بِمَعْلَمِ

أَوْ عَاتِقًا مِنْ أَذْرِعَاتٍ مُعْتَقًا   مِمَّا تُعَتِّقُهُ مُلُوكُ ٱلْأَعْجَمِ

جَادَتْ عَلَيْهَا كُلُّ عَيْنٍ ثَرَّةٍ   فَتَرَكْنَ كُلَّ حَدِيقَةٍ كَٱلدِّرْهَمِ

سَحًّا وَتَسْكَابًا فَكُلَّ عَشِيَّةٍ   يَجْرِي عَلَيْهَا ٱلْمَاءُ لَمْ يَتَصَرَّمِ

فَتَرَى ٱلذُّبَابَ بِهَا يُغَنِّي وَحْدَهُ   هَزِجًا كَفِعْلِ ٱلشَّارِبِ ٱلْمُتَرَنِّمِ

غَرِدًا يَسُنُّ ذِرَاعَهُ بِذِرَاعِهِ   فِعْلَ ٱلْمُكِبِّ عَلَى ٱلزِّنَادِ ٱلْأَجْذَمِ

تُمْسِي وَتُصْبِحُ فَوْقَ ظَهْرِ حَشِيَّةٍ   وَأَبِيتُ فَوْقَ سَرَاةِ أَدْهَمَ مُلْجَمِ

وَحَشِيَّتِي سَرْجٌ عَلَى عَبْلِ ٱلشَّوَى   نَهْدٍ مَرَاكِلُهُ نَبِيلِ ٱلْمَحْزِمِ

هَلْ تُبْلِغَنِّي دَارَهَا شَدَنِيَّةٌ   لُعِنَتْ بِمَحْرُومِ ٱلشَّرَابِ مُصَرَّمِ

خَطَّارَةٌ غِبَّ ٱلسُّرَى زَيَّافَةٌ   تَقِصُ ٱلْإِكَامَ بِكُلِّ خُفٍّ مِيثَمِ

وَكَأَنَّمَا أَقِصُ ٱلْإِكَامَ عَشِيَّةً   بِقَرِيبِ بَيْنَ ٱلْمَنْسِمَيْنِ مُصَلَّمِ

يَأْوِي إِلَى حِزَقِ ٱلنَّعَامِ كَمَا أَوَتْ   حِزَقٌ يَمَانِيَةٌ لِأَعْجَمَ طِمْطِمِ

يَتْبَعْنَ قُلَّةَ رَأْسِهِ وَكَأَنَّهُ   زَوْجٌ عَلَى حَرَجٍ لَهُنَّ مُخَيَّمِ

Then a sudden light, a flash
    of teeth sweet to mouth and tongue.
I'm caught—the thought
    of this young fawn and her tender stare,[6]
her scent wafting before her smile,
    sprung from a merchant's musk pouch[7]
or strong Adhriʿāt wine
    which foreign kings like to age
or from a rain-soaked field of flowers
    known to few beasts of the wild[8]
where showers have been kind
    and pools glint like silver coins
in downpours from the clouds—
    evenings when water flows unchecked
and the lone hopper, look,
    screeches its drunken song
scraping out a tune
    leg on leg like a one-arm man
bent over a fire stick.
    By day and dark she lies on her pillow.
My nights I pass in the saddle
    of a black horse, bridled,
its leg strong, flank round, girth lean.

Can I reach her on a shadanī camel,
    her teats snipped, cursed to be dry?[9]
She's a high-stepper, tail still twitching
    after a long night's ride,
feet like mallets as though
    I were smashing stones and hills
on the back of a dock-ear pinch-toe
    ostrich dashing to his flock
as Yemenis rush to a stuttering stranger,[10]
    sprinting to his nest in Dhū l-ʿUshayrah,[11]
his crown like a cover draped
    over bier posts held high

صَعْلٍ يَعُودُ بِذِي ٱلْعُشَيْرَةِ بَيْضَهُ   كَٱلْعَبْدِ ذِي ٱلْفَرْوِ ٱلطَّوِيلِ ٱلْأَصْلَمِ

شَرِبَتْ بِمَاءِ ٱلدُّحْرُضَيْنِ فَأَصْبَحَتْ   زَوْرَاءَ تَنْفِرُ عَنْ حِيَاضِ ٱلدَّيْلَمِ

وَكَأَنَّمَا يَنْأَى بِجَانِبِ دَفِّهَا ٱلْـوَحْشِيِّ بَعْدَ مَخِيلَةٍ وَتَزَغُّمِ

هِرٌّ جَنِيبٌ كُلَّمَا عَطَفَتْ لَهُ   غَضْبَى ٱتَّقَاهَا بِٱلْيَدَيْنِ وَبِٱلْفَمِ

أَبْقَى لَهَا طُولُ ٱلسِّفَارِ مُقَرْمَدًا   سَنَدًا وَمِثْلَ دَعَائِمِ ٱلْمُتَخَيِّمِ

بَرَكَتْ عَلَى مَاءِ ٱلرِّدَاعِ كَأَنَّمَا   بَرَكَتْ عَلَى قَصَبٍ أَجَشَّ مُهَضَّمِ

وَكَأَنَّ رُبًّا أَوْ كُحَيْلًا مُعْقَدًا   حَشَّ ٱلْقِيَانُ بِهِ جَوَانِبَ قُمْقُمِ

يَنْبَاعُ مِنْ ذِفْرَى غَضُوبٍ حُرَّةٍ   زَيَّافَةٍ مِثْلِ ٱلْفَنِيقِ ٱلْمُقْرَمِ

إِنْ تُغْدِفِي دُونِي ٱلْقِنَاعَ فَإِنَّنِي   طَبٌّ بِأَخْذِ ٱلْفَارِسِ ٱلْمُسْتَلْئِمِ

أَثْنِي عَلَيَّ بِمَا عَلِمْتِ فَإِنَّنِي   سَمْحٌ مُخَالَقَتِي إِذَا لَمْ أُظْلَمِ

فَإِذَا ظُلِمْتُ فَإِنَّ ظُلْمِي بَاسِلٌ   مُرٌّ مَذَاقَتُهُ كَطَعْمِ ٱلْعَلْقَمِ

وَلَقَدْ شَرِبْتُ مِنَ ٱلْمُدَامَةِ بَعْدَمَا   رَكَدَ ٱلْهَوَاجِرُ بِٱلْمَشُوفِ ٱلْمُعْلَمِ

بِزُجَاجَةٍ صَفْرَاءَ ذَاتِ أَسِرَّةٍ   قُرِنَتْ بِأَزْهَرَ فِي ٱلشِّمَالِ مُفَدَّمِ

فَإِذَا شَرِبْتُ فَإِنَّنِي مُسْتَهْلِكٌ   مَالِي وَعِرْضِي وَافِرٌ لَمْ يُكْلَمِ

وَإِذَا صَحَوْتُ فَمَا أُقَصِّرُ عَنْ نَدًى   وَكَمَا عَلِمْتِ شَمَائِلِي وَتَكَرُّمِي

وَحَلِيلِ غَانِيَةٍ تَرَكْتُ مُجَدَّلًا   تَمْكُو فَرِيصَتُهُ كَشِدْقِ ٱلْأَعْلَمِ

tiny head and thin neck
    a dock-eared slave wrapped in furs.

She drinks at Duḥruḍān, and sprints
    from Daylam's wells with a mad stare,[12]
swaggering to and fro, groaning
    as if fleeing a cat strapped
to her right flank, against whose claw
    and fang she wheels in a rage.[13]
At the ride's end, she looms, massive
    as a fortress, kneeling at Ridāʿ's well
long legs like hoarse bass horns[14]
    sweat oozing from her neck like syrup
or the tar blacksmiths boil for pots—
    an angry, noble tail-switcher,[15]
bulky, big as a bite-scarred stud.

Turn away, if you wish, ʿAblah
    hide behind your veil!
I crush knights in armor and mail.
    Praise me for what you know me to be—
easy when not wronged
    but when wronged, savage in wrath,
bitter as a desert gourd.
    After the midday heat I drink
good wine from a streaked yellow glass
    strained from a gleaming jug
held fast in my left hand,
    paid for with minted gold.
I squander all I have on drink—
    keeping my honor whole.
Sober again, I'm lavish still
    ʿAblah, as you know.

عَجِلَتْ يَدَايَ لَهُ بِمَارِنِ طَعْنَةٍ   وَرَشَاشِ نَافِذَةٍ كَلَوْنِ ٱلْعَنْدَمِ

هَلَّا سَأَلْتِ ٱلْقَوْمَ يَا ٱبْنَةَ مَالِكٍ   إِنْ كُنْتِ جَاهِلَةً بِمَا لَمْ تَعْلَمِي

إِذْ لَا أَزَالُ عَلَى رِحَالَةِ سَابِحٍ   نَهْدٍ تَعَاوَرُهُ ٱلْكُمَاةُ مُكَلَّمِ

طَوْرًا يُعَرَّضُ لِلطِّعَانِ وَتَارَةً   يَأْوِي إِلَى حَصِدِ ٱلْقِسِيِّ عَرَمْرَمِ

يُخْبِرْكِ مَنْ شَهِدَ ٱلْوَقَائِعَ أَنَّنِي   أَغْشَى ٱلْوَغَى وَأَعِفُّ عِنْدَ ٱلْمَغْنَمِ

وَمُدَجَّجٍ كَرِهَ ٱلْكُمَاةُ نِزَالَهُ   لَا مُمْعِنٍ هَرَبًا وَلَا مُسْتَسْلِمِ

جَادَتْ يَدَايَ لَهُ بِعَاجِلِ طَعْنَةٍ   بِمُثَقَّفٍ صَدْقِ ٱلْقَنَاةِ مُقَوَّمِ

بِرَحِيبَةِ ٱلْفَرْغَيْنِ يَهْدِي جَرْسُهَا   بِٱللَّيْلِ مُعْتَسَّ ٱلسِّبَاعِ ٱلضُّرَّمِ

كَمَّشْتُ بِٱلرُّمْحِ ٱلطَّوِيلِ ثِيَابَهُ   لَيْسَ ٱلْكَرِيمُ عَلَى ٱلْقَنَا بِمُحَرَّمِ

وَتَرَكْتُهُ جَزَرَ ٱلسِّبَاعِ يَنُشْنَهُ   مَا بَيْنَ قُلَّةِ رَأْسِهِ وَٱلْمِعْصَمِ

وَمَشَكِّ سَابِغَةٍ هَتَكْتُ فُرُوجَهَا   بِٱلسَّيْفِ عَنْ حَامِي ٱلْحَقِيقَةِ مُعْلِمِ

رَبِذٍ يَدَاهُ بِٱلْقِدَاحِ إِذَا شَتَا   هَتَّاكِ غَايَاتِ ٱلتِّجَارِ مُلَوَّمِ

With quick thrust of my pliant spear
I felled a decent man
his jugular hissing, split like a harelip,[16]
spurting ʿandam resin red.
ʿAblah, Daughter of Mālik, ask
the riders if you want to hear
how I live in my horse's saddle,
swimming through troops
exposed to spear thrusts
wound after wound
charging the great harvest of bows.
The riders will tell you—
I enter the fray
then decline the spoils.

I gave the iron-mail warrior
relentless, feared by his foes,
a swift thrust with my war-tested spear,
straight and true.
A gash opened, wide as a bucket
the thud a signal
to hungry hyenas—
nobles like this are fair game.
My spear mucked him up.
He didn't look so fancy
lying there, a feast for night
predators ripping him head to wrist.[17]

Next came the standard-bearer
that fierce champion—
My sword split
the ripples of his mail!
He was nimble
gambling in winter
and blamed for his largesse
with the year's stock of wine—[18]

بَطَلٍ كَأَنَّ ثِيَابَهُ فِي سَرْحَةٍ   يُحْذَى نِعَالَ ٱلسِّبْتِ لَيْسَ بِتَوْأَمِ
لَمَّا رَآنِي قَدْ قَصَدْتُ أُرِيدُهُ   أَبْدَى نَوَاجِذَهُ لِغَيْرِ تَبَسُّمِ
فَطَعَنْتُهُ بِٱلرُّمْحِ ثُمَّ عَلَوْتُهُ   بِمُهَنَّدٍ صَافِي ٱلْحَدِيدَةِ مِخْذَمِ
عَهْدِي بِهِ شَدَّ ٱلنَّهَارِ كَأَنَّمَا   خُضِبَ ٱللَّبَانُ وَرَأْسُهُ بِٱلْعِظْلِمِ
يَا شَاةَ مَا قَنَصٍ لِمَنْ حَلَّتْ لَهُ   حَرُمَتْ عَلَيَّ وَلَيْتَهَا لَمْ تَحْرُمِ
فَبَعَثْتُ جَارِيَتِي فَقُلْتُ لَهَا ٱذْهَبِي   فَتَحَسَّسِي أَخْبَارَهَا لِي وَٱعْلَمِي
قَالَتْ رَأَيْتُ مِنَ ٱلْأَعَادِي غِرَّةً   وَٱلشَّاةُ مُمْكِنَةٌ لِمَنْ هُوَ مُرْتَمِ
فَكَأَنَّمَا ٱلْتَفَتَتْ بِجِيدِ جَدَايَةٍ   رَشَإٍ مِنَ ٱلْغِزْلَانِ حُرٍّ أَرْثَمِ
نُبِّئْتُ عَمْرًا غَيْرَ شَاكِرِ نِعْمَتِي   وَٱلْكُفْرُ مَخْبَثَةٌ لِنَفْسِ ٱلْمُنْعِمِ
وَلَقَدْ حَفِظْتُ وَصَاةَ عَمِّي بِٱلضُّحَى   إِذْ تَقْلِصُ ٱلشَّفَتَانِ عَنْ وَضَحِ ٱلْفَمِ
فِي حَوْمَةِ ٱلْمَوْتِ ٱلَّتِي لَا تَشْتَكِي   غَمَرَاتِهَا ٱلْأَبْطَالُ غَيْرَ تَغَمْغُمِ
إِذْ يَتَّقُونَ بِيَ ٱلْأَسِنَّةَ لَمْ أَخِمْ   عَنْهَا وَلَوْ أَنِّي تَضَايَقَ مُقْدَمِي

a hero born for battle
    sarḥah-tree tall
an only child
    in soft leather boots.[19]
He saw me charging and bared
    his teeth without a smile.
I speared him and finished him off
    with a keen, hard Indian blade.[20]
That morning his chest and head lay
    dyed dark in indigo.

Why, my doe, is it lawful for others
    to hunt you, but not for me?[21]
I said to my slave girl, "Go!
    Find out what you can."
Her news: "Your enemy's lulled.
    The freeborn doe is yours for the taking—
a snub-nosed gazelle offering
    her tender neck."

'Amr, I hear, didn't like my gift—
    ingratitude blights the soul.
When battered by waves of war
    heroes do not gripe,
their teeth aglint in a grimace
    as the fighters grunt
in a sea of battlerage.
    I heeded my uncle's counsel.
The soldiers used me as a shield
    against lances—
even sore pressed, I wouldn't flinch.[22]
    The army was on the march.
I wheeled and charged—
    true to my code.
"'Antar!" they roared—
    spears taut as well ropes

لَمَّا رَأَيْتُ ٱلْقَوْمَ أَقْبَلَ جَمْعُهُمْ   يَتَذَامَرُونَ كَرَرْتُ غَيْرَ مُذَمَّمِ
يَدْعُونَ عَنْتَرَ وَٱلرِّمَاحُ كَأَنَّهَا   أَشْطَانُ بِئْرٍ فِي لَبَانِ ٱلْأَدْهَمِ
مَا زِلْتُ أَرْمِيهِمْ بِثُغْرَةِ نَحْرِهِ   وَلَبَانِهِ حَتَّى تَسَرْبَلَ بِٱلدَّمِ
فَٱزْوَرَّ مِنْ وَقْعِ ٱلْقَنَا بِلَبَانِهِ   وَشَكَا إِلَيَّ بِعَبْرَةٍ وَتَحَمْحُمِ
لَوْ كَانَ يَدْرِي مَا ٱلْمُحَاوَرَةُ ٱشْتَكَى   أَوْ كَانَ يَدْرِي مَا جَوَابُ تَكَلُّمِي
وَٱلْخَيْلُ تَقْتَحِمُ ٱلْخَبَارَ عَوَابِسًا   مِنْ بَيْنِ شَيْظَمَةٍ وَأَجْرَدَ شَيْظَمِ
وَلَقَدْ شَفَى نَفْسِي وَأَبْرَأَ سُقْمَهَا   قِيلُ ٱلْفَوَارِسِ وَيْكَ عَنْتَرَ قَدِّمِ
ذُلُلٌ جِمَالِي حَيْثُ شِئْتُ مُشَايِعِي   لُبِّي وَأَحْفِزُهُ بِرَأْيٍ مُبْرَمِ
إِنِّي عَدَانِي أَنْ أَزُورَكِ فَٱعْلَمِي   مَا قَدْ عَلِمْتِ وَبَعْضُ مَا لَمْ تَعْلَمِي
حَالَتْ رِمَاحُ بَنِي بَغِيضٍ دُونَكُمْ   وَزَوَتْ جَوَانِي ٱلْحَرْبِ مَنْ لَمْ يُجْرِمِ
وَلَقَدْ كَرَرْتُ ٱلْمُهْرَ يَدْمَى نَحْرُهُ   حَتَّى ٱتَّقَتْنِي ٱلْخَيْلُ بِٱبْنَيْ حِذْيَمِ
وَلَقَدْ خَشِيتُ بِأَنْ أَمُوتَ وَلَمْ تَدُرْ   لِلْحَرْبِ دَائِرَةٌ عَلَى ٱبْنَيْ ضَمْضَمِ
ٱلشَّاتِمَيْ عِرْضِي وَلَمْ أَشْتِمْهُمَا   وَٱلنَّاذِرَيْنِ إِذَا لَمَ ٱلْقَهُمَا دَمِي
إِنْ يَفْعَلَا فَلَقَدْ تَرَكْتُ أَبَاهُمَا   جَزَرًا لِخَامِعَةٍ وَنَسْرٍ قَشْعَمِ

pierced my black steed's chest.[23]
    Again I battered them, and then
again. My horse, its withers and chest
    robed in blood, withdrew
from the spearclash grumbling softly
    —if he could speak
he'd have grumbled more—
    as the steeds
and giant mares
    scowled and sank
in the soft soil
    and the knights shouted
"Ho 'Antar, Onward!"
    How it healed my soul.

My camels go where I wish.
    My heart and will comply.
You think you know why I've been unable
    to visit you, 'Ablah
with Baghīḍ barring the way with spears,
    petty warmongers picking a fight?
I wheeled my bloodied colt.
    The knights cowered
behind Ḥidhyam's sons.[24]

I feared I'd die before war's mill
    could grind Ḍamḍam's sons to dust.[25]
Unprovoked, they vowed revenge
    and stained my honor.
There's still time for them to act!
    I killed their father—[26]
carrion for gimpy hyenas
    and grizzled vultures!

~ 2 ~

Damn the ruins!

In this victory chant, the poet sings of his tribe's military might and inveighs against the cowardice of their enemies, routed in battle. The first two lines banish ideas of desolation and its attendant emotions (dhikr al-aṭlāl), notions drowned out by eleven lines of raucous vaunt (mufākharah) in which warriors find fulfillment in the nihilism of victory. The heat of battle refashions reality, twisting it into grotesquery: the vanquished foes are zoomorphized into locusts, dogs, and old camels; women are gazelles; horses have manes like women's lice-ridden hair. While the poem is stalked by Death the transformer, to whom ʿAntarah and his warriors yield their souls as stakes in a grim game of chance, everything is overshadowed by Time the destroyer, who inflicts Death at whim.

أَلا قاتَلَ ٱللهُ ٱلطُّلولَ ٱلبَوالِيا   وَقاتَلَ ذِكْراكَ ٱلسِّنينَ ٱلخَوالِيا

وَقَوْلَكَ لِلشَّيْءِ ٱلَّذي لا تَنالُهُ   إِذا ما هُوَ ٱحْلَوْلَى أَلا لَيْتَ ذا لِيا

وَنَحْنُ مَنَعْنا بِٱلْفَرُوقِ نِساءَنا   نُطَرِّفُ عَنْها مُشْعِلاتٍ غَواشِيا

حَلَفْنا لَهُمْ وَٱلْخَيْلُ تَرْدِي بِنا مَعًا   نُزايِلُكُمْ حَتَّى تَهِرُّوا ٱلْعَوالِيا

عَوالِيَ زُرْقًا مِنْ رِماحِ رُدَيْنَةٍ   هَرِيرَ ٱلْكِلابِ يَتَّقِينَ ٱلْأَفاعِيا

تَفادَيْتُمُ أَسْتاهَ نِيبٍ تَجَمَّعَتْ   عَلَى رِمَّةٍ مِنَ ٱلْعِظامِ تَفادِيا

أَلَمْ تَعْلَمُوا أَنَّ ٱلْأَسِنَّةَ أَحْرَزَتْ   بَقِيَّتَنا لَوْ أَنَّ لِلدَّهْرِ باقِيا

أَبَيْنا أَبَيْنا أَنْ تَضِبَّ لِثاتُكُمْ   عَلَى مُرْشِقاتٍ كَٱلظِّباءِ عَواطِيا

وَقُلْتُ لِمَنْ قَدْ أَخْطَرَ ٱلْمَوْتَ نَفْسَهُ   أَلا مَنْ لِأَمْرٍ حازِمٍ قَدْ بَدا لِيا

وَقُلْتُ لَهُمْ رُدُّوا ٱلْمُغِيرَةَ عَنْ هَوًى   سَوابِقِها وَأَقْبِلُوها ٱلنَّواصِيا

فَما وَجَدُونا بِٱلْفَرُوقِ أُشابَةً   وَلا كُشُفًا وَلا دُعِينا مَوالِيا

وَإِنّا نَقُودُ ٱلْخَيْلَ حَتَّى رُؤُوسُها   رُؤُوسُ نِساءٍ لا يَجِدْنَ فَوالِيا

تَعالَوْا إِلَى ما تَعْلَمُونَ فَإِنَّنِي   أَرَى ٱلدَّهْرَ لا يُنْجِي مِنَ ٱلْمَوْتِ ناجِيا

البحر: الطويل.

Damn the ruins! Damn you!
    Stop dwelling on the past again.
Damn you! Stop all this talk—you
    won't ever get the sweet times back.
At al-Farūq we shielded our women,
    trampled the locusts underfoot
when the armies collided.
    "No retreat!" we swore.
"Our spears are from Rudaynah,[27]
    hard iron to make you whine
like dogs at the sight of vipers!"
    You bolted, rumps in the air
like old camels sniffing a corpse.[28]
    Couldn't you see—
our spears protect us?
    You're not going to drool
over our
    soft-necked gazelles.
Still, Time
    takes us all.[29]

Death appeared.
    I said to my men
"Who's up for a wager?
    Who'll face Death with me?[30]
Turn your horses
    the raiders are here.
Don't let them win
    the prize." They met
warriors, not slaves
    at al-Farūq.
We drive our horses
    hard, their manes
matted like lice-ridden hair.[31]
    Come back for more
now that you know—
    Time damns us all.

~ 3 ~

The Battle of ʿUrāʿir

A victory chant in which the poet intones his successful allegiance to the cause of Death. Despite his tribe's victory in battle, his soul's thirst for blood—its sickness—is unappeased. His warriors remain constantly at war so their wounds have neither opportunity nor time to heal. They derive their nourishment, contentment, and strength (ʿulālah, specifically the milk gathering in the camel's udder) from their swords, and the standards of the squadrons cast shadows that resemble the shadows of birds circling overhead, i.e., vultures, those grisly avatars of Death.

أَلَا هَلْ أَتَاهَا أَنَّ يَوْمَ عُرَاعِرٍ شَفَى سَقَمًا لَوْ كَانَتِ ٱلنَّفْسُ تَشْتَفِي
فَجِئْنَا عَلَى عَمْيَاءَ مَا جَمَعُوا لَنَا بِأَرْعَنَ لَا خَلٍّ وَلَا مُتَكَشِّفِ
تَمَارَوْا بِنَا إِذْ يَمْدُرُونَ حِيَاضَهُمْ عَلَى ظَهْرِ مَقْضِيٍّ مِنَ ٱلْأَمْرِ مُحْصَفِ
وَمَا نَذِرُوا حَتَّى غَشِينَا بُيُوتَهُمْ بِغَيْبَةِ مَوْتٍ مُسْبِلِ ٱلْوَدْقِ مُزْعِفِ
فَظِلْنَا نَكُرُّ ٱلْمَشْرَفِيَّةَ فِيهِمُ وَخِرْصَانَ لَدْنِ ٱلسَّمْهَرِيِّ ٱلْمُثَقَّفِ
عُلَالَتُنَا فِي كُلِّ يَوْمِ كَرِيهَةٍ بِأَسْيَافِنَا وَٱلْقَرْحُ لَمْ يَتَقَرَّفِ
أَبَيْنَا فَلَا نُعْطِي ٱلسَّوَاءَ عَدُوَّنَا قِيَامًا بِأَعْضَادِ ٱلسَّرَاءِ ٱلْمُعَطَّفِ
بِكُلِّ هَتُوفٍ عَجْسُهَا رَضَوِيَّةٍ وَسَهْمٍ كَسَيْرِ ٱلْحِمْيَرِيِّ ٱلْمُؤَنَّفِ
فَإِنْ يَكُ عِزٌّ فِي قُضَاعَةَ ثَابِتٌ فَإِنَّ لَنَا بِرَحْرَحَانَ وَأَسْقُفِ
كَتَائِبَ شُهْبًا فَوْقَ كُلِّ كَتِيبَةٍ لِوَاءٌ كَظِلِّ ٱلطَّائِرِ ٱلْمُتَصَرِّفِ

البحر: الطويل.

The Battle of ʿUrāʿir was a healing.
    Has she heard?
        Can my soul ever be cured?
We came upon a mighty army
    serried and drilled
        bigger than a mountain[32]
and digging the trough of war.[33]
    Our raid, a brutal storm of death,
        ended their dispute.
Charges of Mashraf blades and pliant
    Samhar spears[34]
        took them by surprise.

Nourished by grim battleswords
    our wounds still fresh
        we'll never cede to our foes!
We line up our taut Raḍwā bows
    grips groaning
        arrows tapered
            like tongues of Ḥimyar leather.

Let Quḍāʿah revel in glory.
    Our squadrons stand ready
        in Asquf and Raḥraḥān,
armor burnished
    arrayed for battle
        banners flapping
            like vultures' shadows.[35]

~ 4 ~

Your sorry ass

In this personal invective, the poet first humiliates his opponent through the grotesque physicality of the opening couplet. He then sings of his weapons: sword, bow, arrows, and spear. These are no ordinary weapons, however: his sword is his spouse, and it can never be blunted; it is held in a hand that never relaxes its grip (implying also that it never leaves his hand); the arrows are as light as leaves; the bow is so taut that its arc seems to form a sharp edge; the spear shafts are perfect; the glow of the spearheads (as they thirst for blood) light up the night sky like fires assuring travelers of a hospitable welcome. A pastoral scene taken from camel herding is used as a threat against ʿUmārah, though its exact meaning is obscure. The poet ends with a warning that ʿUmārah and his comrades will be torn to shreds by the mighty lions under the poet's command.

أَحَوْلِي تَنْفُضُ ٱسْتُكَ مِذْرَوَيْهَا   لِتَقْتُلَنِي فَهَا أَنَا ذَا عُمَارَا
مَتَى مَا نَلْتَقِي فَرْدَيْنِ تَرْجُفْ   رَوَانِفُ أَلْيَتَيْكَ وَتُسْتَطَارَا
وَسَيْفِي صَارِمٌ قَبَضَتْ عَلَيْهِ   أَشَاجِعُ لَا تَرَى فِيهَا ٱنْتِشَارَا
وَسَيْفِي كَٱلْعَقِيقَةِ وَهْوَ كِمْعِي   سِلَاحِي لَا أَفَلَّ وَلَا فُطَارَا
وَكَٱلْوَرَقِ ٱلْخِفَافِ وَذَاتُ غَرْبٍ   تَرَى فِيهَا عَنِ ٱلشِّرْعِ ٱزْوِرَارَا
وَمُطَّرِدُ ٱلْكُعُوبِ أَحَصُّ صَدْقٌ   تَخَالُ سِنَانَهُ بِٱللَّيْلِ نَارَا
سَتَعْلَمُ أَيُّنَا لِلْمَوْتِ أَدْنَى   إِذَا دَانَيْتَ بِي ٱلْأَسَلَ ٱلْحِرَارَا
وَلَلرُّعْيَانُ فِي لُقُحٍ ثَمَانٍ   تُهَادِنُهُنَّ صَرًّا أَوْ غِرَارَا
أَقَامَ عَلَى خَسِيسَتِهِنَّ حَتَّى   لَقِحْنَ وَنَتَّجَ ٱلْأُخَرَ ٱلْعِشَارَا
وَقَطَنَ عَلَى لَصَافِ وَهُنَّ غُلْبٌ   تُرِنُّ مُتُونُهَا لَيْلًا ظُؤَارَا
وَمَنْجُوفٌ لَهُ مِنْهُنَّ صِرْعٌ   يَمِيلُ إِذَا عَدَلْتَ بِهِ ٱلشِّوَارَا
أَقَلُّ عَلَيْكَ ضُرًّا مِنْ قَرِيحٍ   إِذَا أَصْحَابُهُ ذَمَرُوهُ سَارَا
وَخَيْلٍ قَدْ زَحَفْتُ لَهَا بِخَيْلٍ   عَلَيْهَا ٱلْأُسْدُ تَهْتَصِرُ ٱهْتِصَارَا

البحر: الوافر.

Has your sorry ass come to kill me?
'Umārah, I'm right here!
Shall we have a go at it, you and I?
Or will you run, butt shaking with fear?
My sword cuts deep
with a sure-sinewed hand
my sparkling bride is a weapon
never dented or dull,[36]
my arrowheads glint,[37]
my bow's strung taut,
my spear shaft straight and true—[38]
its head burns bright in the night.

Are you so sure I'll be the first
to die when thirsty spears close in?
Shepherds have their tricks to get
milk from a dried-out camel.
They tend the weaklings till they're heavy
with young and deliver the others in season
by summering them in Laṣāfi,
grunting all night to adopted foals.
That's how they get two skins full of milk
so the saddle lists beneath the load.[39]

The wounded cannot harm you
even if their comrades goad.
I lead the charge of mounted lions
who snap the necks of their prey.

~ 5 ~

Raqāshi is gone

This dense victory chant is unique in the al-Aṣmaʿī tradition for its declaration of the poet's mixed race in the final line. (For an expanded version, consisting of twenty-one lines, see Poem 29). In this poem, a complex narrative emerges. The poet's ties with tribal society, symbolized by the woman (women?) the poet loves, are cut, signaling that the poet has entered the warrior state, ready to sacrifice his life in the pursuit of glory. He emerges from the warrior state (insofar as ʿAntarah could ever be said to leave the warrior state behind) in his exultant return to the tribe, a celebration of his mixed race. The battle narrative begins with victory. At the end of the battle, with victory won, the poet and his comrades look to find where the women of the tribe have fled to, to avoid capture. Proverbial wisdom communicates the transition from one state to the next: dalliance with women is illusory—it does not bring fame, so fortify your soul for bloodshed. The poet then rehearses his feats of valor in keeping the women safe, exploits that led to the tribe's victory.

نَأَتْكَ رَقَاشِ إِلَّا عَنْ لِمَامِ ... وَأَمْسَى حَبْلُهَا خَلَقَ ٱلرِّمَامِ
وَمَا ذِكْرِي رَقَاشِ إِذَا ٱسْتَقَرَّتْ ... لَدَى ٱلطَّرْفَاءِ عِنْدَ ٱبْنَيْ شَمَامِ
وَمَسْكِنُ أَهْلِهَا مِنْ بَطْنِ جِزْعٍ ... تَبِيضُ بِهِ مَصَائِفُ ٱلْحَمَامِ
وَقَفْتُ وَصُحْبَتِي بِأُرَيْنِبَاتٍ ... عَلَى أَقْتَادِ عُوجٍ كَٱلسَّمَامِ
فَقُلْتُ تَبَيَّنُوا ظُعُنًا أَرَاهَا ... تَحُلُّ شُوَاحِطًا جُنْحَ ٱلظَّلَامِ
وَقَدْ كَذَبَتْكَ نَفْسُكَ فَاكْذِبَنْهَا ... لِمَا مَنَّتْكَ تَغْرِيرًا قَطَامِ
وَمُرْقِصَةٍ رَدَدْتُ ٱلْخَيْلَ عَنْهَا ... وَقَدْ هَمَّتْ بِإِلْقَاءِ ٱلزِّمَامِ
فَقُلْتُ لَهَا ٱقْصِرِي مِنْهُ وَسِيرِي ... وَقَدْ قُرِعَ ٱلْجَرَائِرُ بِٱلْخِدَامِ
أَكُرُّ عَلَيْهِمُ مُهْرِي كَلِيمًا ... قَلَائِدُهُ سَبَائِبُ كَٱلْقِرَامِ
كَأَنَّ دُفُوفَ مَرْجِعِ مَرْفِقَيْهِ ... تَوَارَثَهَا مَنَازِيعُ ٱلسِّهَامِ
تَقَعَّسَ وَهْوَ مُضْطَمِرٌ مُضِرٌّ ... بِقَارِحِهِ عَلَى فَأْسِ ٱللِّجَامِ
يُقَدِّمُهُ فَتًى مِنْ خَيْرِ عَبْسٍ ... أَبُوهُ وَأُمُّهُ مِنْ آلِ حَامِ

البحر: الوافر.

Raqāshi is gone, our ties frayed.
    Her wraith now visits me at night.
I think of her standing by the peaks
    of Shamāmi, beneath the tamarisk,
her people camped in the valley
    where, in summer, the doves nest.[40]

Our lean camels like swallows in flight
    came to a halt at Uraynibāt.
"Look," I said. "Night's falling.
    The litters stop at Shuwāḥiṭ."[41]
About Qaṭāmi, your desires lied to you.
    Go now, lie to them in turn.[42]

In panic my woman fled on her camel
    anklets jangling against the saddle.
"Pull on the rein!" I cried, keeping
    the raiders at bay.
I turned my wounded horse
    his flanks shredded by arrows
his halter red with blood
    like the fringes of a rug.[43]
He charged full tilt, gripping the bit
    drilled for battle by a bold warrior.

My mother descends from Ham
    but my father's the finest of the clan!

~ 6 ~

I know Death

A vivid bipartite battle song, comprising evocation of ruins (dhikr al-aṭlāl) and personal vaunt (mufākharah). The poem explores the worth of noble lineage, metaphors of thirst and drinking (always evocative of war in the cosmic economy of water),[44] *and the transformations of experience in battle, where, in a magnificent line, the poet fights with such ferocity that Death assumes the form of the poet—the poet becomes an avatar of Death, and embodies Death. Once again, the structure of the ode is destabilized by the poet's rejection of the carper (ʿādhilah) in the boast: the carper is customarily, though admittedly not always, encountered in the amatory episode (nasīb).*

طَالَ ٱلثَّوَاءُ عَلَى رُسُومِ ٱلْمَنْزِلِ   بَيْنَ ٱللَّكِيكِ وَبَيْنَ ذَاتِ ٱلْحَرْمَلِ
فَوَقَفْتُ فِي عَرَصَاتِهَا مُتَحَيِّرًا   أَسَلُ ٱلدِّيَارَ كَفِعْلِ مَنْ لَمْ يَذْهَلِ
لَعِبَتْ بِهَا ٱلْأَنْوَاءُ بَعْدَ أَنِيسِهَا   وَٱلرَّامِسَاتُ وَكُلُّ جَوْنٍ مُسْبِلِ
أَفَمِنْ بُكَاءِ حَمَامَةٍ فِي أَيْكَةٍ   ذَرَفَتْ دُمُوعُكَ فَوْقَ ظَهْرِ ٱلْمَحْمَلِ
كَٱلدُّرِّ أَوْ فَضَضِ ٱلْجُمَانِ تَقَطَّعَتْ   مِنْهُ عَقَائِدُ سِلْكِهِ لَمْ يُوصَلِ
لَمَّا سَمِعْتُ دُعَاءَ مُرَّةَ إِذْ دَعَا   وَدُعَاءَ عَبْسٍ فِي ٱلْوَغَى وَمُحَلَّلِ
نَادَيْتُ عَبْسًا فَٱسْتَجَابُوا بِٱلْقَنَا   وَبِكُلِّ أَبْيَضَ صَارِمٍ لَمْ يَنْحَلِ
حَتَّى ٱسْتَبَاحُوا آلَ عَوْفٍ عَنْوَةً   بِٱلْمَشْرَفِيِّ وَبِٱلْوَشِيجِ ٱلذُّبَّلِ
إِنِّي ٱمْرُؤٌ مِنْ خَيْرِ عَبْسٍ مَنْصِبًا   شَطْرِي وَأَحْمِي سَائِرِي بِٱلْمُنْصُلِ
إِنْ يُلْحَقُوا أَكْرُرْ وَإِنْ يُسْتَلْحَمُوا   أَشْدُدْ وَإِنْ يُلْفَوْا بِضَنْكٍ أَنْزِلِ
حِينَ ٱلنُّزُولُ يَكُونُ غَايَةَ سَيْرِنَا   وَيَفِرُّ كُلُّ مُضَلَّلٍ مُسْتَوْهَلِ
وَلَقَدْ أَبِيتُ عَلَى ٱلطَّوَى وَأَظَلُّهُ   حَتَّى أَنَالَ بِهِ كَرِيمَ ٱلْمَأْكَلِ
وَإِذَا ٱلْكَتِيبَةُ أَحْجَمَتْ وَتَلَاحَظَتْ   أُلْفِيتُ خَيْرًا مِنْ مُعَمٍّ مُخْوَلِ
وَٱلْخَيْلُ تَعْلَمُ وَٱلْفَوَارِسُ أَنَّنِي   فَرَّقْتُ جَمْعَهُمُ بِطَعْنَةِ فَيْصَلِ
إِذْ لَا أُبَادِرُ فِي ٱلْمَضِيقِ فَوَارِسِي   وَلَا أُوَكَّلُ بِٱلرَّعِيلِ ٱلْأَوَّلِ
وَلَقَدْ غَدَوْتُ أَمَامَ رَايَةِ غَالِبٍ   يَوْمَ ٱلْهِيَاجِ وَمَا غَدَوْتُ بِأَعْزَلِ
بَكَرَتْ تُخَوِّفُنِي ٱلْحُتُوفَ كَأَنَّنِي   أَصْبَحْتُ عَنْ غَرَضِ ٱلْحُتُوفِ بِمَعْزِلِ

البحر: الكامل.

I lingered around the camp[45]
    past al-Lakīk
before Dhāt al-Ḥarmal,
    where wind and rain and cloud
danced in a barren stretch
    where my quest
brought only sadness.
    A dove cooed in the trees
and on my swordbelt
    I shed my tears—
silver balls or pearls
    that scatter when string-
knots unravel.

Murrah, ʿAbs, and Muḥallil
    cried for help.[46]
I mustered my tribe for War.
    With high spears and sabers
sharp with thirst[47]
    hardened lances and keen
Mashraf blades
    they brought ʿAwf to ruins
and left them there to rot.
    The noble line of my tribe
accounts for some of what I am—
    my sword takes care of the rest.
Close in on us, I'll fight.
    Surround me, and I'll charge.
Hand to hand—I'm your man.[48]
    Dismount and square up
to fight—or run for your life.

I've spent nights in twisting hunger
    and killed foes who'd eaten their fill.[49]
If they flinched or showed flashes of fear,
    highborn or low,

فَأَجَبْتُهَا إِنَّ ٱلْمَنِيَّةَ مَنْهَلٌ   لَا بُدَّ أَنْ أُسْقَى بِكَأْسِ ٱلْمَنْهَلِ
فَٱقْنَيْ حَيَاءَكِ لَا أَبَا لَكِ وَٱعْلَمِي   أَنِّي ٱمْرُؤٌ سَأَمُوتُ إِنْ لَمْ أُقْتَلِ
إِنَّ ٱلْمَنِيَّةَ لَوْ تُمَثَّلُ مُثِّلَتْ   مِثْلِي إِذَا نَزَلُوا بِضَنْكِ ٱلْمَنْزِلِ
وَٱلْخَيْلُ سَاهِمَةُ ٱلْوُجُوهِ كَأَنَّمَا   تُسْقَى فَوَارِسُهَا نَقِيعَ ٱلْحَنْظَلِ
وَإِذَا حَمَلْتُ عَلَى ٱلْكَرِيهَةِ لَمْ أَقُلْ   بَعْدَ ٱلْكَرِيهَةِ لَيْتَنِي لَمْ أَفْعَلِ

I'd stare them down.[50]

The cavalry knew I'd break the line
with a brutal strike[51]
flanked by my men
into the fray.
Armor-clad, I rode at the head
of Ghālib's banner.
"Stay back," my woman pleaded
as though I could cheat Death.[52]
Death is a cup we all must drink of.
No more fuss. If I live today
tomorrow brings another draft.
Death I know—it looks like me[53]
grim as battle, when riders wince
and horses flinch
from bitter colocynth.
With no qualm or care
I embrace the terrors of War.

~ 7 ~

Blade-thin, war-spent

This, the second-longest poem in al-Aṣmaʿī's redaction, is a meditation on the difficulties experienced by the soldier upon returning home from campaign. ʿAntarah has been on campaign so long (he has even come face to face with Death itself) that he is more weapon than human. Rejected by ʿAblah upon his return to the tribe, he addresses the whole poem to her, intoning his successes on the battlefield. The boast contains a gripping battle narrative and an urgent description of a magnificent warhorse. The entire poem is subordinate to the impassioned challenge to ʿAblah ("Look me in the eye"), exhorting her to see past his shocking appearance and treat him with the respect his exploits demand.

عَجِبَتْ عُبَيْلَةُ مِنْ فَتًى مُتَبَذِّلٍ   عَارِي ٱلْأَشَاجِعِ شَاحِبٍ كَٱلْمُنْصُلِ
شَعِثِ ٱلْمَفَارِقِ مُنْهِجٍ سِرْبَالُهُ   لَمْ يَدَّهِنْ حَوْلًا وَلَمْ يَتَرَجَّلِ
لَا يَكْتَسِي إِلَّا ٱلْحَدِيدَ إِذَا ٱكْتَسَى   وَكَذَاكَ كُلُّ مُغَاوِرٍ مُسْتَبْسِلِ
قَدْ طَالَ مَا لَبِسَ ٱلْحَدِيدَ فَإِنَّمَا   صَدَأُ ٱلْحَدِيدِ بِجِلْدِهِ لَمْ يُغْسَلِ
فَتَضَاحَكَتْ عَجَبًا وَقَالَتْ قَوْلَةً   لَا خَيْرَ فِيكَ كَأَنَّهَا لَمْ تَحْفِلِ
فَعَجِبْتُ مِنْهَا كَيْفَ زَلَّتْ عَيْنُهَا   عَنْ مَاجِدٍ طَلْقِ ٱلْيَدَيْنِ شَمَرْدَلِ
لَا تَصْرِمِينِي يَا عُبَيْلَ وَرَاجِعِي   فِيَّ ٱلْبَصِيرَةَ نَظْرَةَ ٱلْمُتَأَمِّلِ
فَلَرُبَّ أَمْلَحَ مِنْكِ دَلًّا فَٱعْلَمِي   وَأَقَرَّ فِي ٱلدُّنْيَا لِعَيْنِ ٱلْمُجْتَلِي
وَصَلَتْ حِبَالِي بِٱلَّذِي أَنَا أَهْلُهُ   مِنْ وُدِّهَا وَأَنَا رَخِيُّ ٱلْمِطْوَلِ
يَا عَبْلَ كَمْ مِنْ غَمْرَةٍ بَاشَرْتُهَا   بِٱلنَّفْسِ مَا كَادَتْ لَعَمْرُكِ تَنْجَلِي
فِيهَا لَوَامِعُ لَوْ شَهِدْتِ زُهَاءَهَا   لَسَلَوْتِ بَعْدَ تَخَضُّبٍ وَتَكَحُّلِ

البحر: الكامل.

Blade-thin, war-spent
    he shocked ʿAblah
with sinewy hands
    and matted hair
in a year's grime
    and coat of mail
its battered iron
    so long worn
he had turned to rust.
    And looked a wreck.
"You're worthless,"
    ʿAblah said
shocking me
    by the laugh she got
from gathered friends
    as she cast
a scant glance
    at this glorious warrior
this brave lion
    famed for largesse.

Look me in the eye, ʿAblah.
    Don't leave—
I've had better flirts than you
    and far prettier, too.
I've had my way
    and then roamed free.
Get that into your head.
    My soul has been mired
in battlemurk—
    the blade's glister
would make you forget
    all your henna
and your kohl.
    Who cares if I'm thin?
I've been hard at it,
    dodging spears.

إِمَّا تَرَيْنِي قَدْ نَحَلْتُ وَمَنْ يَكُنْ   غَرَضًا لِأَطْرَافِ ٱلْأَسِنَّةِ يَنْحَلِ
فَلَرُبَّ أَبْلَجَ مِثْلِ بَعْلِكِ بَادِنٍ   ضَخْمٍ عَلَى ظَهْرِ ٱلْجَوَادِ مُهَبَّلِ
غَادَرْتُهُ مُتَعَفِّرًا أَوْصَالُهُ   وَٱلْقَوْمُ بَيْنَ مُجَرَّحٍ وَمُجَدَّلِ
فِيهِمْ أَخُو ثِقَةٍ يُضَارِبُ نَازِلًا   بِٱلْمَشْرَفِيِّ وَفَارِسًا لَمْ يَنْزِلِ
وَرِمَاحُنَا تَكِفُ ٱلنَّجِيعَ صُدُورُهَا   وَسُيُوفُنَا تَخْلِي ٱلرِّقَابَ فَتَخْتَلِي
وَٱلْهَامُ تَنْدُرُ بِٱلصَّعِيدِ كَأَنَّمَا   تَلْقَى ٱلسُّيُوفُ بِهَا رُؤُوسَ ٱلْحَنْظَلِ
وَلَقَدْ لَقِيتُ ٱلْمَوْتَ يَوْمَ لَقِيتُهُ   مُتَسَرْبِلًا وَٱلسَّيْفُ لَمْ يَتَسَرْبَلِ
فَرَأَيْتُنَا مَا بَيْنَنَا مِنْ حَاجِزٍ   إِلَّا ٱلْمِجَنُّ وَنَصْلُ أَبْيَضَ مِقْصَلِ
ذَكَرٍ أَشُقُّ بِهِ ٱلْجَمَاجِمَ فِي ٱلْوَغَى   وَأَقُولُ لَا تُقْطَعْ يَمِينُ ٱلصَّيْقَلِ
وَلَرُبَّ مُشْعَلَةٍ وَزَعْتُ رِعَالَهَا   بِمُقَلِّصٍ نَهْدِ ٱلْمَرَاكِلِ هَيْكَلِ
سَلِسِ ٱلْمُعَذَّرِ لَاحِقٍ أَقْرَابُهُ   مُتَقَلِّبٍ عَبَثًا بِفَأْسِ ٱلْمِسْحَلِ
نَهْدِ ٱلْقَطَاةِ كَأَنَّهَا مِنْ صَخْرَةٍ   مَلْسَاءَ يَغْشَاهَا ٱلْمَسِيلُ بِمَحْفِلِ

I've floored many a warrior
    like your precious lord
posh lumps of flesh in the saddle
    sprawled in dirt
mid wounded soldiers
    and unhorsed riders
while we, mounted
    or dismounted,
fought on to the kill,
    our spears bloodied
black to the haft
    our swords reaping
skulls like gourds.
    In full armor
weapons in hand
    I went face to face with Death
up close, with only a shield
    and burnished saber
to keep us apart.
    I blessed the smith
who forged
    the skull-splitter.
Raid after raid
    I've held the line
on my hill of a horse.
    Light to the hand
he rolls the bit
    inside his lip
tight in the flank
    his croup muscled
like a rock
    in a flash flood
his mane as if
    from a palm's
stripped trunk
    he snorts from nostrils

وَكَأَنَّ هَادِيَهُ إِذَا ٱسْتَقْبَلْتَهُ   جِذْعٌ أُذِلَّ وَكَانَ غَيْرَ مُذَلَّلِ
وَكَأَنَّ مَخْرَجَ رَوْحِهِ فِي وَجْهِهِ   سَرَبَانِ كَانَا مَوْلِجَيْنِ لِجَيْأَلِ
وَكَأَنَّ مَتْنَيْهِ إِذَا جَرَّدْتَهُ   وَنَزَعْتَ عَنْهُ ٱلْجُلَّ مَتْنَا إِيَّلِ
وَلَهُ حَوَافِرُ مُوثَقٌ تَرْكِيبُهَا   صُمُّ ٱلنُّسُورِ كَأَنَّهَا مِنْ جَنْدَلِ
وَلَهُ عَسِيبٌ ذُو سَبِيبٍ سَابِغٌ   مِثْلِ ٱلرِّدَاءِ عَلَى ٱلْغَنِيِّ ٱلْمُفْضِلِ
سَلِسُ ٱلْعِنَانِ إِلَى ٱلْقِتَالِ فَعَيْنُهُ   قَبْلَاءُ شَاخِصَةٌ كَعَيْنِ ٱلْأَحْوَلِ
وَكَأَنَّ مِشْيَتَهُ إِذَا نَهْنَهْتَهُ   بِٱلنِّكْلِ مِشْيَةُ شَارِبٍ مُسْتَعْجِلِ
فَعَلَيْهِ أَقْتَحِمُ ٱلْهِيَاجَ تَقَحُّمًا   فِيهَا وَأَنْقَضُّ ٱنْقِضَاضَ ٱلْأَجْدَلِ

deep and round
    as a hyena's den.
Saddlecloth removed
    he has the back
of an ibex,
    rock-hard hooves
and soles made of stone.
    Tail thick
as a rich man's robe.
    In combat he answers
my touch,
    fierce squint in his eye
stumbling like a drunk
    as I pull on the reins.
A proud falcon
    he swoops into war.

~ 8 ~

The crow croaked

A gem of a poem that brings to mind "The Raven" by Edgar Allan Poe (1845). The poet brilliantly explores the motif of the ill-omened cawing of the crow and reflects on the worth of human endeavor in the face of inexorable Fate. If, as the poet knows, Death is ineluctable, valor in combat is the warrior's only viable life choice. Note the poet's rebuke of the crow, and how he anthropomorphizes it as an avatar of destiny.

ظَعَنَ ٱلَّذِينَ فِرَاقَهُمْ أَتَوَقَّعُ   وَجَرَى بِبَيْنِهِمُ ٱلْغُرَابُ ٱلْأَبْقَعُ
حَرِقُ ٱلْجَنَاحِ كَأَنَّ لَحْيَيْ رَأْسِهِ   جَلَمَانِ بِٱلْأَخْبَارِ هَشٌّ مُولَعُ
فَزَجَرْتُهُ أَلَّا يُفَرِّخَ عُشَّهُ   أَبَدًا وَيُصْبِحَ وَاحِدًا يَتَفَجَّعُ
إِنَّ ٱلَّذِينَ نَعَيْتَ لِي بِفِرَاقِهِمْ   قَدْ أَسْهَرُوا لَيْلِي ٱلتِّمَامَ فَأَوْجَعُوا
وَمُغِيرَةٍ شَعْوَاءَ ذَاتِ أَشِلَّةٍ   فِيهَا ٱلْفَوَارِسُ حَاسِرٌ وَمُقَنَّعُ
فَزَجَرْتُهَا عَنْ نِسْوَةٍ مِنْ عَامِرٍ   أَفْخَاذُهُنَّ كَأَنَّهُنَّ ٱلْخِرْوَعُ
وَعَرَفْتُ أَنَّ مَنِيَّتِي إِنْ تَأْتِنِي   لَا يُنْجِنِي مِنْهَا ٱلْفِرَارُ ٱلْأَسْرَعُ
فَصَبَرْتُ عَارِفَةً لِذٰلِكَ حُرَّةً   تَرْسُو إِذَا نَفْسُ ٱلْجَبَانِ تَطَلَّعُ

البحر: الكامل.

The crow,
beak like a pair of shears,
croaked.[54]
I was afraid
they'd leave
and now they're gone.
"Don't let your chicks fly the nest
and leave you
lost and bereft"
I warned him, but his news
inspired my fear
the long night through.[55]
Often I've defended
the women of ʿĀmir,
their legs slim
and tender as stalks,
from the onslaught of
armed raiders.
I won't be able
to outrun Fate
when she comes.
Cowards run.
I stand
my ground.[56]

~ 9 ~

Traced like tattoos

A dense piece of invective and threat, embroiled in the toil and moil of clan conflict among the various branches of the Ṭayyiʾ lineage group. The treachery of clans Jarm, Sulām, and Thuʿal against clan ʿAdī has brought about the state of collapse described in the first two lines, where the poet's world is in chaos, because the signs that are identifiable and that should normally be decipherable, like bridal tattoos, can no longer be deciphered and understood, but rather resemble incomprehensible Pahlavi writings read out at the court of Khusro (Kisrā). The poet's bellicosity on behalf of clan ʿAdī is intended to set right what is wrong and bring order back to the world.

أَلَا يَا دَارَ عَبْلَةَ بِٱلطَّوِيِّ   كَرَجْعِ ٱلْوَشْمِ فِي رُسْغِ ٱلْهَدِيِّ
كَوَحْيِ صَحَائِفٍ مِنْ عَهْدِ كِسْرَى   فَأَهْدَاهَا لِأَعْجَمَ طِمْطِمِيِّ
أَمِنْ زَوِّ ٱلْحَوَادِثِ يَوْمَ تَسْمُو   بَنُو جَرْمٍ لِحَرْبِ بَنِي عَدِيِّ
إِذَا ٱضْطَرَبُوا سَمِعْتَ ٱلصَّوْتَ فِيهِمْ   خَفِيًّا غَيْرَ صَوْتِ ٱلْمَشْرَفِيِّ
وَغَيْرَ نَوَافِذٍ يَخْرُجْنَ مِنْهُمْ   بِطَعْنٍ مِثْلِ أَشْطَانِ ٱلرَّكِيِّ
وَقَدْ خَذَلَتْهُمُ ثُعَلُ بْنُ عَمْرٍو   سُلَامِيُّوهُمُ وَٱلْجَرْوَلِيُّ

البحر: الوافر.

ʿAblah's camp at Ṭawī,
traced like tattoos
on a bride's wrists,
engraved now
like Persian mumbled
at Kisrā's court.[57]

Jarm raided ʿAdī.
Fate decreed the clash—
the clang of swords
the whoosh of spears
like well ropes
taut in the throw.
ʿAdī were left
in the lurch by their kin—
the Sulām,
Clan Jarwal,
and Thuʿal
ibn ʿAmr.[58]

~ 10 ~

The eyes of an ʿUsfān gazelle

An obscure poem, which appears to have been composed in response to an incident alluded to in the phrase "when the staff was thrown." The commentators locate its provenance as part of the story of how ʿAntarah won formal recognition by his father, and set it within a seduction scenario reminiscent of the story of Joseph (Yūsuf) in the eponymous twelfth surah of the Qurʾan.

أَمِنْ سُهَيَّةَ دَمْعُ ٱلْعَيْنِ تَذْرِيفُ   لَوْ أَنَّ ذَا مِنْكِ قَبْلَ ٱلْيَوْمِ مَعْرُوفُ
كَأَنَّهَا يَوْمَ صَدَّتْ مَا تُكَلِّمُنِي   ظَبْيٌ بِعُسْفَانَ سَاجِي ٱلطَّرْفِ مَطْرُوفُ
تَجَلَّلَتْنِيَ إِذْ أَهْوَى ٱلْعَصَا قِبَلِي   كَأَنَّهَا صَنَمٌ يُعْتَادُ مَعْكُوفُ
أَلْمَالُ مَالُكُمُ وَٱلْعَبْدُ عَبْدُكُمُ   فَهَلْ عَذَابُكَ عَنِّي ٱلْيَوْمَ مَصْرُوفُ
تَنْسَى بَلَائِيَ إِذَا مَا غَارَةٌ لَقِحَتْ   تَخْرُجُ مِنْهَا ٱلطُّوَالَاتُ ٱلسَّرَاعِيفُ
يَخْرُجْنَ مِنْهَا وَقَدْ بُلَّتْ رَحَائِلُهَا   بِٱلْمَاءِ يَرْكُضُهَا ٱلْمُرْدُ ٱلْغَطَارِيفُ
قَدْ أَطْعَنُ ٱلطَّعْنَةَ ٱلنَّجْلَاءَ عَنْ عُرُضٍ   تَصْفَرُّ كَفُّ أَخِيهَا وَهْوَ مَنْزُوفُ

البحر: البسيط.

Is Suhayyah weeping
    for me? I wish
she'd let me know before
    refusing to speak,
entrancing me with
    the eyes of an ʿUsfān gazelle.
When the staff was thrown
    she towered above me,
a precious idol
    swarmed by its priests.[59]

You are my lord and master,
    I am yours.
Will you show mercy today?[60]
    You forget my prowess
when the battle's in rut[61]
    and the sleek mares swarm
like locusts, sweat-flecked saddles
    ridden by hawks,
and my lance driven deep
    till the blood spurts.[62]

~ 11 ~

Shut up about my horse

A wonderful vignette full of grim irony, in which ʿAntarah responds to his wife who begrudged the milk he was giving his horse: You complain about what I feed my horse but he is what prevents you from being taken captive and is what will enable me to defend you when another tribe comes on a raid. If you persist I will abandon you and you will be taken prisoner by other men. Then you will need me and my horse, the (Son of the) Ostrich, to come to your rescue.

لَا تَذْكُرِي مُهْرِي وَمَا أَطْعَمْتُهُ   فَيَكُونَ جِلْدُكِ مِثْلَ جِلْدِ ٱلْأَجْرَبِ
إِنَّ ٱلْغَبُوقَ لَهُ وَأَنْتِ مَسُوءَةٌ   فَتَأَوَّهِي مَا شِئْتِ ثُمَّ تَحَوَّبِي
كَذَبَ ٱلْعَتِيقُ وَمَاءُ شَنٍّ بَارِدٌ   إِنْ كُنْتِ سَائِلَتِي غَبُوقًا فَٱذْهَبِي
إِنَّ ٱلرِّجَالَ لَهُمْ إِلَيْكِ وَسِيلَةٌ   إِنْ يَأْخُذُوكِ تَكَحَّلِي وَتَخَضَّبِي
وَيَكُونُ مَرْكَبُكِ ٱلْقَعُودَ وَرَحْلَهُ   وَٱبْنُ ٱلنَّعَامَةِ يَوْمَ ذٰلِكَ مَرْكَبِي
إِنِّي أُحَاذِرُ أَنْ تَقُولَ ظَعِينَتِي   هٰذَا غُبَارٌ سَاطِعٌ فَتَلَبَّبِ
وَأَنَا ٱمْرُؤٌ إِنْ يَأْخُذُونِي عَنْوَةً   أُقْرَنْ إِلَى شَرِّ ٱلرِّكَابِ وَأُجْنَبِ

البحر: الكامل.

Shut up about my horse
    or else I'll leave you looking
like a mangy camel.
    I'll feed him what I want.
He can have all the milk
    he needs. Go,
scream and moan
    to your heart's content.
If you think I'll waste
    his milk on you,
think again. Water and dates
    are plenty for you.
If you're captured in a raid
    and bundled onto a camel's back
you can wear all the makeup you like—
    but that's when you'll be glad
the Ostrich is mine.[63]
    Trust me,
no woman will ever say
    "It's a raid. Grab your weapons!"
My enemies cower before me.
    They'd have to kill me
or drag me in chains behind
    their ugliest camel.

~ 12 ~

A cavalry charge

A victory ode celebrating the outcome of a skirmish occasioned by internal squabbles between member groups of Ṭayyi' and their confederates. The poem is terse, yet brims with 'Antarah's indomitable spirit, and has some fine lines narrating a raid and describing the bellicose virility of the poet's troop.

وَفَوَارِسٍ لِي قَدْ عَلِمْتُهُمُ　　صُبُرٍ عَلَى ٱلتَّكْرَارِ وَٱلْكَلَمِ
يَمْشُونَ وَٱلْمَاذِيُّ فَوْقَهُمُ　　يَتَوَقَّدُونَ تَوَقُّدَ ٱلنَّجْمِ
كَمْ مِنْ فَتًى فِيهِمْ أَخِي ثِقَةٍ　　حُرٍّ أَغَرَّ كَغُرَّةِ ٱلرِّئْمِ
لَيْسُوا كَأَقْوَامٍ عَلِمْتُهُمُ　　سُودِ ٱلْوُجُوهِ كَمَعْدِنِ ٱلْبُرْمِ
عَجِلَتْ بَنُو شَيْبَانَ مُدَّتَهُمْ　　وَٱلْبُقْعُ أَسْتَاهًا بَنُو لَأْمِ
كُنَّا إِذَا نَفَرَ ٱلْمَطِيُّ بِنَا　　وَبَدَا لَنَا أَحْوَاضُ ذِي ٱلرَّضْمِ
نُعْدِي فَنَطْعُنُ فِي أُنُوفِهِمُ　　نَخْتَارُ بَيْنَ ٱلْقَتْلِ وَٱلْغُنْمِ
إِنَّا كَذٰلِكَ يَا سُهَيَّ إِذَا　　غَدَرَ ٱلْحَلِيفُ نَمُورُ بِٱلْخُطْمِ
وَبِكُلِّ مُرْهَفَةٍ لَهَا نَفَذٌ　　بَيْنَ ٱلضُّلُوعِ كَطُرَّةِ ٱلْفَدْمِ

البحر: الكامل.

A cavalry charge
    of war-bitten riders
bloodied in slaughter
    armor glinting,[64]
free warriors
    with brows as bright
as rhim gazelles,
    unlike Shaybān and La'm
those sorry tribes
    with leprous butts
and brows black as pots.

We harried their fate
    and fearless, raced
our mounts
    through rock-strewn wastes,[65]
charging deep in their midst
    and spearing them hard.
The choice was ours—
    kill, or clap them in irons.[66]

When allies renege, Suhayyah,
    we attack with bows
piercing ribs and ripping flanks
    into ribbons of red.[67]

~ 13 ~

Between Qaww and Qārah

A brilliant and vividly concise victory ode celebrating the death of a foe. The raid, combat, and death of the Tamīm chieftain are capped with a line in which the cavalry of ʿAbs is lined up, ever on the alert, ready to charge and bring Death to the next enemy to oppose them. The sensory complexity and power of the image of the spears screaming in the loins of the foe as if gripped in the spear straightener, are startlingly sonorous.

كَأَنَّ ٱلسَّرَايَا بَيْنَ قَوٍّ وَقَارَةٍ   عَصَائِبُ طَيْرٍ يَنْتَحِينَ لِمَشْرَبِ
وَقَدْ كُنْتُ أَخْشَى أَنْ أَمُوتَ وَلَمْ تَقُمْ   قَرَائِبُ عَمْرٍو وَسْطَ نَوْحٍ مُسَلِّبِ
شَفَى ٱلنَّفْسَ مِنِّي أَوْ دَنَا مِنْ شِفَائِهَا   تَرَدِّيهِمُ مِنْ حَالِقٍ مُتَصَوِّبِ
تَصِيحُ ٱلرُّدَيْنِيَّاتُ فِي جَجَبَاتِهِمْ   صِيَاحَ ٱلْعَوَالِي فِي ٱلثِّقَافِ ٱلْمُثَقَّبِ
كَتَائِبُ تُزْجَى فَوْقَ كُلِّ كَتِيبَةٍ   لِوَاءٌ كَظِلِّ ٱلطَّائِرِ ٱلْمُتَقَلِّبِ

البحر: الطويل.

Between Qaww and Qārah
  the troops flocked like grouse
to a spring. I feared I'd die
  before ʿAmr's women
could keen his death. We charged
  the foe from on high
and my soul sick with bloodlust
  was nearly healed—
we skewered their loins
  with Rudaynah spears
that screamed as if
  squeezed in a vise.

Our squadrons stand
  arrayed for battle
banners flapping
  like vultures' shadows.

~ 14 ~

The hostage you offered up

A pithy lament (marthiyah) for a fallen chieftain that mixes praise with invective and the threat of vengeance. Unlike the fallen chieftain, who would never have behaved with such treachery, ʿAmr ibn Jābir and the "cowardly bastard" are guilty of a violation of customary propriety: the dead hero should not have been killed, but offered for ransom. Poems are now the most powerful weapon ʿAntarah has at his disposal for vengeance, and they will memorialize their shame. From this moment on, his poems of invective will clothe his foes and become their distinctive mark.

هَدِيُّكُمُ خَيْرٌ أَبًا مِنْ أَبِيكُمُ   أَعَفُّ وَأَوْفَى بِٱلْجِوَارِ وَأَحْمَدُ
وَأَطْعَنُ فِي ٱلْهَيْجَا إِذَا ٱلْخَيْلُ صَدَّهَا   غَدَاةَ ٱلصِّيَاحِ ٱلسَّمْهَرِيُّ ٱلْمُقَصَّدُ
فَهَلَّا وَفَى ٱلْفَوْغَاءُ عَمْرُو بْنُ جَابِرٍ   بِذِمَّتِهِ وَٱبْنُ ٱللَّقِيطَةِ عِصْيَدُ
سَيَأْتِيكُمُ عَنِّي وَإِنْ كُنْتُ نَائِيًا   دُخَانُ ٱلْعَلَنْدَى دُونَ بَيْتِيَ مِذْوَدُ
قَصَائِدُ مِنْ قِيلِ ٱمْرِئٍ يَحْتَدِيكُمُ   بَنِي ٱلْعُشَرَاءِ فَٱرْتَدُوا وَتَقَلَّدُوا

البحر: الطويل.

The hostage you offered up
was nobler than any of you—
more honorable and admired,
an abler warrior in the dawn din
when the scarred Samhar spear
scatters horses.[68]

Why was he betrayed
by loudmouth ʿAmr
ibn Jābir and that other
cowardly bastard?[69]
Like a volcano, I'll spew
poems that long
after my death
will find and hold you
up to shame.[70]

They suit you,
Clan ʿUsharāʾ.
Wear them with pride.

~ 15 ~

I planted my cold arrow

This vaunt with invective, commemorating the poet's attack on a foe during a raid, is a fine example of ʿAntarah at his poetic and brutal best. The vivid imagery of the poem, drawn from cultic practice, the natural world, weaponry, and the cosmic economy of water (here: well ropes), crackles with inventiveness.

تَرَكْتُ جُرَيَّةَ ٱلْعَمْرِيَّ فِيهِ   سَدِيدُ ٱلْعَيْرِ مُعْتَدِلٌ شَدِيدُ
جَعَلْتُ بَنِي ٱلْهُجَيْمِ لَهُ دَوَارًا   إِذَا يَمْضِي جَمَاعَتَهُمْ يَعُودُ
إِذَا تَقَعُ ٱلرِّمَاحُ بِجَانِبَيْهِ   تَوَلَّى قَابِعًا فِيهِ صُدُودُ
فَإِنْ يَبْرَأْ فَلَمْ أَنْفِثْ عَلَيْهِ   وَإِنْ يُفْقَدْ فَحُقَّ لَهُ ٱلْفُقُودُ
وَهَلْ يَدْرِي جُرَيَّةُ أَنَّ نَبْلِي   يَكُونُ حَفِيرَهَا ٱلْبَطَلُ ٱلنَّجِيدُ
كَأَنَّ رِمَاحَهُمْ أَشْطَانُ بِئْرٍ   لَهَا فِي كُلِّ مَدْلَجَةٍ خُدُودُ

البحر: الوافر.

I planted my cold
    arrow in Jurayyah[71]
forcing the Hujaym
    to swarm around him
like worshipers rushing
    round an idol.[72]
As the spears flew fast
    he'd advance
then retreat, like a hedgehog
    cowering and shrinking.[73]
Who cares if he lives?
    If he dies, better still!
Many a warrior
    knows what it's like
to be a grave
    for my arrows[74]
when enemy lances fly
    taut as ropes
gouging the edges
    of trough and well.[75]

~ 16 ~

Primed for battle

A brusque and aggressive vaunt commemorating the poet's exploits during a raid. In a chiaroscuro effect, the poet's generosity to, and care for, his own people is set beside his brutality to enemies, as three foes are dispatched by sword, spear, and arrow, the full armory of the elite cavalryman.

خُذُوا مَا أَسْأَرَتْ مِنْهَا قِدَاحِي   وَرِسْلُ ٱلضَّيْفِ وَٱلْأَنَسُ ٱلْجَمِيعُ ١
فَلَوْ لَاقَيْتَنِي وَعَلَيَّ دِرْعِي   عَلِمْتَ عَلَامَ تُحْتَمَلُ ٱلدُّرُوعُ
تَرَكْتُ جُبَيْلَةَ بْنَ أَبِي عَدِيٍّ   يَبُلُّ ثِيَابَهُ عَلَقٌ نَجِيعُ
وَآخَرَ مِنْهُمُ أَجْرَرْتُ رُمْحِي   وَفِي ٱلْبَجَلِيِّ مِعْبَلَةٌ وَقِيعُ ٤

البحر: الوافر.

I feed my tribe as befits my honor.
Take whatever meat is left,
the share reserved for guests.[76]
Should you meet me primed for battle
you'd know why armor is worn.
I stained the clothes
of Jubaylah ibn Abī ʿAdī
with a thick coat of gore,
I skewered a warrior
on my spear, and a Bajlī
welcomed my arrow.

~ 17 ~

Your last gasp is near!

A fierce challenge issued to an adversary, mixing threat with invective. The ignobility and unworthiness of the poet's opponents are reflected in their paltry weaponry and in the brilliant final insult.

قَدْ أَوْعَدُونِي بِأَرْمَاحٍ مُعَلَّبَةٍ   سُودٍ لُقِطْنَ مِنَ ٱلْحَوْمَانِ أَخْلَاقِ   ١
لَمْ يَسْلُبُوهَا وَلَمْ يُعْطُوا بِهَا ثَمَنًا   أَيْدِي ٱلنَّعَامِ فَلَا أَسْقَاهُمُ ٱلسَّاقِي
عَمْرُو بْنَ أَسْوَدَ فَا زَبَّاءَ قَارِبَةٍ   مَاءَ ٱلْكُلَابِ عَلَيْهَا ٱلظِّنْءُ مِعْنَاقِ   ٣

البحر: البسيط.

They're threatening me now
with their dirty old spears
picked up when the battle was done[77]
not won as plunder, or earned
as hire at the wellhead.[78]
May they die of thirst!
'Amr ibn Aswad, you
foul-breathed clan of shabby old camels—
Your last gasp is near![79]

~ 18 ~

Jostled by horses

An obscure boast with taunts of withering irony, addressed to an unnamed individual. The poet (unintentionally and thus ironically) does a good deed to an opponent in battle by letting him escape, thereby ensuring that he does not lie unburied on the battlefield. The poet then addresses this runaway, who is invited to accept and celebrate the poet's act of kindness, rather than seek vengeance for the death of a kinsman ('Abd Allāh), because as the unnamed addressee of the poem has already learned to his cost, he is no match for the poet and his warriors.

نَحَا فَارِسُ ٱلشَّهْبَاءِ وَٱلْخَيْلُ جُنَّحٌ   عَلَى فَارِسٍ مِنَ ٱلْأَسِنَّةِ مُقْصَدِ
وَلَوْ لَا يَدٌ نَالَتْهُ مِنَّا لَأَصْبَحَتْ   سِبَاعٌ تَهَادَى شِلْوَهُ غَيْرَ مُسْنَدِ
فَلَا تَكْفُرِ ٱلنُّعْمَى وَأَثْنِ بِفَضْلِهَا   وَلَا تَأْمَنَنْ مَا يُحْدِثِ ٱللهُ فِي غَدِ
فَإِنْ يَكُ عَبْدُ ٱللهِ لَاقَى فَوَارِسًا   يَرُدُّونَ خَالَ ٱلْعَارِضِ ٱلْمُتَوَقِّدِ
فَقَدْ أَمْكَنَتْ مِنْكَ ٱلْأَسِنَّةُ عَانِيًا   فَلَمْ تُجْزِ إِذْ تَسْعَى فَتِيلًا بِمَعْبَدِ

البحر: الطويل.

Jostled by horses
I aimed my mare's
star-front toward
a rider skewered
in a thicket of spears.[80]
Scavengers would
have feasted on
your corpse unbiered,[81]
but for my mercy.
Don't ignore our kindness.
Are you so sure that God
will give you life tomorrow?

In the heat of War
our cavalry routed
'Abd Allāh's banners.
Don't forget
the bite of our spears
when your revenge
for Maʿbad wasn't
worth a damn.[82]

~ 19 ~

I didn't start this war

A declaration of uncompromising fealty in time of conflict, this short piece is typical of much pre-Islamic poetry that is not composed in the qasida tradition: it is terse, laconic, occasional (in that it is clearly tied to a specific incident), and conveys a message (here to both sides of the conflict).

إِنْ تَكُ حَرْبُكُمْ أَمْسَتْ عَوَانًا   فَإِنِّي لَمْ أَكُنْ مِمَّنْ جَنَاهَا ١
وَلٰكِنْ وُلْدُ سَوْدَةَ أَرَّثُوهَا   وَشَبُّوا نَارَهَا لِمَنِ ٱصْطَلَاهَا
فَإِنِّي لَسْتُ خَاذِلَكُمْ وَلٰكِنْ   سَأَسْعَى ٱلْآنَ إِذْ بَلَغَتْ إِنَاهَا ٣

البحر: الوافر.

I didn't start this
    war that engulfs you.[83]
For generations
    Sawdah's sons
fanned its flames.
    Friend and foe—
all feel the heat.
    War is at
fever pitch.
    I won't desert you.

~ 20 ~

That dung beetle, Ja'd

A curse of an opponent whose perfidious conduct has deformed reality: it has turned him into a dung beetle and turned the poet into a warrior without a spear (ajamm, the epithet used for "naked in battle," can also refer to a ram without horns). The piece may be ironic—the poet has speared Ja'd in battle, but Ja'd has survived and escaped, perhaps with the spear still fixed in him.

إِذَا لَاقَيْتَ جَمْعَ بَنِي أَبَانٍ   فَإِنِّي لَائِمٌ لِلْجَعْدِ لَاحِ
كَأَنَّ مُؤَشَّرَ ٱلْعَضُدَيْنِ جَحْلًا   هَدُوجًا بَيْنَ أَقْلِبَةٍ مِلَاحِ
تَضَمَّنَ نِعْمَتِي فَعَدَا عَلَيْهَا   بُكُورًا أَوْ تَعَجَّلَ فِي ٱلرَّوَاحِ
أَلَمْ تَعْلَمْ لَحَاكَ ٱللّٰهُ أَنِّي   أَجَمُّ إِذَا لَقِيتُ ذَوِي ٱلرِّمَاحِ
كَسَوْتُ ٱلْجَعْدَ جَعْدَ بَنِي أَبَانٍ   سِلَاحِي بَعْدَ عُرْيٍ وَٱفْتِضَاحِ

البحر: الوافر.

Tell Abān if you meet them
how I despise
that dung beetle, Jaʿd,
jaggy legs
hobbling among
brackish wells.
He took advantage
of my good nature
making off with
what is mine,
a thief in the night.

God damn it!
Don't you realize
I was naked[84]
in battle facing
the spear lords?
Jaʿd of Abān wore
my weapons in
brazen dishonor.

~ 21 ~

Who'll side with you?

Another poem very typical of the non-qasida tradition, and clearly occasional in that it is tied to an imminent or present conflict. This threat is expressed in the form of an injunction to the listener to convey a message to other tribes on behalf of the poet.

١ سَائِلْ عَمِيرَةَ حَيْثُ حَلَّتْ جَمْعَهَا   عِنْدَ ٱلْحُرُوبِ بِأَيِّ حَيٍّ تَلْحَقُ
أَبِحَيِّ قَيْسٍ أَمْ بِعُذْرَةَ بَعْدَمَا   رُفِعَ ٱللِّوَاءُ لَهَا وَبِئْسَ ٱلْمَلْحَقُ
وَٱسْأَلْ حُذَيْفَةَ حِينَ أَرَّشَ بَيْنَنَا   حَرْبًا ذَوَائِبُهَا بِمَوْتٍ تَخْفِقُ
٤ فَلَتَعْلَمَنَّ إِذَا ٱلْتَقَتْ فُرْسَانُنَا   بِلِوَى ٱلنُّجَيْرَةِ أَنَّ ظَنَّكَ أَحْمَقُ

البحر: الكامل.

Who'll side with you
in the war to come?
With the banners raised
what good will Qays
or ʿUdhrah do?
Ask the ʿAmīrah
when they turn up,
Ḥudhayfah too.
In the breeze
our pennants signal[85]
death. At Nujayrah
when the knights clash
you'll see
your hopes are vain!

~ 22 ~

Grasping at spears

A victory chant commemorating the killing in battle of an opponent by ʿAntarah's kinsman. Reality is mutated when humans become beasts in the distorting heat of war—ʿAntarah's kinsman Ward ibn Ḥābis adopts the behavior of a wolf to hunt down his foe, Abū Nawfal Naḍlah of Asad. In the final line, the effulgent saber is defeated by the rocklike hardness of the arrow.

١ غَادَرْنَ نَضْلَةَ فِي مَعْرَكٍ   يَجُرُّ ٱلْأَسِنَّةَ كَٱلْمُحْتَطِبْ
فَمَنْ يَكُ عَنْ شَأْنِهِ سَائِلًا   فَإِنَّ أَبَا نَوْفَلٍ قَدْ شَجِبْ
تَذَاءَبَ وَرْدٌ عَلَى إِثْرِهِ   وَأَدْرَكَهُ وَقْعُ مُرْدٍ خَشِبْ
٤ تَدَارَكَ لَا يَتَّقِي نَفْسَهُ   بِأَبْيَضَ كَٱلْقَبَسِ ٱلْمُلْتَهِبْ

البحر: المتقارب.

Naḍlah died on the field of battle
grasping at spears
like a slave girl
gathering wood for a fire.
Should anyone ask—
Abū Nawfal's dead!
Ward stalked him
like a wolf
and felled him with
a dark blow[86]
before he could draw
his blazing sword.

~ 23 ~

A panicked leader

In old age, the poet looks back on his exploits in battle and sings of his tribe's success in eliminating its foes. The battle description is visually acute and has a cinematic feel: the poet's eye zooms in on how he comes to the rescue of a comrade and defeats a foe. The opening of the poem is exceptional for its description of altered sensory perception in the din of war; the graphic image of vultures (Death's avatars) as bridal attendants waiting on the corpse-bride while the fallen hero gives his last twitch in death is brilliant; and the phrase "commanding Death" is powerful.

وَمَكْرُوبٍ كَشَفْتُ ٱلْكَرْبَ عَنْهُ   بِطَعْنَةِ فَيْصَلٍ لَمَّا دَعَانِي
دَعَانِي دَعْوَةً وَٱلْخَيْلُ تَرْدِي   فَمَا أَدْرِي أَبِٱسْمِي أَمْ كَنَانِي
فَلَمْ أُمْسِكْ بِسَمْعِي إِذْ دَعَانِي   وَلٰكِنْ قَدْ أَبَانَ لَهُ لِسَانِي
فَكَانَ إِجَابَتِي إِيَّاهُ أَنِّي   عَطَفْتُ عَلَيْهِ خَوَّارَ ٱلْعِنَانِ
بِأَسْمَرَ مِنْ رِمَاحِ ٱلْخَطِّ لَدْنٍ   وَأَبْيَضَ صَارِمٍ ذَكَرٍ يَمَانِ
وَقِرْنٍ قَدْ تَرَكْتُ لَدَى مَكَرٍّ   عَلَيْهِ سَبَائِبٌ كَٱلْأُرْجُوَانِ
تَرَكْتُ ٱلطَّيْرَ عَاكِفَةً عَلَيْهِ   كَمَا تَرْدِي إِلَى ٱلْعُرُسِ ٱلْبَوَانِي
وَيَمْنَعُهُنَّ أَنْ يَأْكُلْنَ مِنْهُ   حَيَاةُ يَدٍ وَرِجْلٍ تَرْكُضَانِ
فَمَا أَوْهَى مِرَاسُ ٱلْحَرْبِ رُكْنِي   وَلٰكِنْ مَا تَقَادَمَ مِنْ زَمَانِ
وَقَدْ عَلِمَتْ بَنُو عَبْسٍ بِأَنِّي   أَهَشُّ إِذَا دُعِيتُ إِلَى ٱلطِّعَانِ
وَأَنَّ ٱلْمَوْتَ طَوْعُ يَدِي إِذَا مَا   وَصَلْتُ بَنَانَهَا بِٱلْهُنْدُوَانِي

البحر: الوافر.

A panicked leader
    called to me.[87]
I broke the line,
    drove fear away.
The horses charged.
    He called out once.
Did he ask my name?
    I couldn't hear
in the din of War
    but answered, blazing
through the soldiers
    like a lightning bolt,
urging my horse on,
    and with hard Khaṭṭī
lance and manly
    Yemeni steel
left my challenger
    dead—his hair
a bloody redbud,
    the vultures praying
over him,
    dancing their bridal
dance, held
    back from feasting
by the thrum
    and twitching of
his hands and feet.

Time, not War,
    has made me weak.
A hero, I advance
    on that coward, Death.
My tribe, summoned
    to fight, knows
how I smile,
    commanding Death,

وَنِعْمَ فَوَارِسُ ٱلْهَيْجَاءِ قَوْمِي   إِذَا عَلِقُوا ٱلْأَعِنَّةَ بِٱلْبَنَانِ
هُمُ قَتَلُوا لَقِيطًا وَٱبْنَ حُجْرٍ   وَأَرْدَوْا حَاجِبًا وَٱبْنَيْ أَبَانِ

my hand wielding
    the Indian blade.

In War my clan
    are the finest riders
gripping the reins
    in hands that killed
Laqīṭ and Ibn Ḥujr,
    Ḥājib and
the sons of Abān.[88]

~ 24 ~

The antelopes sprinted right and left

A classic bipartite qasida, with the chiaroscuro technique of juxtaposition of an evocation of ruins (dhikr al-aṭlāl) and past love (nasīb), and a victory chant intoning a vividly narrated raid on Ḍabbah. The poet struggles to determine the significance of the portents in the opening lines, but as the denouement of the poem indicates, the poet's augury was successful, accurately depicting the triumphant destruction of Ḍabbah and the slaughter of its chieftains and champions.

طَرِبْتَ وَهَاجَتْكَ ٱلظِّبَاءُ ٱلسَّوَانِحُ   غَدَاةَ غَدَتْ مِنْهَا سَنِيحٌ وَبَارِحُ
فَمَالَتْ بِيَ ٱلْأَهْوَاءُ حَتَّى كَأَنَّمَا   بِزَنْدَيْنِ فِي جَوْفِي مِنَ ٱلْوَجْدِ قَادِحُ
تَعَزَّيْتَ عَنْ ذِكْرَى سُهَيَّةَ حِقْبَةً   فَبُحْ عَنْكَ مِنْهَا بِٱلَّذِي أَنْتَ بَائِحُ
لَعَمْرِي لَقَدْ أَعْذَرْتُ لَوْ تَعْذِرِينَنِي   وَخَشَّنْتِ صَدْرًا غَيْبُهُ لَكِ نَاصِحُ
أَعَاذِلَ كَمْ مِنْ يَوْمِ حَرْبٍ شَهِدْتُهُ   لَهُ مَنْظَرٌ بَادِي ٱلنَّوَاجِذِ كَالِحُ
فَلَمْ أَرَ حَيًّا صَابَرُوا مِثْلَ صَبْرِنَا   وَلَا كَافَحُوا مِثْلَ ٱلَّذِينَ نُكَافِحُ
إِذَا شِئْتُ لَاقَانِي كَمِيٌّ مُدَجَّجٌ   عَلَى أَعْوَجِيٍّ بِٱلطِّعَانِ مُسَامِحُ
نُزَاحِفُ زَحْفًا أَوْ نُلَاقِي كَتِيبَةً   تُطَاعِنُنَا أَوْ يَذْعَرُ ٱلسَّرْحَ صَائِحُ
فَلَمَّا ٱلْتَقَيْنَا بِٱلْجِفَارِ تَصَعْصَعُوا   وَرُدَّتْ عَلَى أَعْقَابِهِنَّ ٱلْمَسَالِحُ
وَسَارَتْ رِجَالٌ نَحْوَ أُخْرَى عَلَيْهِمُ ٱلْـ   ـحَدِيدُ كَمَا تَمْشِي ٱلْجِمَالُ ٱلدَّوَالِحُ

البحر: الطويل.

The antelopes sprinted right and left
in the morning light.[89]
Passion flared
desire took hold.
I'd absorbed
the loss of Suhayyah
but now it's time
to reveal my thoughts.
You were cruel
to one who wished
you well, and I
forgave you.
Why wouldn't you
forgive me?

Enough! I've seen too many
snarling days,
when our clan was unbowed
our foes unrivaled.[90]
Bring on the warriors
brandishing their spears
on Aʿwaj stallions.
We march on armies
attack the cavalry
under a salvo,
in dawn raids
scattering herds of women.[91]

Our armies met by the wells of Jifār.
Their scouts turned tail
the soldiers breaking
ranks in fear—
the iron-weight warriors
fought to the death
in chain mail flowing
like sheets of raging

إِذَا مَا مَشَوْا فِي ٱلسَّابِغَاتِ حَسِبْتَهُمْ   سُيُولًا وَقَدْ جَاشَتْ بِهِنَّ ٱلْأَبَاطِحُ
فَأُشْرِعَ رَايَاتٌ وَتَحْتَ ظِلَالِهَا   مِنَ ٱلْقَوْمِ أَبْنَاءُ ٱلْحُرُوبِ ٱلْمَرَاجِحُ
وَدُرْنَا كَمَا دَارَتْ عَلَى قُطْبِهَا ٱلرَّحَى   وَدَارَتْ عَلَى هَامِ ٱلرِّجَالِ ٱلصَّفَائِحُ
بِهَاجِرَةٍ حَتَّى تَغَيَّبَ نُورُهَا   وَأَقْبَلَ لَيْلٌ يَقْبِضُ ٱلطَّرْفَ سَائِحُ
تَدَاعَى بَنُو عَبْسٍ بِكُلِّ مُهَنَّدٍ   حُسَامٍ يُزِيلُ ٱلْهَامَ وَٱلصَّفُّ جَانِحُ
وَكُلِّ رُدَيْنِيٍّ كَأَنَّ سِنَانَهُ   شِهَابٌ بَدَا فِي ظُلْمَةِ ٱللَّيْلِ وَاضِحُ
فَخَلَّوْا لَنَا عُوذَ ٱلنِّسَاءِ وَجَبَّبُوا   عَبَادِيدَ مِنْهَا مُسْتَقِيمٌ وَجَامِحُ
وَكُلَّ كَعَابٍ خَدْلَةِ ٱلسَّاقِ فَخْمَةٍ   لَهَا مَنْصِبٌ فِي آلِ ضَبَّةَ طَامِحُ
تَرَكْنَا ضِرَارًا بَيْنَ عَانٍ مُكَبَّلٍ   وَبَيْنَ قَتِيلٍ غَابَ عَنْهُ ٱلنَّوَائِحُ
وَعَمْرًا وَحَيَّانًا تَرَكْنَا بِقَفْرَةٍ   تَعُودُهُمَا فِيهَا ٱلضِّبَاعُ ٱلْكَوَالِحُ
يُجَرِّرْنَ هَامًا فَلَّقَتْهُ رِمَاحُنَا   تُزَيِّلُ مِنْهُنَّ ٱللِّحَى وَٱلْمَسَائِحُ

floodwater, lumbering
    like laden camels.
The banners cast shadows
    over war-bitten troops
and like a millstone
    on its pivot[92]
we turned, swinging
    our broad blades
overhead in the heat of day
    until the light was hidden
in black night, robbing
    the eye of sight.[93]
The swords of the ʿAbs
    answered each other—
Indian blades severing skulls,
    Rudaynah spears
with iron heads,
    comets against the darkness.
Some froze to the spot.
    Others panicked, abandoning
mothers, children, and Ḍabbah's
    pert-breasted maids.
We clapped Ḍirār in irons
    slaying others, unmourned.
In the wilderness the corpses
    of ʿAmr and Ḥayyān
played host to snarling hyenas
    that tore at beards and curls
and dragged heads
    our swords split open.

~ 25 ~

An enemy squadron attacked

A personal boast with a description of brave comrades, followed by a raid narrative, continuing with a celebration of the exemplariness of the poet's ethical conduct, which ends on a surprising note when the poet declares his undying love for ʿAblah.

وَكَتِيبَةٍ لَبَّسْتُهَا بِكَتِيبَةٍ   شَهْبَاءَ بَاسِلَةٍ يُخَافُ رَدَاهَا
خَرْسَاءَ ظَاهِرَةِ ٱلْأَدَاةِ كَأَنَّهَا   نَارٌ يُشَبُّ وَقُودُهَا بِلَظَاهَا
فِيهَا ٱلْكُمَاةُ بَنُو ٱلْكُمَاةِ كَأَنَّهُمْ   وَٱلْخَيْلُ تَعْثُرُ فِي ٱلْوَغَى بِقَنَاهَا
شُهُبٌ بِأَيْدِي ٱلْقَابِسِينَ إِذَا بَدَتْ   بِأَكُفِّهِمْ بَهَرَ ٱلظَّلَامَ سَنَاهَا
صُبُرٌ أَعَدُّوا كُلَّ أَجْرَدَ سَابِحٍ   وَنَجِيبَةٍ ذَبَلَتْ وَخَفَّ حَشَاهَا
يَعْدُونَ بِٱلْمُسْتَلْئِمِينَ عَوَابِسًا   قُودًا تَشَكَّى أَيْنَهَا وَوَجَاهَا
يَحْمِلْنَ فِتْيَانًا مَدَاعِسَ بِٱلْقَنَا   وُقُرًا إِذَا مَا ٱلْحَرْبُ خَفَّ لِوَاهَا
مِنْ كُلِّ أَرْوَعَ مَاجِدٍ ذِي صَوْلَةٍ   مَرِسٍ إِذَا لَحِقَتْ خُصًى بِكُلَاهَا
وَصَحَابَةٍ شُمِّ ٱلْأُنُوفِ بَعَثْتُهُمْ   لَيْلًا وَقَدْ مَالَ ٱلْكَرَى بِطُلَاهَا
وَسَرَيْتُ فِي وَعْثِ ٱلظَّلَامِ أَقُودُهُمْ   حَتَّى رَأَيْتُ ٱلشَّمْسَ زَالَ ضُحَاهَا
وَلَقِيتُ فِي قُبُلِ ٱلْهَجِيرِ كَتِيبَةً   فَطَعَنْتُ أَوَّلَ فَارِسٍ أُولَاهَا
وَضَرَبْتُ قَرْنَيْ كَبْشِهَا فَتَجَدَّلَا   وَحَمَلْتُ مُهْرِي وَسْطَهَا فَمَضَاهَا

البحر: الكامل.

An enemy squadron attacked.[94]
My cavalry crushed it,
arms aglitter, hearts high—
silent agents of death
as sudden to strike as dry
wood bursting
into flame,
their horses wading
into battle, stumbling
over lances—
spawn of soldiers,
well-armed troops blazing
through the darkness
like embers
stirred to life—
steadfast men, trainers
of sleek stallions and lean mares
grimacing and galloping
stretching their long necks
grumbling of weary hooves
freighted with armor,
carrying the spearmen
trained not to flee
when banners feel light in battle.
Fearsome heroes, noble and strong
leaping into the fray
when testicles tighten.

This proud troop I roused,
heads heavy with sleep.
We traveled through the talcy sands
of night till dawn spread into day.
With the sun at its hottest pitch
I fell upon an enemy knight
and hacked him down at the head of his column
then locked horns with their chief

حَتَّى رَأَيْتُ ٱلْخَيْلَ بَعْدَ سَوَادِهَا   حُمْرَ ٱلْجُلُودِ خُضِبْنَ مِنْ جَرْحَاهَا
يَعْثُرْنَ فِي وَقْعِ ٱلنَّجِيعِ جَوَافِلاً   وَيَطَأْنَ مِنْ حَمْيِ ٱلْوَغَى قَتْلَاهَا
فَرَجَعْتُ مَحْمُودًا بِرَأْسِ عَظِيمِهَا   وَتَرَكْتُهَا جَزَرًا لِمَنْ نَاوَاهَا
مَا ٱسْتَمْتُ أُنْثَى نَفْسَهَا فِي مَوْطِنٍ   حَتَّى أُوَفِّيَ مَهْرَهَا مَوْلَاهَا
وَلَمَا رَزَأْتُ أَخَا حِفَاظٍ سِلْعَةً   إِلَّا لَهُ عِنْدِي بِهَا مِثْلَاهَا
أَغْشَى فَتَاةَ ٱلْحَيِّ عِنْدَ حَلِيلِهَا   وَإِذَا غَزَا فِي ٱلْجَيْشِ لَا أَغْشَاهَا
وَأَغُضُّ طَرْفِي مَا بَدَتْ لِيَ جَارَتِي   حَتَّى يُوَارِيَ جَارَتِي مَأْوَاهَا
إِنِّي ٱمْرُؤٌ سَمْحُ ٱلْخَلِيقَةِ مَاجِدٌ   لَا أُتْبِعُ ٱلنَّفْسَ ٱللَّجُوجَ هَوَاهَا
وَلَئِنْ سَأَلْتَ بِذَاكَ عَبْلَةَ خَبَّرَتْ   أَنْ لَا أُرِيدُ مِنَ ٱلنِّسَاءِ سِوَاهَا
وَأُجِيبُهَا إِمَّا دَعَتْ لِعَظِيمَةٍ   وَأُعِينُهَا وَأَكُفُّ عَمَّا سَاهَا

and slashed my way into their midst
    as the black horses ran red with wounds,
wading through a swamp of blood,
    in their war lust trampling the dead.
Covered in glory, I returned
    with the head of their mighty chief—
all defiance strewn behind me,
    hacked to pieces.

I've never set out to seduce a woman
    but always paid the full dowry.
I've never robbed a comrade of riches
    without repaying him twofold.
I never visit a tribeswoman
    unless her husband's near—
when our tribe is off on a raid
    I stay away.
A woman's modesty in my care
    I preserve.

I am a man of glorious deeds
    in all things charitable,
no slave to his desire.
    If you ask ʿAblah about me
she'll say I want her, and her alone.
    She demands great things of me
and I don't disappoint—
    I keep ruin at bay.

~ 26 ~

Jirwah is mine

In this concise tribal boast embroiled in the mundanities of clan conflict, clearly a response to an invective directed at the poet and his clan by the kin group of al-ʿUsharāʾ, part of Fazārah, the poet's praise of his warhorse is also a threat of attack, and is in keeping with the spirit of Poem 11.

مَنْ يَكُ سَائِلًا عَنِّي فَإِنِّي وَجِرْوَةَ لَا تَرُودُ وَلَا تُعَارُ
مُقَرَّبَةُ ٱلشِّتَاءِ وَلَا تَرَاهَا وَرَاءَ ٱلْحَيِّ يَتْبَعُهَا ٱلْمِهَارُ
لَهَا بِٱلصَّيْفِ أَصْبِرَةٌ وَجُلٌّ وَنِيبٌ مِنْ كَرَائِمِهَا غِزَارُ
أَلَا أَبْلِغْ بَنِي ٱلْعُشَرَاءِ عَنِّي عَلَانِيَةً فَقَدْ ذَهَبَ ٱلسِّرَارُ
قَتَلْتُ سَرَاتَكُمْ وَخَسَلْتُ مِنْكُمْ خَسِيلًا مِثْلَ مَا خُسِلَ ٱلْوِبَارُ
وَلَمْ نَقْتُلْكُمُ سِرًّا وَلٰكِنْ عَلَانِيَةً وَقَدْ سَطَعَ ٱلْغُبَارُ
فَلَمْ يَكُ حَقُّكُمْ أَنْ تَشْتُمُونَا بَنِي ٱلْعُشَرَاءِ إِذْ جَدَّ ٱلْفَخَارُ

البحر: الوافر.

If anyone asks
    Jirwah is mine.
In winter
    I don't let her roam.
I keep her foals
    close to the tribe.
In summer
    she gets camel's milk
and fine fodder.

Give 'Usharā' this message—
    the time for secrets is gone.
I slew your chief
    and sent you scurrying
like rabbits into your holes.[95]
    In the dust of battle
we slaughtered you in
    broad daylight.
When men clamor
    and boast you have
no right
    to insult us.

~ 27 ~

War ripped out Ghaṭafān's spine

The poet bewails the start of the War of Dāḥis and al-Ghabrā' that led to the death of Mālik ibn Zuhayr, brother of the 'Abs commander Qays ibn Zuhayr.

لِلّٰهِ عَيْنَا مَنْ رَأَى مِثْلَ مَالِكٍ   عَقِيرَةَ قَوْمٍ أَنْ جَرَى فَرَسَانِ
فَلَيْتَهُمَا لَمْ يَجْرِيَا نِصْفَ غَلْوَةٍ   وَلَيْتَهُمَا لَمْ يُرْسَلَا لِرِهَانِ
وَلَيْتَهُمَا مَاتَا جَمِيعًا بِبَلْدَةٍ   وَأَخْطَاهُمَا قَيْسٌ فَلَا يُرَيَانِ
لَقَدْ جَلَبَا حَيْنًا وَحَرْبًا عَظِيمَةً   تُبِيدُ سَرَاةَ ٱلْقَوْمِ مِنْ غَطَفَانِ
وَكَانَ فَتَى ٱلْهَيْجَاءِ يَحْمِي ذِمَارَهَا   وَيَضْرِبُ عِنْدَ ٱلْكَرِّ كُلَّ بَنَانِ

البحر: الطويل.

The grim sight of such a hero
    slaughtered for a race, God.
The bets should have never been placed,[96]
    Qays should never have watched,
the horses should never have run
    but died in a far-off land!
They raised hell and War ripped out
    Ghaṭafān's spine—
keeper of their honor in battle,
    hacker of limbs.[97]

Two Qasidas from Ibn Maymūn's Anthology

~ 28 ~

The East Wind blew

An epic boast addressed to ʿAblah, this poem is clearly inspired by the address to ʿAblah and the battle scenes in the Muʿallaqah, and by key lines in ʿAntarah's corpus, such as the final line of Poem 5. The poem is also included in The Epic of ʿAntar. The enumeration of the tribes is not typical of the style of the poems in al-Aṣmaʿī's redaction. The Iraqi location of the Battle of Shibāk is also more in keeping with the topography of The Epic of ʿAntar.

عَفَّى ٱلرُّسُومَ وَبَاقِيَ ٱلْأَطْلَالِ   رِيحُ ٱلصَّبَا وَتَجَرُّمُ ٱلْأَحْوَالِ
لَعِبَتْ بِعَافِيهَا وَأَخْلَقَ رَسْمُهَا   وَوَكِيفُ كُلِّ مُجَلْجَلٍ هَطَّالِ
كَانَتْ بَنُو هِنْدٍ فَشَطَّ مَزَارُهَا   وَتَبَدَّلَتْ خَيْطًا مِنَ ٱلْآجَالِ
فَلَئِنْ صَرَمْتِ ٱلْحَبْلَ يَا ٱبْنَةَ مَالِكٍ   وَسَمِعْتِ فِيَّ مَقَالَةَ ٱلْعُذَّالِ
فَلَعَمْرُ جَدِّكِ إِنَّنِي لَمُشَايِعِي   لُبِّي وَإِنِّي لِلْمُلُوكِ لَقَالِي
وَسَلِي لِكَيْمَا تُخْبَرِي بِفَعَالِنَا   عِنْدَ ٱلْوَغَى وَمَوَاقِفِ ٱلْأَهْوَالِ
وَٱلْخَيْلُ تَعْثُرُ بِٱلْقَنَا فِي جَاحِمٍ   تَهْفُو بِهِ وَيَجُلْنَ كُلَّ مَجَالِ
وَأَنَا ٱلْمُجَرَّبُ فِي ٱلْمَوَاطِنِ كُلِّهَا   مِنْ آلِ عَبْسٍ مَنْصِبِي وَفَعَالِي
مِنْهُمْ أَبِي حَقًّا فَهُمْ لِي وَالِدٌ   وَٱلْأُمُّ مِنْ حَامٍ فَهُمْ أَخْوَالِي

البحر: الكامل.

The years passed
and the East Wind blew.[98]
Even the ruins
fell into ruin—
tired playthings
of Time
and the thunder
and rain.
Clan Hind lived here once.
You can't visit them now—
Fate has spun
their thread.

If you heed the gossipers,
Daughter of Mālik,
and sever the ties
that we share,
I swear by your ancestors
my mind is a match
for my mettle.
I'm no friend of kings!
Ask about my deeds
when Fear stood
primed for battle
and the horses waded
through the blaze of spears.
War has steeled my nerve.
Is there any fray
I haven't fought in?
I yield my fame
to my father's clan—
my mother descends
from the sons of Ham.
In the forest of lances
one thrust from me
and your Fate is changed.

وَأَنَا ٱلْمَنِيَّةُ حِينَ تَشْتَجِرُ ٱلْقَنَا   وَٱلطَّعْنُ مِنِّي سَابِقُ ٱلْآجَالِ
وَلَرُبَّ قِرْنٍ قَدْ تَرَكْتُ مُجَدَّلًا   بِلَبَانِهِ كَنَوَاضِحِ ٱلْجِرْيَالِ
تَنْتَابُهُ طُلْسُ ٱلسِّبَاعِ مُغَادَرًا   فِي قَفْرَةٍ مُتَمَزِّقَ ٱلْأَوْصَالِ
أَوْجَرْتُهُ لَدْنَ ٱلْمَهَزَّةِ ذَابِلًا   مَرَنَتْ عَلَيْهِ أَشَاجِعِي وَخِصَالِي
وَلَرُبَّ خَيْلٍ قَدْ وَزَعْتُ رَعِيلَهَا   بِأَقَبَّ لَا ضَغِنٍ وَلَا مِجْفَالِ
وَمُسَرْبَلٍ حَلَقَ ٱلْحَدِيدِ مُدَجَّجٍ   كَٱللَّيْثِ بَيْنَ عَرِينَةِ ٱلْأَشْبَالِ
غَادَرْتُهُ لِلْجَنْبِ غَيْرَ مُوَسَّدٍ   مُتَثَنِّيَ ٱلْأَوْصَالِ عِنْدَ مَجَالِ
وَلَرُبَّ شَرْبٍ قَدْ صَبَحْتُ مُدَامَةً   لَيْسُوا بِأَنْكَاسٍ وَلَا أَوْغَالِ

I am Death.
    I've felled many
        a foe, their chests
dyed in rivers of red jiryāl,
    their bodies unburied
        on the open plain,
their limbs torn
    to shreds
        by dusky wolves,
            aortas pierced
by the pliant spear
    gripped tight
        as I closed in.

On a lean warhorse,
    hard to spook,
        unflinching,
I've held the line
    at the head of my troops.
        I've left mighty
lions lying
    in chain mail
        in the dirt,
clutching guts
    limbs spasmed
        with pain
heads
    unpillowed
        by the hard plain.

I've served wine
    to high-born and brave
        at dawn,
bewitched
    pert-breasted girls
        with a flicker of shyness

وَكَوَاعِبٍ مِثْلِ ٱلدُّمَى أَصْبَيْتُهَا   يَنْظُرْنَ فِي خَفَرٍ وَحُسْنِ دَلَالِ

وَسَلِي بِنَا عَكًّا وَخَثْعَمَ تُخْبَرِي   وَسَلِي ٱلْمُلُوكَ وَطَيِّئَ ٱلْأَجْبَالِ

أَوْ آلَ ضَبَّةَ بِٱلشِّبَاكِ إِذِ ٱسْلَمَتْ   بَكْرٌ حَلَائِلَهَا وَرَهْطَ عِقَالِ

وَبَنِي صَبَاحٍ قَدْ تَرَكْنَا مِنْهُمُ   جَزَرًا بِذَاتِ ٱلرِّمْثِ فَوْقَ أُثَالِ

زَيْدًا وَسُودًا وَٱلْمُقَطَّعَ أَقْصَدَتْ   أَرْمَاحُنَا وَمُجَاشِعَ بْنَ هِلَالِ

رُعْنَاهُمُ بِٱلْخَيْلِ تَرْدِي بِٱلْقَنَا   وَبِكُلِّ أَبْيَضَ صَارِمٍ قَصَّالِ

يَوْمَ ٱلشِّبَاكِ فَأَسْلَمُوا أَبْنَاءَهُمْ   وَنَوَاعِمًا كَٱلرَّبْرَبِ ٱلْأَطْفَالِ

in their eyes,
    white as the marble
        effigies of goddesses.

Ask Khathʿam and ʿAkk
    about our feats.
        Ask the kings.
            Ask Ṭayyiʾ of the Mountains.
Ask Ḍabbah's folk about Shibāk
    when in the fray
        the Bakr yielded
            their wives and ʿIqāl's kin.
Ask Clan Ṣabāḥ
    how we butchered them
        at Dhāt al-Rimth
            above Uthāl.
Ask Zayd and Sūd.
    Ask al-Muqaṭṭaʿ
        and Mujāshiʿ ibn Hilāl
how our spears
    sought them out
        how our horses
            filled them with fear
as we wielded
    swords
        keen and bright
            harvesting limbs.
Ask how
    they yielded their sons
        and pampered women
like a herd of young
    oryx
        at the Battle of Shibāk.

مَنْ مِثْلُ قَوْمِي حِينَ تَخْتَلِفُ ٱلْقَنَا   وَإِذَا تَـزُولُ مَـقَادِمُ ٱلْأَبْطَالِ
فَفِدًى لِقَوْمِي عِنْدَ كُلِّ عَظِيمَةٍ   نَفْسِي وَرَاحِلَتِي وَسَائِرُ مَالِي
قَوْمِي ٱلصِّمَامُ لِمَنْ أَرَادُوا ضَيْمَهُمْ   وَٱلْقَاهِرُونَ لِكُلِّ أَغْلَبَ خَالِي
وَٱلْمُطْعِمُونَ وَمَا عَلَيْهِمْ نِعْمَةٌ   وَٱلْأَكْرَمُونَ أَبًا وَمَحْتِدَ خَالِ
نَحْنُ ٱلْحَصَى عَدَدًا وَسَطْنَا قَوْمَنَا   وَرِجَالُنَا فِي ٱلْحَرْبِ غَيْرُ رِجَالِ
مِنَّا ٱلْمُعِينُ عَلَى ٱلنَّدَى بِفَعَالِهِ   وَٱلْبَذْلِ فِي ٱللَّزَبَاتِ بِٱلْأَمْوَالِ
إِنَّا إِذَا حَمِسَ ٱلْوَغَى نُرْوِي ٱلْقَنَا   وَنَعِفُّ عِنْدَ مَقَاسِمِ ٱلْأَنْفَالِ
نَأْتِي ٱلصَّرِيخَ عَلَى جِيَادٍ ضُمَّرٍ   قُبِّ ٱلْبُطُونِ كَأَنَّهُنَّ مَغَالِ

When spears clash
and the mighty fall
the men in my command
are unrivaled.
My life, my camel—
when disaster strikes
I'd give everything
I possess
for my fighters
of noble descent
heroes who crush
every opponent
destroying lion-
necked warriors,
feeding the hungry,
refusing to yield.

We are the heart of the tribe
multitudinous
as the desert sands
no ordinary soldiers
generous to a fault
we give what we have
in times of drought.
We let our lances
drink deep
from the fires of War
but show restraint
dividing the spoils.
Our battle-drilled steeds
are quick to answer
cries for help—
long-legged mares
swift as arrows
strong in the stretch

مِنْ كُلِّ شَوْهَاءِ ٱلْيَدَيْنِ طِمِرَّةٍ   وَمُقَلِّصٍ عَبْلِ ٱلشَّوَى ذَيَّالِ

لَا تَأْسَيَنَّ عَلَى خَلِيطٍ زَايَلُوا   بَعْدَ ٱلْأُلَى قُتِلُوا بِذِي أَخْتَالِ

كَانُوا يَشُبُّونَ ٱلْحُرُوبَ إِذَا خَبَتْ   قُدُمًا بِكُلِّ مُهَنَّدٍ قَصَّالِ

وَبِكُلِّ مَحْبُوكِ ٱلسَّرَاةِ مُقَلِّصٍ   تَنْمِي مَنَاسِبُهُ لِذِي ٱلْعُقَّالِ

وَمُعَاوِدِ ٱلتَّكْرَارِ طَالَ مَضِيُّهُ   طَعْنًا بِكُلِّ مُثَقَّفٍ عَسَّالِ

مِنْ كُلِّ أَرْوَعَ لِلْكُمَاةِ مُنَازِلٍ   نَاجٍ مِنَ ٱلْغَمَرَاتِ كَٱلرِّئْبَالِ

يُعْطِي ٱلْمِئِينَ إِلَى ٱلْمِئِينَ مُرَزَّأً   حَمَّالَ مُفْظِعَةٍ مِنَ ٱلْأَثْقَالِ

and hard-muscled stallions
solid of limb
thick of tail.

I'll no longer grieve
that tribe of men
slain in Dhū Akhtāl
gone to join our kin.
They would stoke
the fires of War
if its flames
flickered low.
They would attack
with Indian blades
and harvest limbs
astride the bloodline
of Dhū l-ʿUqqāl—[99]
hard-muscled steeds
with welded spines.
They were trained
to wheel and charge
in a phalanx of fighters
to hurl vise-
straightened spears
aquiver in
their grip. They
were a terror
to behold
leaping at their foes
like angry lions
sprung from the dust of War.
They were nobles
who bore the burden
of calamity

وَإِذَا ٱلْأُمُورُ تَحَوَّلَتْ أَلْفَيْتَهُمْ   عِصَمَ ٱلْهَوَالِكِ سَاعَةَ ٱلزِّلْزَالِ
وَهُمُ ٱلْحُمَاةُ إِذَا ٱلنِّسَاءُ تَحَسَّرَتْ   يَوْمَ ٱلْحِفَاظِ وَكَانَ يَوْمَ نِزَالِ
يَقِصُونَ ذَا ٱلْأَنْفِ ٱلْحَمِيِّ وَفِيهِمِ   حِلْمٌ وَلَيْسَ حَرَامُهُمْ بِحَلَالِ
وَٱلْمُطْعِمُونَ إِذَا ٱلسِّنُونَ تَتَابَعَتْ   مَحْلًا وَضَنَّ سَحَابُهَا بِسِجَالِ

providing camels
    by the thousand
        when famine struck
protecting the dying
    when the wind changed
        or earth quaked.
They would parry
    dawn raiders
        in hand-to-hand
combat, keeping
    their wives safe
        and unstained,
dispatching proud foes
    fighting desperately
        to save their women.
They were the men
    who fed the tribe
        during long
years of drought
    when the clouds allowed
        not a bucket of rain.

~ 29 ~

Between shock and grief

A bipartite poem, classic in structure, consisting of an amatory episode followed by a boast celebrating the poet's exploits in repelling a raid. In this expanded version of the shorter piece edited and translated as Poem 5, the motif of the women departing in their litters is cast as part of the remembrance of the departure of the poet's beloved, whereas in the short version of the poem, the motif forms part of the battle narrative proper. As in the Muʿallaqah, the poem culminates in the death of a foe—on this occasion, however, the corpse is not prey to savage predators but, in a dramatic image of trauma, the fallen warrior is surrounded by grief-stricken womenfolk.

نَأَتْكَ رَقَاشِ إِلَّا عَنْ لِمَامِ وَأَمْسَى حَبْلُهَا خَلَقَ ٱلرِّمَامِ
وَمَا ذِكْرِي رَقَاشِ قَدْ أَبَنَّتْ رَحَى ٱلْأَدَمَاتِ عِنْدَ ٱبْنَيْ شَمَامِ
وَمَسْكَنُ أَهْلِهَا مِنْ نَخْلِ جِزْعٍ تَبِيضُ بِهِ مَصَائِيفُ ٱلْحَمَامِ
وَقَفْتُ وَصُحْبَتِي بِشُعَيْلِبَاتٍ عَلَى أَقْتَادِ عُوجٍ كَٱلسَّمَامِ
فَقُلْتُ تَبَيَّنُوا ظُعُنًا سِرَاعًا تَأُمُّ شُوَاحِطًا مَلَثَ ٱلظَّلَامِ
لَقَدْ مَنَّتْكَ نَفْسُكَ يَوْمَ قَوٍّ أَحَادِيثَ ٱلْفُؤَادِ ٱلْمُسْتَهَامِ
وَقَدْ كَذَبَتْكَ نَفْسُكَ فَٱصْدُقَنْهَا بِمَا مَنَّتْكَ تَغْرِيرًا قَطَامِ
وَمُرْقِصَةٍ رَدَدْتُ ٱلْخَيْلَ عَنْهَا وَقَدْ هَمَّتْ بِإِلْقَاءِ ٱلزِّمَامِ
فَقُلْتُ لَهَا أَقِصْرِي مِنْهُ وَسِيرِي وَقَدْ عَلِقَ ٱلرَّجَائِزُ بِٱلْخِدَامِ

البحر: الوافر.

Raqāshi is gone,
our ties are frayed.[100]
Her wraith now visits
me at night.
I think of her leaving
Raḥā l-Adamāt[101]
standing by
the peaks of Shamāmi,
her people camped
in the valley
where the doves
in summer nest.

Our lean camels
like swallows in flight
stopped at Thuʿaylibāt.
"Look," I said.
"Night is falling.
I see the litters
racing for Shuwāḥiṭ."
At Qaww, your soul
told you tales
of a lovelorn heart,
lying about Qaṭāmi.
Go now—be
true to your soul.

In panic my woman
fled in her litter
its curtains flapping.
"Rein her in!"
I cried, keeping
the raiders at bay.
Fear ruled the day.
The riders attacked

وَخَيْلٍ تَحْمِلُ ٱلْأَبْطَالَ شُعْثٍ   غَدَاةَ ٱلرَّوْعِ أَمْثَالَ ٱلزِّلَامِ
عَنَاجِيجٍ تَخُبُّ عَلَى وَجَاهَا   تُثِيرُ ٱلنَّقْعَ بِٱلْمَوْتِ ٱلزُّؤَامِ
إِلَى خَيْلٍ مُسَوَّمَةٍ عَلَيْهَا   حُمَاةُ ٱلرَّوْعِ فِي رَهَجِ ٱلْقَتَامِ
بِأَيْدِيهِمْ مُهَنَّدَةٌ وَسُمْرٌ   كَأَنَّ ظُبَاتِهَا شُعَلُ ٱلضِّرَامِ
فَجَاؤُوا عَارِضًا بَرِدًا وَجِئْنَا   حَرِيقًا فِي غَرِيفٍ ذِي ٱضْطِرَامِ
وَأُسْكِتَ كُلُّ صَوْتٍ غَيْرُ ضَرْبٍ   وَعَتْرَسَةٍ وَمَرْمِيٍّ وَرَامِ
وَزَعْتُ رَعِيلَهَا بِٱلرُّمْحِ شَزْرًا   عَلَى رَبِذٍ كَسِرْحَانِ ٱلظَّلَامِ
أَكُرُّ عَلَيْهِمِ مُهْرِي كَلِيمًا   قَلَائِدُهُ سَبَائِبُ كَٱلْقِرَامِ

in a sandstorm
    of sudden death
on disheveled horses
    thin as arrows
long-necked sprinters
    ignoring the ache
in their hooves.
    In the murk of battle
fearsome fighters
    wielding Indian
blades and brown
    lances tipped
with iron flames
    attacked from one side.
Then we countered
    their feeble charge
with a rush
    exploding in
the cramped field.
    Silence fell.

Listen—then,
    swords clashing
arrows thwacking
    warriors grunting
in dread combat.
    Thrusting my spear
right and left
    I held the line
against a nimble-
    handed champion
attacking like
    a wolf in the night.
Hemmed in
    I wheeled my wounded

إِذَا شَكَّتْ بِنَافِذَةٍ يَدَاهُ   تَعَرَّضَ مَوْقِفًا ضَنْكَ ٱلْمُقَامِ
كَأَنَّ دُفُوفَ مَرْجِعِ مِرْفَقَيْهِ   تَوَارَدَهَا مَنَازِعُ ٱلسِّهَامِ
تَقَدَّمَ وَهْوَ مُضْطَبِرٌ مُصِرٌّ   بِقَارِحِهِ عَلَى فَأْسِ ٱللِّجَامِ
يُقَدِّمُهُ فَتًى مِنْ آلِ قَيْسٍ   أَبُوهُ وَأُمُّهُ مِنْ آلِ حَامِ
عَجُوزٌ مِنْ بَنِي حَامِ بْنِ نُوحٍ   كَأَنَّ جَبِينَهَا حَجَرُ ٱلْمَقَامِ
وَقِرْنٍ قَدْ تَرَكْتُ لَدَى مَكَرٍّ   صَرِيعًا بَيْنَ أَصْدَاءٍ وَهَامِ
تَرَكْتُ ٱلطَّيْرَ عَاكِفَةً عَلَيْهِ   كَمَا تَرْدِي إِلَى ٱلْعُرُسَاتِ آمِ
تَبِيتُ نِسَاؤُهُ عُجُلًا عَلَيْهِ   يُرَاوِحْنَ ٱلتَّفَجُّعَ بِٱلنِّدَامِ

horse, his flanks
    shredded by arrows
his legs gashed
    by spears
his halter tipped
    with blood
fringed like a rug.
    He charged full tilt
gripping the bit
    trained for battle
by a bold warrior
    whose father is
the best of his tribe
    though his mother
descends from Ham
    her brow dark
as the Black Stone.[102]

I felled him
    that champion
amid rusty armor
    and severed heads.
The vultures waited
    on him like maids
attending a bride.
    That night his women
caught between
    shock and grief
prepared his corpse
    for the soil.

Poems from al-Baṭalyawsī's Recension

~ 30 ~

Why are you fat as camels' humps?

A pithy and testy rebuke of his brothers for putting their own needs before those of their warhorses (see Poem 11 above). The commentators situate the poem in a rather obscure narrative, in which ʿAntarah is cast as the resourceful trickster who devises a stratagem to establish in the eyes of his tribe the honorable status of his humble family.

أَبَنِي زَبِيبَةَ مَا لِمُهْرِكُمُ   مُتَخَدِّدًا وَبُطُونُكُمْ عُجْرُ ١
أَأَلَكُمْ بِآلَاءِ ٱلْوَشِيجِ إِذَا   مَرَّ ٱلشِّيَاهُ بِوَقْعِهِ خُبْرُ
إِذْ لَا تَزَالُ لَكُمْ مُغَرْغِرَةٌ   تَغْلِي وَأَعْلَى لَوْنِهَا صَهْرُ
لَمَّا غَدَوْا وَغَدَتْ سَطِيحَتُهُمْ   مَلْأَى وَبَطْنُ جَوَادِهِمْ صِفْرُ ٤

البحر: الكامل.

Sons of Zabībah, brothers, why
    are you fat as camels' humps
        when your colt's so thin?
Have you forgotten the good things
    that stiff spears bring
        when you kill
the nimble oryx
    and the fat bubbles
        at the cauldron's rim?
Your horses starve
    while you wake
        to buckets of milk.

~ 31 ~

Spears adrip with gore

A pithy victory chant, a miniature masterpiece of war poetry, in which exploit and incident charge at the listener. The poem is packed with detail and is remarkable for the verve of its battle scene.

بَرَّحَ بِٱلْعَيْنَيْنِ كُلُّ مُغْبِرَةٍ أَسِنَّتُهَا مِنْ قَانِي ٱلدَّمِ تَرْدُمُ ١
أُمَارِسُ فِيهَا ٱبْنَيْ قُشَيْرٍ كِلَيْهِمَا بِرُمْحِيَ حَتَّى بَلَّ عَامِلَهُ ٱلدَّمُ
أُمَارِسُ خَيْلاً لِلْهُجَيْمِ كَأَنَّهَا سَعَالَى بِأَيْدِيهَا ٱلْوَشِيجُ ٱلْمُقَوَّمُ ٣

البحر: الطويل.

Spears adrip with gore
    the raiders charge.
My eyes smart
    in the murk.
Spearhaft steeped
    in black blood
I fight the sons
    of Qushayr[103]
and the troops
    of the Hujaym—
She-devils
    brandishing
battle-stiff spears.

~ 32 ~

The crow croaked

This extended version of Poem 8 converts the ruminations on Fate expressed in that poem into a glorious bipartite battle chant, with a fine raid narrative that culminates in a majestic image of a mighty eagle. This new version of the poem, especially in view of the dawn raid, is closely interwoven with Ibn al-Sikkīt's account of the occasion of its composition, quoted by both al-Shantamarī and al-Baṭalyawsī.

ظَعَنَ ٱلَّذِينَ فِرَاقَهُمْ أَتَوَقَّعُ   وَجَرَى بِبَيْنِهِمُ ٱلْغُرَابُ ٱلْأَبْقَعُ
حَرِقُ ٱلْجَنَاحِ كَأَنَّ لَحْيَيْ رَأْسِهِ   جَلَمَانِ بِٱلْأَخْبَارِ هَشٌّ مُولَعُ
فَزَجَرْتُهُ أَلَّا يُفَرِّخَ عُشَّهُ   أَبَدًا وَيُصْبِحَ وَاحِدًا يَتَفَجَّعُ
إِنَّ ٱلَّذِينَ نَعَيْتَ لِي بِفِرَاقِهِمْ   هُمْ أَسْهَرُوا لَيْلِي ٱلتِّمَامَ فَأَوْجَعُوا
وَمُغِيرَةٍ شَعْوَاءَ ذَاتِ أَشِلَّةٍ   فِيهَا ٱلْفَوَارِسُ حَاسِرٌ وَمُقَنَّعُ
فَزَجَرْتُهَا عَنْ نِسْوَةٍ مِنْ عَامِرٍ   أَفْخَاذُهُنَّ كَأَنَّهُنَّ ٱلْخِرْوَعُ
وَعَرَفْتُ أَنَّ مَنِيَّتِي إِنْ تَأْتِنِي   لَا يُنْجِنِي مِنْهَا ٱلْفِرَارُ ٱلْأَسْرَعُ
فَصَبَرْتُ عَارِفَةً لِذَٰلِكَ حُرَّةً   تَرْسُو إِذَا نَفْسُ ٱلْجَبَانِ تَطَلَّعُ
كَمْ فِيهِمُ لِي مِنْ صَدِيقٍ مَاجِدٍ   أَمْسَى تَوَى وَلِكُلِّ جَنْبٍ مَصْرَعُ
وَلَقَدْ صَبَحْنَا جَعْفَرًا وَضِبَابَهَا   وَبَنِي ٱلْوَحِيدِ بِكُلِّ حِزْقٍ يُرْوِعُ

البحر: الكامل.

The crow,
beak like a pair of shears,
croaked.
I was afraid
they'd leave
and now they're gone.
"Don't let your chicks fly the nest
and leave you lost
and bereft"
I warned him, but his news
inspired my fear
the long night through.
Yet I've often defended
the women of ʿĀmir,
their legs slim
and tender as stalks,
from the onslaught of
armed raiders.
I won't be able
to outrun Fate
when she comes.
Cowards run.
I stand
my ground,
despite my comrades
my men of honor
dead by dusk.

At dawn we raided
Jaʿfar,
Ḍabāb, and Waḥīd,
a fearsome troop
of ʿAbs riders
rallying to our cry.

بِفَوَارِسٍ مِنْ آلِ عَبْسٍ إِنَّهُمْ سَجَلُوا لَكُمْ فِي ٱلْحَرْبِ حِينَ تَسَمَّعُوا
مِنْ طُولِ مَا سَعَرُوا ٱلْحُرُوبَ وَطِئْتُكُمْ يَا آلَ كَعْبٍ فَٱصْبِرُوا لَا تَجْزَعُوا
وَعَلَيَّ سَابِغَةٌ تَمُورُ فُضُولُهَا مَجْدُولَةٌ مِمَّا تَخَيَّرَ تُبَّعُ
زَغْفٌ أُكَفِّتُهَا بِأَبْيَضَ صَارِمٍ عَضْبٍ إِذَا مَسَّ ٱلْكَرِيهَةَ يَقْطَعُ
فَغَدَوْتُ تَحْمِلُ شِكَّتِي خَيْفَانَةٌ مَرَطَى ٱلْجِرَاءِ لَهَا تَلِيلٌ أَتْلَعُ
كَمُدِلَّةٍ عَجْزَاءَ تُلْحِمُ نَاهِضاً فِي ٱلْوَكْرِ مَوْقِعُهَا ٱلشَّظَاءُ ٱلْأَرْفَعُ
تَرْعَى ٱلنَّهَارَ مَبِيتُهَا فِي شَاهِقٍ صُلْبٍ أَشَمَّ مِنَ ٱلذُّرَى مُتَمَنِّعُ

How we engulfed you
in floods of War,[104]
fires stoked high!
We crushed you. Stop
sniveling, Kaʿb!
Accept your fate.
Clad in the garb
of Yemen's kings,
a long coat of mail
rippling like the sea,
I wielded a keen
white blade
answering War's
touch with slash
and cut, astride
my nimble steed—
a long-necked colossus
swift to charge,
a mighty white-tailed
eagle feeding
her chick in
her cliff-top aerie.

~ 33 ~

Pay for my blood

A short piece threatening vengeance on a foe in return for an arrow injury, consistent with the occasional, responsive, and belligerent features of non-qasida poetry.

إِنَّ ٱبْنَ سَلْمَى فَٱعْلَمُوا عِنْدَهُ دَمِي   وَهَيْهَاتَ لَا يُرْجَى ٱبْنُ سَلْمَى وَلَا دَمِي ١
يَحُلُّ بِأَكْنَافِ ٱلشِّعَابِ وَيَنْتَمِي   مَكَانَ ٱلثُّرَيَّا لَيْسَ بِٱلْمُتَهَضَّمِ
رَمَانِي وَلَمْ يَدْهَشْ بِأَزْرَقَ لَهْذَمٍ   عَشِيَّةَ حَلُّوا بَيْنَ نَعْفٍ وَمَخْرَمِ ٣

البحر: الطويل.

Listen! Ibn Salmā
    has to pay
for my blood.
    But how make him?
He's holed up
    in his fortress
near the stars.

The night my men
    set up camp
between the peak
    and the pass
he shot an arrow
    at me and
its iron flange
    sliced me to
the quick.

~ 34 ~

My horse Blaze

A splendid example of pre-Islamic war poetry, with some proud praise of a magnificent warhorse. The attribution of the poem to ʿAntarah is as early as the lifetime of Ibn Qutaybah, who quotes two lines in his Major Treatise on Qurʾanic Motifs (Kitāb al-Maʿānī al-kabīr). The topography of the battles listed in the final line (to be found in the region of the southern Euphrates) would be more in keeping with The Epic of ʿAntar than with the poetry of ʿAntarah, which is predominantly focused on the topography of Najd and Yamāmah.

جَزَى ٱللهُ ٱلْأَغَرَّ جَزَاءَ صِدْقٍ   إِذَا مَا أُوقِدَتْ نَارُ ٱلْحُرُوبِ

يَقِينِي بِٱلْجَبِينِ وَمَنْكِبَيْهِ   وَأَنْصُرُهُ بِمُطَّرِدِ ٱلْكُعُوبِ

وَأُدْفِئُهُ إِذَا هَبَّتْ شَمَالًا   بَلِيلًا حَرْجَفًا بَعْدَ ٱلْجَنُوبِ

أَرَاهُ أَهْلَ ذٰلِكَ حِينَ يَسْعَى   رِعَاءُ ٱلْحَيِّ فِي طَلَبِ ٱلْحَلُوبِ

فَيُخْفِقُ تَارَةً وَيُفِيدُ أُخْرَى   وَيَفْجَعُ ذَا ٱلضَّغَائِنِ بِٱلْأَرِيبِ

إِذَا سَمِنَ ٱلْأَغَرُّ دَنَا لِقَاءٌ   يُغِصُّ ٱلشَّيْخَ بِٱللَّبَنِ ٱلْحَلِيبِ

شَدِيدُ مَجَالِزِ ٱلْكَتِفَيْنِ نَهْدٌ   بِهِ أَثَرُ ٱلْأَسِنَّةِ كَٱلْعُلُوبِ

البحر: الوافر.

God, reward
    my horse Blaze!
He was a true
    comrade, shielding me
with muzzle and shoulder
    when we plunged
through fires of War.
    I protected him
with my sword.
    When the South Wind
had blown over
    and the rains arrived
from the bitter north
    I kept him warm—
he deserved no less—
    I gave him milk
though the drovers struggled
    to find any
among the herds.

Our raids would sometimes
    fail but Blaze
often helped
    the skilled warrior
conquer the spite
    of foes and gain
his spoils. In his prime,
    withers taut
and mighty spear-
    scarred barrel chest,
we faced a conflict
    so fierce it made
tribal elders
    choke on their milk.

وَأُكْرِهُـهُ عَلَى ٱلْأَبْطَالِ حَـتَّى   يُـرَى كَـٱلْأُرْجُوَانِيِّ ٱلْمُجُوبِ

أَلَسْتَ بِصَاحِبِي يَوْمَ ٱلْتَقَـيْنَا   بِسِيفَ وَصَاحِبِي يَوْمَ ٱلْكَثِيبِ

We charged the foe
    till Blaze seemed robed
in crimson blood.
    At the battles of Sīf and Kathīb
he was a comrade true.

~ 35 ~

My steeds live for War

A distillation of ʿAntarah's ethos and poetry: weaponry, horses, military prowess, valor, and savagery.

لَا أَمْلِكُ ٱلسَّيْفَ إِلَّا قَدْ ضَرَبْتُ بِهِ   وَلَا تَمُوتُ جِيَادِي وَهْيَ أَغْمَارُ ١
وَلَا أُعَوِّدُ مُهْرِي أَنْ أُوَقِّفَهُ   وَسْطَ ٱلْكُمَاةِ وَلَا يَشْقَى بِيَ ٱلْجَارُ
ضَرَبْتُ عَمْرًا عَلَى ٱلْخَيْشُومِ مُقْتَدِرًا   بِصَارِمٍ مِثْلِ لَوْنِ ٱلْمِلْحِ بَتَّارِ ٣

البحر: البسيط.

My steeds live for War.
My swords are not for show.
My colt's trained not to stop
short on the battlefield.
My shield gives
no cause for complaint.

A slash of my saber
clean as salt
and off came 'Amr's nose![105]

~ 36 ~

Death and Revenge

The poet addresses another famous warrior-poet of ʿAbs in a short poem that is obscure and difficult to understand in the absence of further information and context.

يَا عُرْوَةَ بْنَ ٱلْوَرْدِ خَيْرَ عَبْسِ ١
أَمَا تَرَانِي قَدْ بَذَلْتُ نَفْسِي
لِلْمَوْتِ وَٱلثَّارَاتِ دُونَ عِرْسِي

البحر: الرجز.

Look, ʿUrwah ibn al-Ward
prince of Clan ʿAbs!
To protect my wife
I've lavished my soul
on Death and Revenge.

~ 37 ~

Escape if you can

An epigrammatic exhortation to war, expressed, as so often, in terms of the cosmic economy of water.

تَقُولُ ٱبْنَةُ ٱلْعَبْسِيِّ قَرِّبْ حِمَالَنَا   وَأَفْرَاسَنَا ثُمَّ ٱنْجُ إِنْ كُنْتَ نَاجِيَا ١
فَقُلْتُ لَهَا مَنْ يَغْنَمِ ٱلْيَوْمَ نَفْسَهُ   وَيُنْظَرْ غَدًا يَلْقَ ٱلَّذِي كَانَ لَاقِيَا

البحر: الطويل.

“Water the horses and camels at the well
then escape if you can.”
So spoke the woman of ‘Abs.

“We can save our souls
and live to tell the tale—
but fate won’t be slipped.”

~ 38 ~

At the Pass of Woe

A bloodthirsty victory chant, with a narrative that showcases several dazzlingly executed conceits.

إِنِّي أَنَا عَنْتَرَةُ ٱلْهَجِينُ
فَجَّ ٱلْأُنَانِ قَدْ عَلَا ٱلْأَنِينُ
تُحْصَدُ فِيهِ ٱلْكَفُّ وَٱلْوَتِينُ
مِنْ وَقْعِ سَيْفِي سَقَطَ ٱلْجَنِينُ
عِنْدَكُمْ مِنْ ذٰلِكَ ٱلْيَقِينُ
عَبْلَةُ قُومِي تَرَكِ ٱلْعُيُونُ
فَيَشْتَفِي مِمَّا بِهِ ٱلْحَزِينُ
دَارَتْ عَلَى ٱلْقَوْمِ رَحَى ٱلْمَنُونُ

البحر: الرجز.

I'm the Half-Blood, ʿAntarah!

At the Pass of Woe[106]
    the groans were deafening.
It was a harvest—
    slashed aortas
severed hands
    women miscarrying
at the roar of my sword—
    you have your proof.

Arise, ʿAblah,
    reveal yourself.
Grief is cured.
    Fate has crushed
the army
    in her mill.

~ 39 ~

Man up, Ḥuṣayn!

A flyting composed in the heat of battle. As a muʿāraḍah (a poem of contestation), ʿAntarah's poem bears the same rhyme and meter as the poem to which it responds. The events of the poem (if we place credence in the narrative they are nestled in) appear to have some bearing on the aftermath of the killing of Ḍamḍam celebrated in the Muʿallaqah, Poem 1.

إِصْبِرْ حُصَيْنُ لِمَنْ تَرَكْتَ بِوَجْهِهِ   أَثَرًا فَإِنِّي لَا أَخَالُكَ تَصْبِرُ ١
مَا سَرَّنِي أَنَّ ٱلْقَنَاةَ تَحَرَّفَتْ   عَمَّا أَصَابَتْ مِنْ حِجَاجِ ٱلْمَحْجِرِ
إِنَّ ٱلْكَرِيمَ نُدُوبُهُ فِي وَجْهِهِ   وَنُدُوبُ مُرَّةَ لَا تُرَى فِي ٱلْمَنْحَرِ
لَكِنَّ فِي أَكْتَافِهِمْ وَظُهُورِهِمْ   فَبِذَاكَ فَٱفْخَرْ بِئْسَ ذَاكَ ٱلْمَفْخَرُ ٤

البحر: الكامل.

Man up, Ḥuṣayn!
    You'll never rise to the task.
Your spear missed my eye
    leaving just a scratch
on my face.
    How can I rejoice?
Noblemen wear their scars
    on their cheeks.
The men of Murrah
    hide their scars
on their rears
    without so much
as a scratch
    on their chests.
What a boast.
    Pathetic!

~ 40 ~

Death always finds a way

A pithy summation of 'Antarah's war ethic, as the warrior welcomes Death and declares his devotion to it.

١ لِكُلِّ جَارٍ حِينَ يَجْرِي مُنْتَهَى

مَا كُلَّ يَوْمٍ تُسْعِفُ ٱلْقَوْمَ ٱلْمُنَى

حَقًّا وَلَا تُخْطِيهِمُ سُبْلُ ٱلرَّدَى

البحر: الرجز.

Wishes rarely
    come true.
Everything takes
    its course.
Death always
    finds a way.

~ 41 ~

In the forest of spears

An obscure poem addressed to Kaʿb that seems to be a battle description. Contrary to the narrative setting furnished by al-Baṭalyawsī, the poem surely describes how ʿAntarah foiled (and not simply averted) a surprise raid on ʿAbs by Kaʿb.

قُلْتُ مَنِ ٱلْقَوْمُ فَقَالُوا سَفَرَهْ
وَٱلْقَوْمُ كُعْبٌ يَبْتَغُونَ ٱلْمُنْكَرَهْ
قُلْتُ لِكَعْبٍ وَٱلْقَنَا مُشْتَجِرَهْ
تَعَلَّمِي يَاكَعْبُ وَٱمْشِي مُبْصِرَهْ
ثُمَّ ٱرْهَبِي مِنِّي وَكُونِي حَذِرَهْ

البحر: الرجز.

"Who goes there?"
I asked.
"Travelers!"
Clan Kaʿb
looking for trouble.
In the forest
of spears, I said,
"Listen to me
Kaʿb, do
not venture
out at night.
Feel fear.
Feel great fear."

~ 42 ~

The Fates claim their due

An exhortation to combat, declaring the poet's devotion to Death.

أَلْيَوْمَ تَبْلُو كُلُّ أُنْثَى بَعْلَهَا
فَٱلْيَوْمَ يَحْمِيهَا وَيَحْمِي رَحْلَهَا
وَإِنَّمَا تَلْقَى ٱلنُّفُوسُ سُبْلَهَا
إِنَّ ٱلْمَنَايَا مُدْرِكَاتٌ أَهْلَهَا
وَخَيْرُ آجَالِ ٱلنُّفُوسِ قَتْلُهَا

البحر: الرجز.

Today, the women on their camels
   will know the mettle
of the men
   who fight for them.
Our souls take their course.
   The Fates claim their due.
The best way to die?
   In battle.

~ 43 ~

The Half-Blood

This obscure and coarse piece, the translation of which is conjectural, is reputedly the poem declaimed by the poet as he charged into battle to win his freedom and gain recognition by his father.

أَنَا ٱلْهَجِينُ عَنْتَرَهْ

كُلُّ ٱمْرِئٍ يَحْمِي حِرَهْ

أَسْوَدَهُ وَأَحْمَرَهْ

وَٱلشَّعَرَاتِ ٱلْمُشْعَرَهْ

أَلْوَارِدَاتِ مِشْفَرَهْ

البحر: الرجز.

I'm the Half-Blood, 'Antarah!

Every man guards
    his woman's cunt,
black or white.
    By the bushy hair,
the thick fuzzy lips—
    This I swear.[107]

Poems from *The Epic of ʿAntar*

~ 44 ~

Did ʿAblah's brightness ignite your heart?

This is an erudite and accomplished pastiche of ʿAntarah's Muʿallaqah (Poem 1), a tour de force of the historical and poetic imagination. Its composer, presenting himself as ʿAntar, recreates the sort of poem he imagines ʿAntar would have composed as a declaration of war and a boast of victory, on the eve of doing battle with Khusro (Kisrā) and the Persians. The poem sensitively explores some of the main themes and structural characteristics of the Muʿallaqah. For example, the desert adventure of the earlier poem becomes here an erotic interlude in a sensual garden, a hortus inclusus, which is itself a reimagining of the water-soaked meadow of the first poem; ʿAntarah's previous enumeration of his ethical accomplishments, his justification to ʿAblah of his conduct, leads in this poem to a two-line conclusion in which the patched garment of poetry becomes the present poem, itself held up as a luminous pattern for all poets henceforth to weave their texts by. The poem is also linguistically lush, replete with unusual quadriliterals and rare vocabulary.

أَشَاقَكَ مِنْ عَبلَ ٱلْخَيَالُ ٱلْمُبَهَّجُ   فَقَلْبُكَ مِنْهُ لَاعِجٌ يَتَوَهَّجُ
فَقَدْتَ ٱلَّتِي بَانَتْ فَبِتَّ مُعَذَّبًا   وَتِلْكَ ٱحْتَوَاهَا عَنْكَ لِلْبَيْنِ هَوْدَجُ
كَأَنَّ فُؤَادِي يَوْمَ قُمْتُ مُوَدِّعًا   عُبَيْلَةَ مِنِّي هَارِبٌ يَتَمَعَّجُ
خَلِيلَيَّ مَا أَنْسَاكُمَا بَلْ فِدَاكُمَا   أَبِي وَأَبُوهَا أَيْنَ أَيْنَ ٱلْمُعَرَّجُ
أَلِمَّا بِمَاءِ ٱلدُّحْرُضَيْنِ فَكَلِّمَا   دِيَارَ ٱلَّتِي فِي حُبِّهَا بِتُّ أَلْهَجُ
دِيَارٌ لِذَاتِ ٱلْخِدْرِ عَبْلَةَ أَصْبَحَتْ   بِهَا ٱلْأَرْبُعُ ٱلْهُوجُ ٱلْعَوَاصِفُ تَرْهَجُ
أَلَا هَلْ تُرَى إِنْ شَطَّ عَنِّي مَزَارُهَا   وَأَزْعَجَهَا عَنْ أَهْلِهَا ٱلْآنَ مُزْعِجُ
فَهَلْ تُبْلِغَنِّي دَارَهَا شَدَنِيَّةٌ   هَمَلَّعَةٌ بَيْنَ ٱلْقِفَارِ تُهَمْلِجُ
تُرِيكَ إِذَا وَلَّتْ سَنَامًا وَكَاهِلًا   وَإِنْ أَقْبَلَتْ صَدْرًا لَهَا يَتَرَجْرَجُ
عُبَيْلَةَ هٰذَا دُرُّ نَظْمٍ نَظَمْتُهُ   وَأَنْتِ لَهُ سِلْكٌ وَحُسْنٌ وَمَبْهَجُ
وَقَدْ سِرْتُ يَا بِنْتَ ٱلْكِرَامِ مُبَادِرًا   وَتَحْتِي مَهْرِيٌّ مِنَ ٱلْإِبْلِ أَهْوَجُ

البحر: الطويل.

Did ʿAblah ignite
your heart?[108]
Night brings pain
now that the camels
have taken her away—
no time for goodbyes,
my heart
at a loss.
"Friends, I'd give
anything, tell me
where she pitched
her tent.
Ask at Duḥruḍān
where I spent
a night of love
in ʿAblah's bower
but where today
the four winds howl."
Is she too far to visit?
Her people bar the way.
Can I reach her on a fleet
shadanī camel
crossing deserts, hump
and withers bulging
chest pounding?
My words, ʿAblah,
are pearls, you
their lustrous string.
I race, Princess,
to you on a pure
mahrī through
hills where rivulets
glisten green,
where myrtle, jujube,
lote, and rose
burst brightly
into bloom.[109]

بِأَرْضٍ تَرَدَّى ٱلْمَاءُ مِنْ هَضَبَاتِهَا   فَأَصْبَحَ فِيهَا نَبْتُهَا يَتَوَهَّجُ
وَأَوْرَقَ فِيهَا ٱلْآسُ وَٱلضَّالُ وَٱلْغَضَا   وَنَبْقٌ وَنِسْرِينٌ وَوَرْدٌ وَعَوْسَجُ
لَئِنْ أَضْحَتِ ٱلْأَطْلَالُ مِنْهَا خَوَالِيًا   كَأَنْ لَمْ يَكُنْ فِيهَا مِنَ ٱلْعَيْشِ مُبْهِجُ
فَيَا طَالَمَا مَازَحْتُ فِيهَا عُبَيْلَةً   وَمَازَحَنِي فِيهَا ٱلْغَزَالُ ٱلْمُغَنَّجُ
أَغَنُّ مَلِيحُ ٱلدَّلِّ أَحْوَرُ أَكْحَلُ   أَزَجُّ نَقِيُّ ٱلْخَدِّ أَبْلَجُ أَدْعَجُ
لَهُ حَاجِبٌ كَٱلنُّونِ فَوْقَ جُفُونِهِ   وَثَغْرٌ كَزَهْرِ ٱلْأُقْحُوَانِ مُفَلَّجُ
وَرِدْفٌ لَهُ ثِقْلٌ وَخَصْرٌ مُهَفْهَفٌ   وَخَدٌّ بِهِ وَرْدٌ وَسَاقٌ خَدَلَّجُ
وَبَطْنٌ كَطَيِّ ٱلسَّابِرِيَّةِ لَيِّنٌ   أَقَبُّ لَطِيفٌ ضَامِرُ ٱلْكَشْحِ مُدْمَجُ
لَهَوْتُ بِهَا وَٱللَّيْلُ أَرْخَى سُدُولَهُ   إِلَى أَنْ بَدَا ضَوْءُ ٱلصَّبَاحِ ٱلْمُبَلَّجُ
أُرَاعِي نُجُومَ ٱللَّيْلِ وَهْيَ كَأَنَّهَا   قَوَارِيرُ فِيهَا زِئْبَقٌ يَتَرَجْرَجُ
وَتَحْتِي مِنْهَا سَاعِدٌ فِيهِ دُمْلُجٌ   مُضِيءٌ وَفَوْقِي آخَرٌ فِيهِ دُمْلُجُ
وَإِخْوَانِ صِدْقٍ صَادِقِينَ صَحِبْتُهُمْ   عَلَى غَارَةٍ مِنْ مِثْلِهَا ٱلْخَيْلُ تُسْرَجُ
تَطُوفُ عَلَيْهِمْ خَنْدَرِيسٌ مُدَامَةٌ   تَرَى حَبَبًا مِنْ فَوْقِهَا حِينَ تُمْزَجُ
أَلَا إِنَّهَا نِعْمَ ٱلدَّوَاءُ لِشَارِبٍ   أَلَا فَٱسْقِنِيهَا قَبْلَ مَا أَنْتَ تَخْرُجُ

No trace of her now.
    How good life was,
how I played
    with that coy gazelle
that sweet-voiced
    dark-eyed flirt—
so serene,
    eyebrows arched
like pen strokes,
    teeth like daisies
in a row,
    shapely, full,
leggy, silky,
    delicate waist,
smooth skin—
    a tender rose
hid by the curtain
    of night, stars
glittering against
    the dark like quicksilver
in a bottle—
    I played with her
till daybreak
    clasped tenderly
in braceleted arms.

In battle I join
    my brothers,
the horses in full fettle,
    then serve up
a frothy wine.
    It cures the thirst!
Pour me another
    before you leave
and in the drunken
    dawn pass

فَنُضْحِي سُكَارَى وَٱلْمُدَامُ مُصَفَّقٌ   يُدَارُ عَلَيْنَا وَٱلطَّعَامُ ٱلْمُطَبْهَجُ
وَمَا رَاعَنِي يَوْمَ ٱلطِّعَانِ زُهُوقُهُ   إِلَيَّ بِمَنْ بِٱلزَّعْفَرَانِ تَضَرَّجُوا
فَأَقْبَلَ مُنْقَضًّا عَلَيَّ بِخَلْقِهِ   يُقَرِّبُ أَحْيَانًا وَحِينًا يُهَمْلِجُ
فَلَمَّا دَنَا مِنِّي قَطَعْتُ وَتِينَهُ   بِحَدِّ حُسَامٍ صَارِمٍ يَتَبَلَّجُ
كَأَنَّ دِمَاءَ ٱلْفُرْسِ حِينَ تَحَدَّرَتْ   خَلُوقُ ٱلْعَذَارَى أَوْ قَبَاءٌ مُدَبَّجُ
فَوَيْلٌ لِكِسْرَى إِنْ حَلَلْتُ بِأَرْضِهِ   وَوَيْلٌ لِجَيْشِ ٱلْفُرْسِ حِينَ أُعَجْعِجُ
وَأَحْمِلُ فِيهِمْ حَمْلَةً عَنْتَرِيَّةً   أَرُدُّ بِهَا ٱلْأَبْطَالَ فِي ٱلْقَفْرِ تَنْبُجُ
وَأَصْدِمُ كَبْشَ ٱلْقَوْمِ ثُمَّ أُذِيقُهُ   مَرَارَةَ كَأْسِ ٱلْمَوْتِ صَبْرًا يُمَجَّجُ
وَآخُذُ ثَأْرَ ٱلنَّدْبِ سَيِّدِ قَوْمِهِ   وَأُضْرِمُهَا فِي ٱلْحَرْبِ نَارًا تُؤَجَّجُ

round the skins
    and roast meats.

I watched the hero
    stride into battle
with his bloodstained
    mob.
A sprint, then
    a feint—he swooped.
At close quarters
    I pierced his heart
with my whetted
    blade, and Persian
blood ran
    like red lace
or henna
    daubed on virgins.

To hell with Kisrā
    and Persia's hosts
when I bellow
    and invade their realm!
'Antarah's onslaught
    drives their heroes
screaming back
    to the wastes.
I ignite
    the blaze of War
smash their chief
    retching on Death's
bitter draft—
    easy revenge!

وَإِنِّي لَحَمَّالٌ لِكُلِّ مُلِمَّةٍ   تَخِرُّ لَهَا شُمُّ ٱلْجِبَالِ وَتُزْعَجُ
وَإِنِّي لَأَحْمِي ٱلْجَارَ مِنْ كُلِّ ذِلَّةٍ   وَأَفْرَحُ بِٱلضَّيْفِ ٱلْمُقِيمِ وَأَبْهَجُ
وَأَحْمِي حِمَى قَوْمِي عَلَى طُولِ مُدَّتِي   إِلَى أَنْ يَرَوْنِي فِي ٱللَّفَائِفِ أُدْرَجُ
فَدُونَكُمُ يَا آلَ عَبْسٍ قَصِيدَةً   يَلُوحُ لَهَا ضَوْءٌ مِنَ ٱلصُّبْحِ أَبْلَجُ
أَلَا إِنَّهَا خَيْرُ ٱلْقَصَائِدِ كُلِّهَا   يُفَصَّلُ مِنْهَا كُلُّ ثَوْبٍ وَيُنْسَجُ

The burdens I bear
    make mountains quake
I shield allies
    against slights,
my guests I delight.
    I'll defend our land
till I'm shrouded
    in Death.

My tribe! This poem
    shields you, brightening
the dawn sky.
    Let other poets
cut their verse
    to its flawless cloth.

~ 45 ~

The murky binge of battle

Powerless and in chains, ʿAntar is unable to rescue his beloved ʿAblah. He prepares to meet his death, recognizing that his end is imminent, that Fate now wants him for itself.

فَخْرُ ٱلرِّجَالِ سَلَاسِلٌ وَقُيُودُ   وَكَذَا ٱلنِّسَاءُ بَخَانِقٌ وَعُقُودُ
وَإِذَا غُبَارُ ٱلْخَيْلِ مَدَّ رُوَاقَهُ   سُكْرِي بِهِ لَا مَا جَنَى ٱلْعُنْقُودُ
يَا دَهْرُ لَا تُبْقِي عَلَيَّ فَقَدْ دَنَا   مَا كُنْتُ أَطْلُبُ قَبْلَ ذَا وَأُرِيدُ
فَٱلْقَتْلُ لِي مِنْ بَعْدِ عَبْلَةَ رَاحَةٌ   وَٱلْعَيْشُ بَعْدَ فِرَاقِهَا مَنْكُودُ
يَا عَبْلَ قَدْ دَنَتِ ٱلْمَنِيَّةُ فَٱنْدُبِي   إِنْ كَانَ جَفْنُكِ بِٱلدُّمُوعِ يَجُودُ
يَا عَبْلَ إِنْ تَبْكِي عَلَيَّ فَقَدْ بَكَى   صَرْفُ ٱلزَّمَانِ عَلَيَّ وَهُوَ حَسُودُ
يَا عَبْلَ إِنْ سَفَكُوا دَمِي فَفَعَائِلِي   فِي كُلِّ يَوْمٍ ذِكْرُهُنَّ جَدِيدُ
لَهْفِي عَلَيْكِ إِذَا بَقِيتِ سَبِيَّةً   تَدْعِينَ عَنْتَرَ وَهْوَ عَنْكِ بَعِيدُ
وَلَقَدْ لَقِيتُ ٱلْفُرْسَ يَا ٱبْنَةَ مَالِكٍ   وَجُيُوشُهَا قَدْ ضَاقَ عَنْهَا ٱلْبِيدُ
وَتَمُوجُ مَوْجَ ٱلْبَحْرِ إِلَّا أَنَّهَا   لَاقَتْ أُسُودًا فَوْقَهُنَّ حَدِيدُ
جَارُوا فَحَكَّمْنَا ٱلصَّوَارِمَ بَيْنَنَا   فَقَضَتْ وَأَطْرَافُ ٱلرِّمَاحِ شُهُودُ
يَا عَبْلَ كَمْ مِنْ جَحْفَلٍ فَرَّقْتُهُ   وَٱلْجَوُّ أَسْوَدُ وَٱلْجِبَالُ تَمِيدُ
فَسَطَا عَلَيَّ ٱلدَّهْرُ سَطْوَةَ غَادِرٍ   وَٱلدَّهْرُ يَبْخَلُ تَارَةً وَيَجُودُ

البحر: الكامل.

Men find glory in chains
    women in strings of pearls.
I get drunk on the murky binge
    of battle, not strong wine.
Fate, don't go easy on me!
    What I seek lies close at hand.
Without ʿAblah
    my comfort is Death.
Death, ʿAblah, is near.
    Weep if you have any tears
and mourn me more
    than jealous Fate does.
Let them kill me—
    my deeds will live.

I weep for your capture, ʿAblah
    calling in vain for ʿAntar to appear.
Daughter of Mālik, I faced
    the Persians in deserts choked
with soldiers, the armies surging
    then dispersing
attacked by lions clad in mail.
    For their criminal acts
our lances bore witness,
    our swords passed sentence.
I drove the enemy back and day
    went dark as mountains quaked.

Now treacherous Fate has struck.
    She gives and then she takes.

~ 46 ~

The fire for you burns in my belly

A love poem typical of the style of the developed tradition known in Arabic as ghazal, in which the estranged lover, psychotic with grief, and paralyzed by injured pride and abjection, explores the physical symptoms of his emotional disintegration and pledges his troth to his ideal, which is so unattainable as to be always already lost.

إِذَا كَانَ دَمْعِي شَاهِدِي كَيْفَ أَجْحَدُ   وَنَارُ ٱشْتِيَاقِي فِي ٱلْحَشَا تَتَوَقَّدُ
وَهَيْهَاتَ يَخْفَى مَا أُكِنُّ مِنَ ٱلْهَوَى   وَثَوْبُ سَقَامِي كُلَّ يَوْمٍ يُجَدَّدُ
أُقَاتِلُ أَشْوَاقِي بِصَبْرِي تَجَلُّدًا   وَقَلْبِيَ فِي قَيْدِ ٱلْغَرَامِ مُقَيَّدُ
إِلَى ٱللهِ أَشْكُو جَوْرَ قَوْمِي وَظُلْمَهُمْ   إِذَا لَمْ أَجِدْ خِلًّا عَلَى ٱلْبُعْدِ يَعْضُدُ
خَلِيلَيَّ أَمْسَى حُبُّ عَبْلَةَ قَاتِلِي   وَبَأْسِي شَدِيدٌ وَٱلْحُسَامُ مُهَنَّدُ
حَرَامٌ عَلَيَّ ٱلنَّوْمُ يَا ٱبْنَةَ مَالِكٍ   وَمَنْ فَرْشُهُ جَمْرُ ٱلْغَضَا كَيْفَ يَرْقُدُ
سَأَنْدُبُ حَتَّى يَعْلَمَ ٱلطَّيْرُ أَنَّنِي   حَزِينٌ وَيَرْثِي لِي ٱلْحَمَامُ ٱلْمُغَرِّدُ

البحر: الطويل.

When the fire for you
    burns in my belly
and I'm in tears
    how could I
deny my love?
    The disease I conceal
lies revealed.
    Stubborn-hearted
tethered by lust
    I steel myself
to do battle
    with my desire.

Friends, God
    knows how my people
wrong me in
    my absence.
My love for ʿAblah
    is driving me
to my grave
    yet my sword
remains steely—
    my courage great.

Daughter of Mālik,
    sleep is forbidden me.
How could I sleep
    on this bed of coals?
I'll weep till the birds
    hear of my misery
and the turtledoves coo
    my elegy.
I'll kiss the ground
    wherever you're camped.

وَأَلْثِمُ أَرْضًا أَنْتِ فِيهَا مُقِيمَةٌ   لَعَلَّ لَهِيبِي مِنْ ثَرَى ٱلْأَرْضِ يَبْرُدُ
رَحَلْتِ وَقَلْبِي يَا ٱبْنَةَ ٱلْعَمِّ تَائِهٌ   عَلَى أَثَرِ ٱلْأَظْعَانِ لِلرَّكْبِ يَنْشُدُ
لَئِنْ يَشْمَتِ ٱلْأَعْدَاءُ يَا بِنْتَ مَالِكٍ   فَإِنَّ وِدَادِي مِثْلَمَا كَانَ يُعْهَدُ

May its tearstained sands
    dampen the fires
that consume me.

ʿAblah, my cousin,
    you traveled off
and left my heart
    to wander the tracks
of your camel train
    and beckon back
your escorts.
    Daughter of Mālik,
my enemies relish
    my defeat
but nothing can
    vanquish my love.

~ 47 ~

A sin ‘Ablah can’t forgive

A melancholy rumination on doomed, tragic love. The poet, for all his masculine vigor and martial prowess, is felled by the dart-like glances of the beloved’s eyes, and a heady night of pleasure in al-Sharabbah ensues. But in spite of the perfidy shown him by all those he loves, the poet declares his never-ending loyalty.

ذَنْبِي لِعَبْلَةَ ذَنْبٌ غَيْرُ مُغْتَفَرِ   لَمَّا تَبَلَّجَ صُبْحُ ٱلشَّيْبِ فِي شَعَرِي
رَمَتْ عُبَيْلَةُ قَلْبِي مِنْ لَوَاحِظِهَا   بِكُلِّ سَهْمٍ غَرِيقِ ٱلنَّزْعِ فِي ٱلْحَوَرِ
فَٱعْجَبْ لَهُنَّ سِهَامًا غَيْرَ طَائِشَةٍ   مِنَ ٱلْجُفُونِ بِلَا قَوْسٍ وَلَا وَتَرِ
كَمْ قَدْ حَفِظْتُ ذِمَامَ ٱلْقَوْمِ مِنْ وَلَهٍ   يَعْتَادُنِي لِبَنَاتِ ٱلدَّلِّ وَٱلْخَفَرِ
مُهَفْهَفَاتٍ يَغَارُ ٱلْغُصْنُ حِينَ يَرَى   قُدُودَهَا بَيْنَ مَيَّادٍ وَمُنْهَصِرِ
يَا مَنْزِلًا أَدْمُعِي تَجْرِي عَلَيْهِ إِذَا   ضَنَّ ٱلسَّحَابُ عَلَى ٱلْأَطْلَالِ بِٱلْمَطَرِ
أَرْضَ ٱلشَّرَبَّةِ كَمْ قَضَيْتُ مُبْتَهِجًا   فِيهَا مَعَ ٱلْغِيدِ وَٱلْأَتْرَابِ مِنْ وَطَرِ
أَيَّامَ غُصْنُ شَبَابِي فِي نُعُومَتِهِ   أَلْهُو بِمَا فِيهِ مِنْ زَهْرٍ وَمِنْ ثَمَرِ
فِي كُلِّ يَوْمٍ لَنَا مِنْ نَشْرِهَا سَحَرًا   رِيحٌ شَذَاهَا كَنَشْرِ ٱلزَّهْرِ فِي ٱلسَّحَرِ
وَكُلُّ غُصْنٍ قَوِيمٍ رَاقَ مَنْظَرُهُ   مَا حَظُّ عَاشِقِهَا مِنْهُ سِوَى ٱلنَّظَرِ
أَخْشَى عَلَيْهَا وَلَوْلَا ذَاكَ مَا وَقَفَتْ   رَكَائِبِي بَيْنَ وِرْدِ ٱلْعَزْمِ وَٱلصَّدَرِ
كَلَّا وَلَا كُنْتُ بَعْدَ ٱلْقُرْبِ مُقْتَنِعًا   مِنْهَا عَلَى طُولِ بُعْدِ ٱلدَّارِ بِٱلْخَبَرِ

البحر: البسيط.

My hair, bright as the silver dawn,
    is a sin ʿAblah can't forgive.
Her flashing eyes shot their darts
    deep into my heart,
marvelous arrows sped
    from eyes, not bows.
Time was I guarded the tribe,
    preserving its honor
and its dignity, hiding my flights
    of love for girls, slender and coy,
who filled even saplings with jealousy
    as they swayed to and fro.[110]

Rain, my tears, on Sharabbah
    where the ruins are denied their rain
where I fulfilled so many desires
    with sweet young companions
when youth was a tree in bloom
    bursting with fruit,
when Sharabbah breathed its fragrance
    heady as the dawn blossom—
and, marvel to behold,
    its plants grew tall and true.

The sincere lover can only gaze.
    I care for her so deeply
it keeps me from our romance
    yet how can I rest easy
with mere news of her
    once so near but now
so many leagues away?

هُمُ ٱلْأَحِبَّةُ إِنْ خَانُوا وَإِنْ نَقَضُوا   عَهْدِي فَمَا حُلْتُ عَنْ وَجْدِي وَلَا فِكَرِي
أَشْكُو مِنَ ٱلْهَجْرِ فِي سِرٍّ وَفِي عَلَنٍ   شَكْوَى تُؤَثِّرُ فِي صَلْدٍ مِنَ ٱلْحَجَرِ

I love those I love.
    Should they break their vow
I wouldn't waver or change my mind.
    In private and in public
I'd lament our separation—
    my plaint carving its name in stone.

~ 48 ~

I was betrayed

A rumination on Fate and the dignity, albeit ultimately the futility, of human effort. Its religious sentiment is very much in keeping with the spirit of The Epic of ʿAntar.

دَهَتْنِي صُرُوفُ ٱلدَّهْرِ وَٱنْتَشَبَ ٱلْغَدْرُ   وَمَنْ ذَا ٱلَّذِي فِي ٱلنَّاسِ يَصْفُولَهُ ٱلدَّهْرُ
وَكَمْ طَرَقَتْنِي نَكْبَةٌ بَعْدَ نَكْبَةٍ   فَفَرَّجْتُهَا عَنِّي وَمَا مَسَّنِي ضُرُّ
وَلَوْلَا سِنَانِي وَٱلْحُسَامُ وَهِمَّتِي   لَمَا ذُكِرَتْ عَبْسٌ وَلَا نَالَهَا فَخْرُ
بَنَيْتُ لَهُمْ بَيْتًا رَفِيعًا مِنَ ٱلْعُلَا   تَخَرُّ لَهُ ٱلْجَوْزَاءُ وَٱلْفَرْغُ وَٱلْغَفْرُ
وَهَا قَدْ رَحَلْتُ ٱلْيَوْمَ عَنْهُمْ وَأَمْرُنَا   إِلَى مَنْ لَهُ فِي خَلْقِهِ ٱلنَّهْيُ وَٱلْأَمْرُ
سَيَذْكُرُنِي قَوْمِي إِذَا ٱلْخَيْلُ أَقْبَلَتْ   وَفِي ٱللَّيْلَةِ ٱلظَّلْمَاءِ يُفْتَقَدُ ٱلْبَدْرُ
يَعِيبُونَ لَوْنِي بِٱلسَّوَادِ جَهَالَةً   وَلَوْلَا سَوَادُ ٱللَّيْلِ مَا طَلَعَ ٱلْفَجْرُ
وَإِنْ كَانَ لَوْنِي أَسْوَدًا فَخَصَائِلِي   بَيَاضٌ وَمِنْ كَفِّيَّ يُسْتَنْزَلُ ٱلْقَطْرُ
مَحَوْتُ بِذِكْرِي فِي ٱلْوَرَى ذِكْرَ مَنْ مَضَى   وَسُدْتُ فَلَا زَيْدٌ يُقَالُ وَلَا عَمْرُو

البحر: الطويل.

Fate struck. I was betrayed.
  Does Fate treat anyone well?
There was a time nothing could touch me
  as I rebuffed Disaster,
as my lance and sword and zeal
  gave ʿAbs their fame.
I raised their tents so high
  the stars bowed low.[111]
But I've left them and now
  my duty is to Creation's Lord.[112]

My men will remember,
  they'll miss my raids on darkness.
Fools may mock my blackness
  but without night there's no day!
Black as night, so be it!
  But what a night
generous and bright!
  All the paltry ʿAmrs and Zayds
my name has eclipsed.
  I am the Lord of War!

~ 49 ~

ʿAblah's wraith

An intense and disturbing exploration of the apparition scene (ṭayf al-khayāl: see Poem 5 for another occurrence). The goddess-beloved appears to the poet and they consummate their love, a love that previously had been beyond the power of the poet, languishing in the conventional solipsism of the unfulfilled male lover. Upon awakening from his reverie, the poet realizes that, for all his military prowess, he remains prey to his enervating emotional psychosis.

زَارَ ٱلْخَيَالُ خَيَالُ عَبْلَةَ فِي ٱلْكَرَى   لِمُتَيَّمٍ نَشْوَانَ مَحْلُولِ ٱلْعُرَى
فَنَهَضْتُ أَشْكُو مَا لَقِيتُ لِبُعْدِهَا   فَتَنَفَّسَتْ مِسْكًا يُخَالِطُ عَنْبَرَا
فَضَمَمْتُهَا كَيْمَا أُقَبِّلَ ثَغْرَهَا   وَٱلدَّمْعُ مِنْ جَفْنَيَّ قَدْ بَلَّ ٱلثَّرَى
وَكَشَفْتُ بُرْقُعَهَا فَأَشْرَقَ وَجْهُهَا   حَتَّىٰ أَعَادَ ٱللَّيْلُ صُبْحًا مُسْفِرَا
عَرَبِيَّةٌ يَهْتَزُّ لِينُ قَوَامِهَا   فَيَخَالُهُ ٱلْعُشَّاقُ رُمْحًا أَسْمَرَا
مَحْجُوبَةٌ بِصَوَارِمٍ وَذَوَابِلٍ   سُمْرٍ وَدُونَ خِبَائِهَا أُسْدُ ٱلشَّرَى

البحر: الكامل.

ʿAblah's wraith
    appeared in sleep
to her wearied slave.
    Losing my grip
I stood and screamed
    "She's far away!"
A breath of musk
    was her response,
and ambergris.

Blinded by tears
    I tried to seize
her flitting shade
    with a kiss.
On the soaked sand
    I exposed
her sun-bright face
    and night became
as hard as day.

Her body a lance,
    battle-true,
supple to
    the grasp,
hidden in her tent
    behind a veil,
lions of Sharā
    on guard
with war-tested pales
    and tempered swords.[113]

يَا عَبْلَ إِنَّ هَوَاكِ قَدْ جَازَ ٱلْمُدَى   وَأَنَا ٱلْمُعَنَّى فِيكِ مِنْ دُونِ ٱلْوَرَى
يَا عَبْلَ حُبُّكِ فِي عِظَامِي مَعَ دَمِي   لَمَّا جَرَتْ رُوحِي بِجِسْمِي قَدْ جَرَى
وَلَقَدْ عَلِقْتُ بِذَيْلِ مَنْ فَخَرَتْ بِهِ   عَبْسٌ وَسَيْفُ أَبِيهِ أَفْنَى حِمْيَرَا
يَا شَأْسُ جِرْنِي مِنْ غَرَامٍ قَاتِلٍ   أَبَدًا أَزِيدُ بِهِ غُرَامًا مُسْعَرَا
يَا شَأْسُ لَوْلَا أَنَّ سُلْطَانَ ٱلْهَوَى   مَاضِي ٱلْعَزِيمَةِ مَا تَمَلَّكَ عَنْتَرَا

ʿAblah, I
    am so far gone
because of you
    locked in lust
like a camel
    in rut. ʿAblah,
my love for you
    is my lifeblood
the very breath
    in my bones.

Time was
    I made war,
the boast of the tribe
    whose father put
Ḥimyar to the sword.

Deliver me, Shaʾs,
    from lust's domain.
I can't escape it.
    It sears me with mange.
Lust is sovereign.
    O my friend,
lust is all.
    Lust has ʿAntar
in its thrall.

~ 50 ~

The birds are jittery

A threnody for his comrade Mālik ibn Zuhayr, which is in fact an amplification of Poem 27. The additional scenes not contained in Poem 27 are the fateful portent of the crow and the apocalyptic collapse of the heavens, a raid narrative that provides the details of Mālik's death in combat, and a capping oath in which the poet declares his eternal fealty to his dead comrade.

أَلَا يَا غُرَابَ ٱلْبَيْنِ فِي ٱلطَّيَرَانِ   أَعِرْنِي جَنَاحًا قَدْ عَدِمْتُ بَنَانِي
تُرَى هَلْ عَلِمْتَ ٱلْيَوْمَ مَقْتَلَ مَالِكٍ   وَمَصْرَعَهُ فِي ذِلَّةٍ وَهَوَانِ
فَإِنْ كَانَ حَقًّا فَٱلنُّجُومُ لِفَقْدِهِ   تَغِيبُ وَيَهْوِي بَعْدَهُ ٱلْقَمَرَانِ
لَقَدْ كَانَ يَوْمًا أَسْوَدَ ٱللَّيْلِ عَابِسًا   يَخَافُ بَلَاهُ طَارِقُ ٱلْحَدَثَانِ
فَلِلَّهِ عَيْنَا مَنْ رَأَى مِثْلَ مَالِكٍ   عَقِيرَةَ قَوْمٍ أَنْ جَرَى فَرَسَانِ
فَلَيْتَهُمَا لَمْ يَجْرِيَا نِصْفَ غَلْوَةٍ   وَلَيْتَهُمَا لَمْ يُرْسَلَا لِرِهَانِ
وَلَيْتَهُمَا مَاتَا جَمِيعًا بِبَلْدَةٍ   وَأَخْطَاهُمَا قَيْسٌ فَلَا يُرَيَانِ
لَقَدْ جَلَبَا حَيْنًا وَحَرْبًا عَظِيمَةً   تُبِيدُ سَرَاةَ ٱلْقَوْمِ مِنْ غَطَفَانِ
وَقَدْ جَلَبَا حَيْنًا لِمَصْرَعِ مَالِكٍ   وَكَانَ كَرِيمًا مَاجِدًا لِهِجَانِ
وَكَانَ لَدَى ٱلْهَيْجَاءِ يَحْمِي ذِمَارَهَا   وَيَطْعَنُ عِنْدَ ٱلْكَرِّ كُلَّ طِعَانِ

البحر: الطويل.

The birds are jittery.
A crow croaks, "Gone!"[114]
I have nothing
to hold on to—
take me
under your wing.
Have you heard
Mālik died
a mean death?
The stars will flicker
and dim if it's true—
moons slide
out of orbit.

A day blacker than night
snarled and roared.
Even the stalker of night,
Fate, cowered.

The grim sight of such a hero
slaughtered for a race, God.
The bets should have never been placed,
Qays should never have watched,
the horses should never have run
but died in a far-off land!
They raised hell and War ripped out
Ghaṭafān's spine.
They brought death to Mālik,
pride of ancestors,
keeper of their honor in battle,
their bravest horseman.
At dawn we'd attack
the Yemeni blades
but a stroke felled me—
my heart's in my mouth.

بِهِ كُنْتُ أَسْطُو حِينَمَا جَدَّتِ ٱلْعِدَا غَدَاةَ ٱللِّقَا نَحْوِي بِكُلِّ يَمَانِي
فَقَدْ هَدَّ رُكْنِي فَقْدُهُ وَمُصَابُهُ وَخَلَّى فُؤَادِي دَائِمَ ٱلْخَفَقَانِ
فَوَا أَسَفَا كَيْفَ ٱنْثَنَى عَنْ جَوَادِهِ وَمَا كَانَ سَيْفِي عِنْدَهُ وَسِنَانِي
رَمَاهُ بِسَهْمِ ٱلْمَوْتِ رَامٍ مُصَمِّمٌ فَيَا لَيْتَهُ لَمَّا رَمَاهُ رَمَانِي
فَسَوْفَ تَرَى إِنْ كُنْتُ بَعْدَكَ بَاقِيًا وَأَمْكَنَنِي دَهْرٌ وَطُولُ زَمَانِ
وَأَقْسِمُ حَقًّا لَوْ بَقِيتَ لِنَظْرَةٍ لَقَرَّتْ بِهَا عَيْنَاكَ حِينَ تَرَانِي

My spear and sword
could not shield
Mālik, tossed
from his saddle
as the archer sped
Death's keen shaft
home to its target.

Why take *him*,
why not me?

If Time spares me,
if ever Mālik
and I meet again,
I'll make him proud.

This oath I swear.

~ 51 ~

That coward, Death

This is a classic example of a format The Epic of ʿAntar excels at: the inhabitation and development of a preexisting piece from the literate tradition. The poem is an amplified version of Poem 23, with a new introduction in which the poet ferociously defies Time, the battle narrative is extended, and the poet's command of Death, voiced in Poem 23, is further intensified by his berserk attack on Death in this poem.

أَرَى لِي كُلَّ يَوْمٍ مَعْ زَمَانِي   عِتَابًا فِي ٱلْبِعَادِ وَفِي ٱلتَّدَانِي
يُرِيدُ مَذَلَّتِي وَيَدُورُ حَوْلِي   بِجَيْشِ ٱلنَّائِبَاتِ إِذَا رَآنِي
كَأَنِّي قَدْ كَبُرْتُ وَشَابَ رَأْسِي   وَقَلَّ تَجَلُّدِي وَوَهَى جَنَانِي
أَلَا يَا دَهْرُ يَوْمِي مِثْلُ أَمْسِي   وَأَعْظَمُ هَيْبَةً لِمَنِ ٱلْتَقَانِي
وَمَكْرُوبٍ كَشَفْتُ ٱلْكَرْبَ عَنْهُ   بِضَرْبَةِ فَيْصَلٍ لَمَّا دَعَانِي
دَعَانِي دَعْوَةً وَٱلْخَيْلُ تَجْرِي   فَمَا أَدْرِي أَبِاسْمِي أَمْ كَنَانِي
فَلَمْ أُمْسِكْ بِسَمْعِي إِذْ دَعَانِي   وَلٰكِنْ قَدْ أَبَانَ لَهُ لِسَانِي
فَفَرَّقْتُ ٱلْمَوَاكِبَ عَنْهُ قَهْرًا   بِطَعْنٍ يَسْبِقُ ٱلْبَرْقَ ٱلْيَمَانِي
وَمَا لَبَّيْتُهُ إِلَّا وَسَيْفِي   وَرُمْحِي فِي ٱلْوَغَى فَرَسَا رِهَانِ
وَكَانَ إِجَابَتِي إِيَّاهُ أَنِّي   عَطَفْتُ عَلَيْهِ مَوَّارَ ٱلْعِنَانِ
بِأَسْمَرَ مِنْ رِمَاحِ ٱلْخَطِّ لَدْنٍ   وَأَبْيَضَ صَارِمٍ ذَكَرٍ يَمَانِ
وَقِرْنٍ قَدْ تَرَكْتُ لَدَى مَكَرٍّ   عَلَيْهِ سَبَائِبًا كَٱلْأُرْجُوَانِ

البحر: الوافر.

Day by day
Time takes aim[115]
and strikes from far
away, then near,
wheeling. I watch
a crush of woes
grind me down.
It thinks I've grown
soft and weak,
old and gray.
Do, Time,
what you will,
today, as yesterday,
I am the terror
of the foe.

A panicked leader
called to me.
I broke the line,
drove fear away.
The horses charged.
He called out once.
Did he ask my name?
I couldn't hear
in the din of War
but answered, blazing
through the soldiers
like a lightning bolt,
urging my horse on,
and with hard Khaṭṭī
lance and manly
Yemeni steel
left my challenger
dead—his hair
a bloody redbud,
the vultures praying

تَرَكْتُ ٱلطَّيْرَ عَاكِفَةً عَلَيْهِ   كَمَا تَرْدِي إِلَى ٱلْعُرُسِ ٱلْبَوَانِي
وَتَمْنَعُهُنَّ أَنْ يَأْكُلْنَ مِنْهُ   حَيَاةُ يَدٍ وَرِجْلٍ تَرْكُضَانِ
فَمَا أَوْهَى مِرَاسُ ٱلْحَرْبِ رُكْنِي   وَلٰكِنْ مَا تَقَادَمَ مِنْ زَمَانِ
وَمَا دَانَيْتُ شَخْصَ ٱلْمَوْتِ إِلَّا   كَمَا يَدْنُو ٱلشُّجَاعُ مِنَ ٱلْجَبَانِ
وَقَدْ عَلِمَتْ بَنُو عَبْسٍ بِأَنِّي   أَهَشُّ إِذَا دُعِيتُ إِلَى ٱلطِّعَانِ
وَأَنَّ ٱلْمَوْتَ طَوْعُ يَدِي إِذَا مَا   وَصَلْتُ بَنَانَهَا بِٱلْهُنْدُوَانِي
وَنِعْمَ فَوَارِسُ ٱلْهَيْجَاءِ قَوْمِي   إِذَا عَلِقُوا ٱلْأَعِنَّةَ بِٱلْبَنَانِ
هُمُ قَتَلُوا لَقِيطًا وَٱبْنَ حُجْرٍ   وَأَرْدَوْا حَاجِبًا وَٱبْنَيْ أَبَانِ

over him,
    dancing their bridal
dance, held
    back from feasting
by the thrum
    and twitching of
his hands and feet.

Time, not War
    has made me weak.
A hero, I advance
    on that coward, Death.
My tribe, summoned
    to fight, knows
how I smile,
    commanding Death,
my hand wielding
    the Indian blade.

In War my clan
    are the finest riders,
gripping the reins
    in hands that killed
Laqīṭ and Ibn Ḥujr,
    Ḥājib and
the sons of Abān.

Appendix 1

Ibn Qutaybah (d. 276/888): Biographical Note on ʿAntarah ibn Shaddād of ʿAbs in *The Book of Poetry and Poets*[116]

ʿAntarah's full name is ʿAntarah ibn ʿAmr ibn Shaddād ibn ʿAmr ibn Qurād ibn Makhzūm ibn ʿAwf ibn Mālik ibn Ghālib ibn Quṭayʿah ibn ʿAbs ibn Baghīḍ. Ibn al-Kalbī states that "Shāddād was his grandfather on his father's side. His name eclipsed that of the father, so ʿAntarah's lineage is traced through his grandfather. ʿAntarah's name is properly ʿAntarah ibn ʿAmr ibn Shaddād." Others, however, contend that Shaddād was his uncle, i.e., his father's brother, and that it was he who raised ʿAntarah, which is why his lineage is traced back through him. 1.1

ʿAntarah's father did not recognize him as his son until he had reached manhood, because his mother was a black slave called Zabībah, and during the *Jāhiliyyah* the Arabs would consider the children of slaves to be slaves, no matter who their father was. Zabībah's other sons, ʿAntarah's brothers, were also slaves. ʿAntarah was recognized by his father after a raid by an Arab tribe that resulted in a number of ʿAbs losses. The men of ʿAbs gave chase, but the raiders fought back and defended the plunder they had taken. ʿAntarah took part in the pursuit, and when his father shouted, "Attack, ʿAntarah!" he replied, "Slaves do not attack. They're much better at milking camels." "Attack and you are a free man," his father said. Then ʿAntarah charged the foe, declaiming: 1.2

Every man guards
his woman's cunt,
black or white.
By the thick fuzzy lips—
This I swear.[117]

He fought bravely that day, and won back the plunder that ʿAbs had lost. From that day on, his father called him his son and gave him his name.

1.3 There were three "Arab ravens": ʿAntarah, whose mother, Zabībah, was black; Khufāf ibn ʿUmayr al-Sharīdī of Sulaym, who traced his lineage through his black mother, Nadbah; and al-Sulayk ibn ʿUmayr al-Saʿdī, who traced his lineage through his black mother, Sulakah.

1.4 ʿAntarah was the fiercest warrior and the most generous of men. He had not composed more than two or three verses of poetry when one day a fellow tribesman launched a vicious verbal attack on him, shaming him for not being a poet and for being the black son of a black mother with black brothers. "It is customary for people," ʿAntarah replied, "to help one another through sharing food, but neither you nor your father nor your grandfather has ever attended such a communal gathering. It is also customary for people to be summoned to take part in raids and thus to win renown, but none of us has ever seen you in the vanguard of a raiding party. In times of confusion, not one of you, neither you nor your father nor your grandfather, has ever attended a tribunal where a decision was to be taken. You are about as much use as a weed growing in a wasteland. I, however, do not shirk from war. I share my spoils and refrain from begging. I am generous with what I possess. My judgment and resolve are unerring. You're about to find out about my skills as a poet." The first major ode he composed was "Did Poetry Die in its War with the Poets?"[118] It is his finest poem, and they called it "the Golden Ode."

1.5 ʿAntarah participated in the War of Dāḥis and al-Ghabrāʾ with exemplary bravery, and distinguished himself in combat.

1.6 According to Abū ʿUbaydah, ʿAntarah was a man who made his living from raiding. When he grew too old and feeble to take part, he found himself destitute in the aftermath of the Battle of Jabalah Ravine, when ʿAbs, laden with the blood monies they had to pay, returned to live among the Ghaṭafān. He was owed some camels by a member of Ghaṭafān, so he decided to go and call in the debt. He had reached a spot between Sharj and Nāẓirah[119] when a cold wind sprang up after a summer rainstorm. The wind gave the old man a chill, and he was found dead on the spot.

Also according to Abū ʿUbaydah, during the War of Dāḥis and al-Ghabrāʾ, ʿAntarah killed Ḍamḍam of Murrah, the father of Ḥuṣayn and Harim, an event he mentions in the following verses: 1.7

I feared I'd die before war's mill
could grind Ḍamḍam's sons to dust.
Unprovoked, they vowed revenge
and stained my honor.
There's still time for them to act!
I killed their father—
carrion for gimpy hyenas
and grizzled vultures![120]

No one can quibble over the assertion that he was the first poet to develop the following motif: 1.8

and the lone hopper, look,
screeches its drunken song
scraping out a tune
leg on leg like a one-armed man
bent over a fire stick.[121]

This is quite simply a truly great image.

This motif too is original: 1.9

I squander all I have on drink—
keeping my honor whole.
Sober again, I'm lavish still,
ʿAblah, as you know.[122]

As is this: 1.10

The noble line of my tribe
accounts for half of my station—
my blade takes care of the rest . . .
When the squadron flinches,

fear in their eyes,
I am better than any man
with nobility on both
sides of his family.[123]

In other words, half of my lineage belongs to ʿAbs, and I use my sword to defend the rest of my lineage, the half that belongs to the blacks, and in this way I bring it honor.

1.11 The following verses are excellent:

"Stay back," my woman pleaded,
as if the Fates were going
to let me step aside and avoid them.
Death is a pool we all must drink from.
Enough fuss! Save face! I may die
tomorrow, if I'm not killed today.
Death I know—it looks like me,
grim as battle, when warriors clash
on a packed field.[124]

1.12 In this line he goes a bit too far:

In all lands
I am Death.
One thrust from me
and your Fate is changed.[125]

1.13 In the following verses he boasts of his black maternal uncles:

In conflict, all know whence I hail.
My battles and exploits I yield to ʿAbs,
my father's clan—
my mother descends
from the sons of Ham.[126]

Appendix 2

Abū l-Faraj al-Iṣbahānī (d. 356/967): "'Antarah: His Lineage and a Few of His Exploits" from *The Book of Songs*[127]

His name is ʿAntarah ibn Shaddād, or ibn ʿAmr ibn Shaddād, ibn ʿAmr ibn Muʿāwiyah ibn Qurād ibn Makhzūm ibn Rabīʿah, or ibn Makhzūm ibn ʿAwf ibn Mālik ibn Ghālib ibn Quṭayʿah ibn ʿAbs ibn Baghīḍ ibn al-Rayth ibn Ghaṭafān ibn Saʿd ibn Qays ibn ʿAylān ibn Muḍar. His nickname was ʿAntarah "the Cleftlip," because of the cleft in his lips. 2.1

His mother was an Ethiopian slave called Zabībah. She had sons who were slaves and ʿAntarah's half brothers because Shaddād was not their father. 2.2

Shaddād refused to recognize him early on, but later came to accept him and give him his lineage. This was Arab custom. The Arabs would consider the sons of female slaves to be slaves and would recognize those sons who achieved notability, but the rest would remain in slavery. 2.3

I was told the following item of information by ʿAlī ibn Sulaymān al-Akhfash the Grammarian, who had it from Abū Saʿīd al-Ḥasan ibn al-Ḥusayn al-Sukkarī, who had it in turn from Muḥammad ibn Ḥabīb. Abū ʿAmr al-Shaybānī also mentions the event. 2.4

[Muḥammad ibn Ḥabīb:] Before he had been formally recognized by his father, Shaddād, ʿAntarah incurred his father's wrath when his wife claimed that ʿAntarah had tried to seduce her. Shaddād gave him a vicious beating and struck him with his sword. But then his wife threw herself upon ʿAntarah and tried to protect him, bursting into tears at the sight of his wounds. Her name 2.5

was Sumayyah, or, according to others, Suhayyah. This is 'Antarah's poem on the subject:

2.6 Song

Is Suhayyah shedding tears
for me? I wish
she'd let me know before
refusing to speak,
entrancing me with
her languid eyes
blinking like an 'Usfān gazelle.
When the staff was stayed
she cast herself upon me,
an idol
precious and adored.
You are my master, lord,
I'm yours.
Will you show mercy today?
You forget my prowess
when the battle's in rut
and the sleek mares swarm
like locusts,
sweat-flecked saddles
ridden by lords,
haughty, swaggering,
and my lance
is driven obliquely
in a deep cut
till the blood spurts.[128]

2.7 The first and second verses were sung by 'Allawayh. His chosen mode was *thaqīl* rhythm number one, played on an open string with the ring finger. Others say that this is by Ibrāhīm al-Mawṣilī. Ibn Surayḥ is said to have sung both verses in *ramal* rhythm played with the median finger, but this is an erroneous attribution made by Ibn al-Makkī.

"Shedding" is said of someone whose eyes "shed" tears in an almost continuous stream of drops; "I wish she'd let me know before," i.e., "I was unaware of such affections and feelings on your part," because he could not not have known them if they had been known prior to this; "languid eyes:" unhurried and at rest, because anything "languid" is unhurried and at rest; "blinking:" blinking means that the eye is most likely to be unhurried and at rest; "cast:" i.e., she threw herself upon me; "stayed:" propped; "a precious idol:" i.e., one that is visited time and again; "adored" is used of anything people cling to in adoration; "sleek" means swift, "mares" here are warhorses, and "saddles" are seats on horses; "haughty" means holding one's nose high; "swaggering" that they are noblemen and chiefs, for a swagger is a way of walking with pride; a "deep cut" is also a wide one, and a deep-cutting spearhead is one that leaves a wide gash when thrust into an object; "obliquely" means from the side, though some say that the phrase "I take him obliquely" means "I kill him." 2.8

I have the following information from Muḥammad ibn al-Ḥasan ibn Durayd who was citing his uncle who was relying on Ibn al-Kalbī. I also have it from Ibrāhīm ibn Ayyūb who had it from Ibn Qutaybah who, in his turn, also relied on Ibn al-Kalbī. 2.9

[Ibn al-Kalbī:] Shaddād was ʿAntarah's grandfather and his lineage is traced back though his grandfather rather than through his father. So, properly, he is ʿAntarah ibn ʿAmr ibn Shaddād. I have heard some say that Shaddād was his father's brother and that ʿAntarah's lineage is traced back through his uncle and not his father because he grew up in his uncle's care. His father did not recognize him as his son until he had reached manhood because his mother was a black slave called Zabībah, and during the *Jāhiliyyah* the Arabs would consider the sons of slaves to be slaves. ʿAntarah had half brothers who were also slaves. The story of how his father came to recognize him as his son is as follows. During a raid on ʿAbs, many men were killed and camels plundered. The men of ʿAbs gave chase and did battle with the raiders, fighting to win back the plunder. ʿAntarah took part in the pursuit. His father said, "Attack, ʿAntarah!" but ʿAntarah replied, "Slaves do not attack. They're much better at milking camels." "Attack and you are a free man," his father said. Then ʿAntarah charged the foe, declaiming: 2.10

I'm the Half-Blood, 'Antarah!
Every man guards
his woman's cunt,
black or white.
By the <bushy> hair,
the thick fuzzy lips—
This I swear.[129]

He fought bravely that day and his father called him his son, giving him his name.[130]

2.11 The version of this narrative that does not have Ibn al-Kalbī as its source runs as follows: 'Abs raided Ṭayyi' and rustled some livestock. When it came to the division of the spoils, they said to 'Antarah, "You are a slave so we are not going to give you a share equal to ours." But they took so long over the division of the spoils that Ṭayyi' had time to attack them. 'Antarah addressed the troops: "The foe stands before you. You are not outnumbered. Ṭayyi' have taken their livestock back." "Attack, 'Antarah!" his father said. "Are slaves good enough to attack?" "You are not the slave here," his father said, and acknowledged him as his son. 'Antarah charged in attack and won the livestock back, then began to recite:

I'm the Half-Blood, 'Antarah!
Every man guards
his woman's cunt

and so on, to the end of the poem.

2.12 There were three "Arab ravens": 'Antarah, whose mother was Zabībah; Khufāf ibn 'Umayr al-Sharīdī of Sulaym, whose mother was Nadbah; and al-Sulayk ibn 'Umayr al-Sa'dī, whose mother was Sulakah. All three traced their lineage back through their mothers.[131]

2.13 'Antarah mentions this in these lines:

The noble line of 'Abs
accounts for one half of my station—
my blade takes care of the rest . . .
When the squadron flinches,

fear in their eyes,
  I am better than any man
with nobility on both
  sides of his family.[132]

What he means by "one half" is "My father is of ʿAbs aristocracy, whereas my sword strokes make up for my mother's ignobility. Therefore, I am better than those in my tribe whose paternal and maternal uncles belong fully to the tribe but who are no match for me." I believe that the poem I will now quote is the ode to which these two verses that have been put to music belong and that he composed during the War of Dāḥis and al-Ghabrāʾ.

According to Abū ʿAmr al-Shaybānī, ʿAbs, under their commander Qays ibn 2.14
Zuhayr, raided Tamīm but were routed and then pursued. ʿAntarah stood his ground and defended the troops when they were overtaken by a squadron of cavalry. Not a single person of the ʿAbs raiding party was killed in the retreat. ʿAntarah's achievements that day annoyed Qays. Back home, he said, "We owe our safety to the negress's son." Qays was a man who liked to eat. When ʿAntarah learned of what he had said, he composed the following poem:[133]

Song 2.15

"Stay back," my woman pleaded,
  as if the Fates were going
to let me step aside and avoid them.
  Death is a pool we all must drink from.
Enough fuss! Save face! I may die
  tomorrow, if I'm not killed today.
Death I know—it looks like me,
  grim as battle, when warriors clash
on a packed field. . . .
  The noble line of ʿAbs
accounts for one half
  of my station—
my blade takes care of the rest. . . .
  When the squadron flinches,
fear in their eyes,
  I am better than any man

with nobility on both
    sides of his family.
With a shout and
    splintering thrust,
riders know I'll break the line.
    Turn, friends, ride hard.
I have your back.
    Move in on us,
I'll fight in the vanguard . . . .
    Surround us, and I'll charge.
Hand to hand—I'm your man.
    Dismount and square up
to fight—or run for life. . . .
    When horses flinch
from a draft of
    bitter colocynth,
I am hunger-twisted,
    night-starved,
so no one can blame me
    for what I eat.[134]

The meter is *kāmil.* ʿArīb sang the first four verses, as well as verse two, to the light *ramal* rhythm with the ring finger, as reported by al-Hishāmī, Ibn al-Muʿtazz, and Abū l-ʿUbays.

2.16 "The Fates" are the nasty and deadly events that befall men; "step aside," i.e., move to one side away from them; "avoid them" means stay in a place far removed from them; a "pool" is a water hole; "save face" means keep up appearances; "a packed field" is a narrow and confined space; the line "Death I know" means: If Death were created with a form, it would take my shape and form; "station": birth; a "blade" is a sword;[135] to "flinch" is to be fainthearted; a "squadron" is a military formation when it keeps its shape and does not disperse; soldiers have "fear in their eyes" when they see others advance on the enemy—the basic notion comes from when people look at one another out of the corners of their eyes; the thrust is "splintering" because it "splinters" the enemy; "I have your back" because I will not be one of the first to flee but I will be the person who defends them; a "vanguard" is a section; they are "surrounded" when the enemy catches up with them: al-Aṣmaʿī quotes the following verse:

Their fleet warhorses
saved ʿIlāj and Bishr
when Death surrounded
the riders of grade horses.

The horses "flinch" because they have grown emaciated, whereas the riders grimace at the fearsome intensity of the fighting; according to al-Aṣmaʿī, the phrase "I am hunger-twisted, night-starved," means "I spend the night twisted in hunger and stay like this during the day so no one can blame me for what I eat," i.e., food that would bring me shame. A similar expression is, "Two days when I do not taste anything, neither food nor drink,"[136] that is, "I do not taste food or drink during them." "Hunger-twisted" means to have a stomach that is empty and thin, so someone can be either "hungry" or "hunger-twisted."

I have the following information from Aḥmad ibn ʿAbd al-ʿAzīz al-Jawharī, who was citing ʿUmar ibn Shabbah, citing in his turn Ibn ʿĀʾishah. 2.17

[Ibn ʿĀʾishah:] Someone recited this line by ʿAntarah to Prophet Muḥammad (God bless and cherish him!): 2.18

I am hunger-twisted,
night-starved,
so no one can blame me
for what I eat.

The Prophet remarked, "Of all the Arabs of the desert I'd like to have seen ʿAntarah."

I have the following information from ʿAlī ibn Sulaymān al-Akhfash, who was citing Abū Saʿīd al-Sukkarī, who had it from Muḥammad ibn Ḥabīb, whose authorities were Ibn al-Aʿrābī and Abū ʿUbaydah. 2.19

[Ibn al-Aʿrābī and Abū ʿUbaydah:] ʿAntarah was one of a number of brothers, all born to the same mother, and he desperately wanted his people to recognize them as equals. He instructed Ḥanbal, the brother who was the most sensible of the lot: "Give your colt milk to drink, and then later this evening 2.20

bring it to me. When I say to you, 'How is it that your colt has lost so much weight and is in prime condition?' you must strike its stomach with your sword, as if you wanted to show everyone how angry you are at my words." He followed his instructions, and 'Antarah asked him, "Ḥanbal, why is your colt thin when its stomach is so full of milk?" His brother jumped up and struck the horse's belly with his sword, at which point the milk streamed forth. This is 'Antarah's poem on the event:[137]

Sons of Zabībah, brothers,
  Why are you fat as camel humps
when your colt is so thin?
  Have you forgotten
the good things
  your slaves bring
when they hunt
  the nimble oryx
in hard times?[138]

(These lines are part of a longer poem.) Some of the people acknowledged him, but others continued to reject him. The following poem is on this subject:

'Ablah's camp at Ṭawī,
  traced like tattoos
    on a bride's wrists.[139]

It is a long composition in which he enumerates his brave exploits in battle and his achievements among his people.

2.21 The following information comes ultimately from al-Haytham ibn 'Adī. I got it from my uncle and he was told it by al-Kurānī, who had it from al-Naṣr ibn 'Amr.

2.22 [Al-Haytham ibn 'Adī:] "Are you the bravest and fiercest Arab alive?" 'Antarah was asked. "No." "Well then, why are you so famous for being so?" "I attack when I think it brave and retreat when I think it resolute," 'Antarah replied. "I make sure I have a way out of anywhere I enter. I get the sniveling coward in my sights and smite him so hard that brave men go weak at the knees. Then I hit him again and kill him."

I have the next item of information from both Ḥabīb ibn Naṣr and Aḥmad ibn ʿAbd al-ʿAzīz al-Jawharī, who both cited ʿUmar ibn Shabbah. 2.23

[ʿUmar ibn Shabbah:] ʿUmar ibn al-Khaṭṭāb asked al-Ḥuṭayʾah, "How many men did you have when you went to war?" "We numbered a thousand doughty knights." "How so?" "We had Qays ibn Zuhayr—he was a redoubtable leader who had our unquestioning loyalty. ʿAntarah was our knight—we attacked when he did, and retreated when he did. We also had al-Rabīʿ ibn Ziyād—he was a clever commander who directed our every action. And then we had ʿUrwah ibn al-Ward, whose poetry made us complete. That's why I said what I did." "Spoken truly." 2.24

The following comes ultimately from Abū ʿUbaydah and Ibn al-Kalbī. I got it from ʿAlī ibn Sulaymān al-Akhfash who cited Abū Saʿīd al-Sukkarī. He was quoting Muḥammad ibn Ḥabīb who was quoting Ibn al-Aʿrābī and he was relying on al-Mufaḍḍal: 2.25

[Al-Mufaḍḍal:] When he was an old man, ʿAntarah raided Nabhān ibn Ṭayyiʾ and rustled some of their livestock. As he was driving them away, he improvised the following verse: 2.26

The achievements of ostriches in a barren plain.[140]

Wizr ibn Jābir[141] of Nabhān, in the flush of youth, fired an arrow, shouting, "Take that! I am Ibn Salmā." The arrow hit ʿAntarah in the back, but he carried on and managed to get back home, where, despite his wound, he declaimed:

Listen! Ibn Salmā
  has to pay
for my blood.
  But how make him?
He's holed up
  in his fortress
near the stars.

The night the men
  set up camp
between the peak
  and the pass

he shot an arrow
at me and
its iron flange
sliced me to
the quick.[142]

2.27 According to Ibn al-Kalbī, the man who killed ʿAntarah was known as "the Crippled Lion."

2.28 Abū ʿAmr al-Shaybānī tells that ʿAntarah joined his tribe in a raid on Ṭayyiʾ, but they were routed. ʿAntarah fell from his horse, but was too old to retreat, so he hid in a copse. The Ṭayyiʾ lookout had been watching him and came down from the hill in pursuit, but he was too afraid to take ʿAntarah prisoner so he shot and killed him with an arrow.[143]

2.29 Abū ʿUbaydah says that ʿAntarah grew old and fell into penury because he was too infirm to take part in any raids. A man from Ghaṭafān owed him a young camel so he went to call in the debt, but when he had reached a spot between Sharj and Nāẓirah, a cold wind picked up after a summer rainstorm. The wind gave the old man a chill and killed him.[144]

2.30 I have this from Abū Khalīfah whose authority was Muḥammad ibn Sallām.

2.31 [Muḥammad ibn Sallām:] ʿAmr ibn Maʿdī Karib said, "I did not care which Arab knight took the field against me, as long as I did not have to face the two freemen and the two men of slave birth." By "freemen" he meant ʿĀmir ibn al-Ṭufayl and ʿUtaybah ibn al-Ḥārith ibn Shihāb, and by the "two slaves" he was referring to ʿAntarah and al-Sulayk ibn al-Sulakah.

2.32 This is all the information I have on the life and times of ʿAntarah.

Appendix 3

Prefaces Provided by al-Shantamarī and al-Baṭalyawsī

This section provides translations of the narratives and comments that the commentators provide as prefaces to the poems they cite. The material is clearly derived ultimately from the "Battle Lore of the Arabs" (*Ayyām al-ʿArab*) and serves to remind us that these poems were read, wherever possible, as part of the historical record of pre-Islamic Arabia.

For six poems, only cursory information is provided, with phrases such as "another poem by ʿAntarah": Poems 7, 21, 25, 35, 42, and 43.[145]

Ibn Maymūn provides no information for Poem 29, however the reader is directed to the prefaces of al-Shantamarī and al-Baṭalyawsī for Poem 5, of which it is an expansion.

Poems 48 and 49 are taken from the Cairene version of *Sīrat ʿAntar*, which was unavailable to me. *Sharḥ dīwān ʿAntarah*, ed. Shalabī, 88, 91 provides the following brief prefaces: "An example of wisdom poetry" (Poem 48); "One night, while on a foray with Prince Sha's ibn Zuhayr, he happened to see ʿAblah's apparition in a dream. He awoke disoriented and in a state of shock. This is the poem he composed" (Poem 49).

Poem 1

Abū l-Ḥajjāj Yūsuf ibn Sulaymān the Teacher said: This is a poem by ʿAntarah. 3.1.1
His name is ʿAntarah ibn Shaddād ibn Muʿāwiyah, though others say it is ʿAntarah ibn Muʿāwiyah ibn Shaddād ibn Qurād ibn Makhzūm ibn Rabīʿah ibn Mālik ibn Quṭayʿah ibn ʿAbs. Shaddād was the Knight of Jirwah, Jirwah being his horse. ʿAntarah's mother was Ethiopian and had other sons, so ʿAntarah and his brothers were slaves. ʿAntarah was the fiercest warrior and the most

generous of men. When ʿAntarah had proved himself in battle, his father recognized him as his son and gave him his freedom. One day at a gathering of ʿAbs, a fellow tribesman launched a vicious verbal attack on ʿAntarah, upbraiding his mother and brothers and denouncing him for being black. ʿAntarah responded ferociously. He riposted: "I do not shirk from war. I yield the spoils I win. I refrain from begging. I am generous with what I own. My judgment and resolve are unerring." "Ah, but I am a better poet than you," the man retorted. "We'll soon see about that," ʿAntarah said, and declaimed the following poem, his first major composition, celebrating how he had slain Muʿāwiyah ibn Nizāl. The Arabs called this "the Golden Ode."

Source: al-Shantamarī, in *Dīwān ʿAntarah*, ed. Mawlawī, 181–82.

3.1.2 The High Functionary Abū Bakr ʿĀṣim ibn Ayyūb al-Baṭalyawsī (God keep and bless him), expert in religious law and chief of the petty courts, commented: This is a poem by ʿAntarah. Now, according to Abū ʿAmr al-Shaybānī, he is ʿAntarah ibn Muʿāwiyah ibn Shaddād ibn Qurād, of Makhzūm ibn Rabīʿah ibn Mālik ibn Quṭayʿah ibn ʿAbs. Shaddād was the Knight of Jirwah, Jirwah being his horse. Others say correctly that Shaddād was in fact his paternal uncle. According to Abū Yūsuf Yaʿqūb ibn al-Sikkīt, ʿAntarah's mother was Ethiopian and had other sons, so ʿAntarah and his brothers were slaves. ʿAntarah was the fiercest warrior and the most generous of men. ʿAntarah had two familiar names, one for warfare and one for peace. His war name was "ʿAblah's Man," his peacetime name was "Man of Discord."[146] Ibn Ḥabīb[147] says that his familiar name was "Man of Battle Murk," though ʿAntarah was also referred to as "Cleftlip," because of the cleft in his lip. Ibn al-Sikkīt notes that the Arabs called the following poem "the Golden Ode."

Source: al-Baṭalyawsī, in *Sharḥ al-ashʿār*, ed. al-Tūmī, 2:191–92.

Poem 2

3.2.1 On the Battle of al-Farūq. ʿAbs left Dhubyān and traveled to Saʿd ibn Zayd Manāt ibn Tamīm, to settle in their territory as allies. Saʿd hatched a plot to steal some thoroughbred horses and prize camels that ʿAbs possessed; however, the ʿAbs commander, Qays ibn Zuhayr, was suspicious of their motives and got wind of what they were up to. Qays was renowned for his strategic ability. He had ʿAbs wait for nightfall and tied lights to the trees, hanging skins full of water from them, so the water could be heard sloshing about inside the skins. At his command, ʿAbs departed under the cover of night. Saʿd, however, could hear noises and see fires all night long. The following morning, when they realized that ʿAbs had left, they gave chase on horseback. They overtook them at al-Farūq, a wadi between Yamāmah and Baḥrayn, but they were routed in the battle that ensued. The conflict lasted all day, without a break, until nightfall. In the battle, ʿAntarah killed Muʿāwiyah ibn al-Nizāl, the grandfather of al-Aḥnaf. ʿAbs returned to Dhubyān and agreed a truce. ʿAntarah commemorated the battle in the following poem.

Source: al-Shantamarī, in *Dīwān ʿAntarah*, ed. Mawlawī, 223.

During the War of Dāḥis, ʿAbs left Dhubyān and traveled to Saʿd ibn Zayd Manāt 3.2.2
ibn Tamīm ibn Murr, to settle in their territory as allies. Saʿd hatched a plot to steal some thoroughbred horses and prize camels that ʿAbs possessed but the commander of ʿAbs, Qays ibn Zuhayr, had become suspicious of their motives and got wind of what they were up to. Qays was renowned for his strategic ability. He had ʿAbs wait for nightfall and tied lights to the trees, hanging skins full of water from them, so the water could be heard sloshing about inside the skins. At his command, ʿAbs departed under the cover of night. Saʿd, however, could hear noises and see fires all night long. The following morning, when they realized that ʿAbs had left, they gave chase on horseback. They overtook them at al-Farūq, a wadi between Yamāmah and Baḥrayn. The moment ʿAbs realized they were there, the men were ordered to endure the trials of battle. Eventually Saʿd were routed in battle. The conflict lasted all day, without a break, until nightfall. In the battle, according to al-Shaybānī, ʿAntarah killed Muʿāwiyah ibn al-Nizāl, the grandfather of al-Aḥnaf.

Source: al-Baṭalyawsī, in *Sharḥ al-ashʿār*, ed. al-Tūmī, 2:260–61.

Poem 3

On the Battle of ʿUrāʿir. ʿAbs were driven out of Yumn[148] by Ḥanīfah and so 3.3.1
decided to travel to Taghlib. Their route took them past a well called ʿUrāʿir, where a Kalb group was camped. A request to use the water was denied. In fact, Kalb attacked them and tried to seize their belongings. Fighting broke

out and Mas'ūd ibn Muṣād, the chief of Kalb, was killed. Both sides held a parley and agreed to a truce: 'Abs would use the water and pay Kalb for doing so. Then 'Abs continued on their way. 'Antarah composed the following poem on the event.

Source: al-Shantamarī, in *Dīwān 'Antarah*, ed. Mawlawī, 228.

3.3.2 According to Ibn al-Sikkīt, after the battle of al-Farūq, 'Abs entered into an alliance and joined forces with Ḥanīfah. One day Qays ibn Zuhayr was out walking with one of the Ḥanīfah when he chanced upon a human skull. Qays kicked it and said, "You were so afraid of dying that you acquiesced to so many injustices—and yet, I see, still you succumbed to death." The man who had been with Qays said to his kinsmen, "You must do as I say!" "What do you mean?" "The chief of our new allies made a comment that made me realize that a man who talks like this would never be prepared to accept even the merest slight. We must drive them out." 'Abs, driven out, decided to travel to Taghlib. Their route took them past a well called 'Urā'ir, where a group was camped. A request to use the water for their camels was denied. The chief of the group was Mas'ūd ibn Muṣād of Kalb. In fact, Kalb attacked them and tried to seize their women, children, and possessions. Fighting broke out and Mas'ūd was killed. Both sides agreed to a truce: 'Abs would use the water and pay Kalb for doing so. Then 'Abs continued on their way. 'Antarah composed the following poem on the event.

Source: al-Baṭalyawsī, in *Sharḥ al-ash'ār*, ed. al-Tūmī, 2:266–67.

Poem 4

3.4.1 A lampoon of 'Umārah ibn Ziyād. 'Umārah envied 'Antarah and would tell his people that they mentioned 'Antarah's name too often. "God, if only I could confront him face to face," he'd say, "I'd show you that he's no more than a slave." 'Umārah owned many camels and it was his habit to be generous and give away all his wealth, whereas 'Antarah had barely a camel to share among his brothers. 'Antarah learned of what 'Umārah had said about him, so he composed the following poem.

Source: al-Shantamarī, in *Dīwān 'Antarah*, ed. Mawlawī, 233.

ʿAntarah addressed the following poem to ʿUmārah ibn Ziyād, who was known as "the Munificent." ʿUmārah envied ʿAntarah and would tell his people that they mentioned his name too often. "God, if only I could confront him face to face," he said, "I'd show you that he's no more than a slave." For all his generosity and his propensity to give everything away, ʿUmārah was a man of great wealth and he owned many camels, whereas ʿAntarah could barely hold on to a camel, for he always gave them away among his brothers. ʿAntarah learned of what ʿUmārah had been saying about him, so he composed the following poem. 3.4.2

Source: al-Baṭalyawsī, in *Sharḥ al-ashʿār*, ed. al-Tūmī, 2:245.

Poem 5

A row broke out between ʿAntarah and Ziyād. ʿAntarah reminded him[149] of all the battles he had participated in during the War of Dāḥis and al-Ghabrāʾ, especially the battle in which ʿAbs were routed and ʿAntarah stood firm and held the line against the enemy soldiers until his own side had regrouped. Ḥudhayfah ibn Badr, chief of Fazārah, attacked when he learned that ʿAbs planned to pitch camp in the basalt lands of Sulaym, and put them to flight, seizing their possessions. However, ʿAntarah stood firm and protected the women from capture until the ʿAbs cavalry came back. Ḥudhayfah and his brother Ḥamal ibn Badr made for al-Habāʾah,[150] a stream where they could wash after battle. The ʿAbs cavalry regrouped and set off in pursuit of Badr. They killed Ḥudhayfah and his brother as they were washing in the stream. This is ʿAntarah's poem on the event. 3.5.1

Source: al-Shantamarī, in *Dīwān ʿAntarah*, ed. Mawlawī, 239–40.

A poem in which ʿAntarah describes his exploits in the War of Dāḥis and al-Ghabrāʾ. He mentions his feats on the battlefield and how he was not found wanting.[151] 3.5.2

Source: al-Baṭalyawsī, in *Sharḥ al-ashʿār*, ed. al-Tūmī, 2:272.

Poem 6

3.6.1 Under their commander Qays ibn Zuhayr ibn Jadhīmah, ʿAbs raided Tamīm but were routed and then pursued. ʿAntarah stood his ground and defended the troops when they were overtaken by a squadron of cavalry. No member of the ʿAbs raiding party was killed in the retreat. ʿAntarah's feats that day annoyed Qays, so when the soldiers made it back home he said, "We owe our safety to the negress's son." Qays was a man who liked to eat. When ʿAntarah learned of what he had said, he composed the following poem.

Source: al-Shantamarī, in *Dīwān ʿAntarah*, ed. Mawlawī, 245–46.

3.6.2 Ibn al-Sikkīt cites Abū ʿUbaydah as follows: Under their commander Qays ibn Zuhayr ibn Jadhīmah ibn Rawāḥah ibn ʿAbs, ʿAbs raided Tamīm but were routed and then pursued. ʿAntarah stood his ground and defended the troops when they were overtaken by a squadron of cavalry. No member of the ʿAbs raiding party was killed in the retreat. ʿAntarah's feats that day annoyed Qays and filled him with envy, so when the soldiers made it back home he said, "We owe our safety to the negress's son. He fought in the vanguard." Qays was a man who liked to eat. When ʿAntarah learned of what he had said, he composed the following poem, alluding to him.

Source: al-Baṭalyawsī, in *Sharḥ al-ashʿār*, ed. al-Tūmī, 2:318.

Poem 8

3.8.1 Ṭayyiʾ raided ʿAbs in the absence of their menfolk. ʿAntarah was tending his camels on horseback. He headed back as soon as he heard the news and single-handedly deprived Ṭayyiʾ of their booty, killing three or four of the raiders in the process. This was when ʿAbs were settled in the territory of ʿĀmir. One day ʿAntarah was upset by some remarks made by a group of young men from ʿĀmir he was sitting with: At the time, he was living among Shakal of al-Ḥarīsh. So he declaimed the following poem.

Source: al-Shantamarī, in *Dīwān ʿAntarah*, ed. Mawlawī, 262.

ʿAbs were settled in the territory of ʿĀmir ibn Ṣaʿṣaʿah. Ṭayyiʾ raided them in the absence of their menfolk and made off with a number of camels. ʿAntarah was tending his camels on horseback. He was never too far away from his horse. He headed back as soon as he heard the news and single-handedly deprived Ṭayyiʾ of their booty, killing three or four of the raiders in the process. According to Ibn al-Sikkīt, ʿAntarah was upset one day by some remarks made by a group of young men from ʿĀmir he was sitting with. He had previously been living among Shakal of al-Ḥarīsh ibn Kaʿb. So he declaimed the following poem. 3.8.2

Source: al-Baṭalyawsī, in *Sharḥ al-ashʿār*, ed. al-Tūmī, 2:254.

Poem 9

A squabble broke out between ʿAntarah and ʿAbs over some camels that ʿAntarah had taken from one of their confederates. ʿAntarah refused to give them back, as ʿAbs wished him to, and fighting broke out. He took his camels and belongings and went to settle in the territory of the Ṭayyiʾ. A fearsome battle took place between Jadīlah and Thuʿal. ʿAntarah fought on the side of Jadīlah, and this proved to be the only time they enjoyed victory in battle. Thuʿal sent a messenger to Ghaṭafān, saying, "The ties that bind us are close and we deserve better than this. No member of Ghaṭafān should have taken the field against us." Ghaṭafān went to ʿAntarah and placated him by letting him keep the camels. He composed the following poem on these events. 3.9.1

Source: al-Shantamarī, in *Dīwān ʿAntarah*, ed. Mawlawī, 267.

ʿAntarah and ʿAbs fell out over some camels that ʿAntarah had taken from one of their allies. ʿAntarah refused to give them back, as ʿAbs wished him to, and fighting broke out. He took his camels and belongings and went to settle in the territory of the Ṭayyiʾ. A fearsome battle took place between Jadīlah and Thuʿal. ʿAntarah fought on the side of Jadīlah, and this proved to be the only time they enjoyed victory in battle. Thuʿal sent a messenger to Ghaṭafān, saying, "The ties that bind us are close and we deserve better than this. Our foes should not be helped by one of our own." Ghaṭafān went to ʿAntarah and 3.9.2

placated him by letting him keep the camels. He composed the following poem on these events.

Source: al-Baṭalyawsī, in *Sharḥ al-ashʿār*, ed. al-Tūmī, 2:278.

Poem 10

3.10.1 Despite his valor in combat, but before he had been formally recognized by his father, ʿAntarah incurred his father's wrath when his father's wife claimed that ʿAntarah had tried to seduce her. His father gave him a sound thrashing but stopped when his wife threw herself upon ʿAntarah and tried to protect him, bursting into tears at the sight of his wounds. This is his poem on the subject.

Source: al-Shantamarī, in *Dīwān ʿAntarah*, ed. Mawlawī, 269.

3.10.2 Before he had been formally recognized by his father Shaddād, but after he had fought with valor, ʿAntarah incurred his father's wrath when his wife claimed that ʿAntarah had tried to seduce her. Shaddād struck him with his sword, but stopped when his wife threw herself upon ʿAntarah and tried to protect him, bursting into tears at the sight of his wounds. Her name was Sumayyah or, according to others, Suhayyah. Abū l-Faraj al-Iṣbahānī is my authority for this. This is ʿAntarah's poem on the subject.[152]

Source: al-Baṭalyawsī, in *Sharḥ al-ashʿār*, ed. al-Tūmī, 2:280.

Poem 11

3.11.1 ʿAntarah was married to a stingy woman (or, according to al-Baṭalyawsī: a woman of Bajīlah), who kept on referring to his horses and nagging him about his favorite steed.

Source: al-Shantamarī, in *Dīwān ʿAntarah*, ed. Mawlawī, 272; al-Baṭalyawsī, in *Sharḥ al-ashʿār*, ed. al-Tūmī, 2:287.

Poem 12

3.12.1 War broke out between ʿAbs and Jadīlah of the Ṭayyiʾ. Jadīlah and Shaybān were confederates and Shaybān supplied Jadīlah with men. ʿAntarah fought ferociously that day, shedding much blood and inflicting many wounds, but received no share of the cattle seized as booty. This is his poem on the event.

Source: al-Shantamarī, in *Dīwān ʿAntarah*, ed. Mawlawī, 275.

War broke out between ʿAbs and Jadīlah of Ṭayyiʾ. Jadīlah and Abū Rabīʿah ibn Dhuhl ibn Shaybān ibn Thaʿlabah were confederates and Shaybān supplied Jadīlah with men. ʿAntarah fought ferociously that day, shedding much blood and inflicting many wounds, but received no share of the cattle seized as booty. This is his poem on the event. 3.12.2

Source: al-Baṭalyawsī, in *Sharḥ al-ashʿār*, ed. al-Tūmī, 2:283.

Poem 13

Ḥanẓalah of Tamīm raided ʿAbs, who killed their chieftain, ʿAmr ibn ʿAmr ibn ʿUdus of Dārim. Tamīm alleged that their chief had in fact died at the Pass of Aqrun when Tamīm were routed in the encounter known as the Battle of the Pass of Aqrun.[153] ʿAntarah's poem on the event. 3.13.1

Source: al-Shantamarī, in *Dīwān ʿAntarah*, ed. Mawlawī, 278.

Ḥanẓalah of Tamīm raided ʿAbs, who killed their chieftain ʿAmr ibn ʿAmr ibn ʿUdus ibn Zayd ibn ʿAbd Allāh ibn Dārim. Anas al-Fawāris claimed his death. Tamīm were routed by ʿAbs. The battle is known as the Battle of the Pass of Aqrun. Jarīr mentions it in his line 3.13.2

Do you recall Anas al-Fawāris at the Pass of Aqrun,
on the day the Leper fell to his death?[154]

"The Leper" is ʿAmr ibn ʿAmr, because he suffered from leprosy. Tamīm claim that ʿAmr died when he fell from the Pass of Aqrun. ʿAbs were under the command of al-Rabīʿ ibn Ziyād, brother to the ʿAmr ibn Ghālib, and they killed Ḥanẓalah ibn ʿAmr and Shurayḥ. According to al-Aṣmaʿī, when Tamīm were routed, they headed for the pass but did not make it and fell to their deaths from a great height. ʿAntarah's poem on the event.

Source: al-Baṭalyawsī, in *Sharḥ al-ashʿār*, ed. al-Tūmī, 2:291.

Poem 14

3.14.1 Qirwāsh ibn Hunayy of ʿAbs killed Ḥudhayfah ibn Badr of Fazārah. Al-ʿUsharāʾ of Māzin captured Qirwāsh and killed him in retaliation for Ḥudhayfah ibn Badr. This is ʿAntarah's poem on the event.

Source: al-Shantamarī, in *Dīwān ʿAntarah*, ed. Mawlawī, 280.

3.14.2 [Al-Baṭalyawsī:] ʿAbs, who were then living among ʿĀmir, raided Ghaṭafān. Qirwāsh ibn Hunayy ibn Usayd ibn Jadhīmah ibn Rawāḥah was one of the ʿAbs raiding party and was taken captive by Māzin, Fazārah, and al-ʿUsharāʾ of Māzin. They did not know who he was, so they asked him and he replied, "I am of al-Bakkāʾ." Khulaydah, a slave belonging to Qirwāsh's wife (she was originally from Māzin) heard them talking. She came out from a house and said, "Heavens above! Qirwāsh,[155] what a doughty warrior you are; what a welcome for the guest on a cold night!" Qirwāsh's mother had lived with Ḥudhayfah ibn Badr and it was Ḥudhayfah who brought him up, so he was not afraid to kill him. "Abū Shurayḥ," she said, "how your luck has changed." When his captors realized who he was they slaughtered him. This is ʿAntarah's poem on the event.

Source: al-Baṭalyawsī, in *Sharḥ al-ashʿār*, ed. al-Tūmī, 2:294.

Poem 15

3.15.1 ʿAbs raided ʿAmr ibn al-Hujaym. In the fierce fighting that ensued, ʿAntarah fired an arrow and hit one of their principal fighters, a man named Jurayyah. He thought he had killed him, though he had not. This is ʿAntarah's poem on the event.

Source: al-Shantamarī, in *Dīwān ʿAntarah*, ed. Mawlawī, 282.

3.15.2 According to al-Baṭalyawsī, ʿAbs raided ʿAmr ibn al-Hujaym. In the fierce fighting that ensued, ʿAntarah fired an arrow and hit one of their leaders, a mighty warrior named Jurayyah. He thought he had killed him, though he had not. ʿAbs did not win any livestock that day. This is ʿAntarah's poem on the event.

Source: al-Baṭalyawsī, in *Sharḥ al-ashʿār*, ed. al-Tūmī, 2:298.

Poem 16

Sulaym raided when ʿAntarah and a slave were tending to his camels. Mounted on horseback, but without his armor, ʿAntarah fought back and broke his lance in the struggle, so he took up his bow and felled a raider from Bajlah of Sulaym. But the raiders rounded up his camels and made off with them. 3.16.1

Source: al-Shantamarī, in *Dīwān ʿAntarah*, ed. Mawlawī, 284.

[Al-Baṭalyawsi:] According to Ibn al-Naḥḥās, one drought year ʿAntarah took his camels in search of fresh pastures and arrived at good pasture land on sacred ground. Sulaym mounted a surprise raid as he and a slave were tending to the camels. ʿAntarah had his horse with him but not his armor, yet he fought back. He broke his lance in the struggle, so he took up his bow and felled a raider from Bajīlah, but he lost the camels that Sulaym made off with. Sulaym claimed that his camels were in fact theirs, being the stolen offspring of dams that they owned. This is ʿAntarah's poem on the event. 3.16.2

Source: al-Baṭalyawsī, in *Sharḥ al-ashʿār*, ed. al-Tūmī, 2:315.

Poem 17

Addressed to ʿAmr ibn Aswad, brother to the kin group of Saʿd ibn ʿAwf ibn Mālik ibn Zayd Manāt ibn Tamīm. 3.17.1

Source: al-Shantamarī, in *Dīwān ʿAntarah*, ed. Mawlawī, 286; al-Baṭalyawsī, in *Sharḥ al-ashʿār*, ed. al-Tūmī, 2:312.

Poem 18

On the killing of Qirwāsh and ʿAbd Allāh ibn al-Ṣimmah. 3.18.1

Source: al-Shantamarī, in *Dīwān ʿAntarah*, ed. Mawlawī, 287; al-Baṭalyawsī, in *Sharḥ al-ashʿār*, ed. al-Tūmī, 2:305.

Poem 19

3.19.1 Addressed to al-Rabʿī ibn Ziyād of ʿAbs.

Source: al-Shantamarī, in *Dīwān ʿAntarah*, ed. Mawlawī, 289; al-Baṭalyawsī, in *Sharḥ al-ashʿār*, ed. al-Tūmī, 2:309.

Poem 20

3.20.1 Someone from Abān ibn ʿAbd Allāh ibn Dārim asked to borrow ʿAntarah's spear and he consented, but the person kept it and did not return it. ʿAntarah's poem on the event.

Source: al-Shantamarī, in *Dīwān ʿAntarah*, ed. Mawlawī, 290.

3.20.2 Al-Jaʿd of Abān of Dārim went on a vendetta during the months of the pilgrimage. At the end of the pilgrimage season, when fighting became permissible again, he found himself without any weapons, so he went to ʿAntarah and said, "Please let me have the use of your spear. There is a task I need to undertake. I'll give it back to you when I return to my people." ʿAntarah let him have the spear, but when Jaʿd got back to his people he kept it and did not give it back. This is ʿAntarah's poem on the event.

Source: al-Baṭalyawsī, in *Sharḥ al-ashʿār*, ed. al-Tūmī, 2:310.

Poem 22

3.22.1 On the killing of Naḍlah of Asad by Ward ibn Ḥābis (al-Baṭalyawsī: Ward ibn Ḥābis ibn Jābir).

Source: al-Shantamarī, in *Dīwān ʿAntarah*, ed. Mawlawī, 293; al-Baṭalyawsī, in *Sharḥ al-ashʿār*, ed. al-Tūmī, 2:342.

Poem 23

3.23.1 This poem is not included in al-Aṣmaʿī's recension. Al-Aṣmaʿī maintained that it is by Kuthayyir ibn ʿUrwah al-Nahshalī.

Source: al-Shantamarī, in *Dīwān ʿAntarah*, ed. Mawlawī, 294.

Al-Baṭalyawsī noted that according to al-Aṣmaʿī this poem was one of those that had been falsely attributed to ʿAntarah, having in fact been composed by the poet Kuthayyir al-Nahshalī. Al-Aṣmaʿī was very critical of this poem. 3.23.2

Source: al-Baṭalyawsī, in *Sharḥ al-ashʿār*, ed. al-Tūmī, 2:336.

Poem 24

The attribution of this poem to ʿAntarah is false. 3.24.1

Source: al-Shantamarī, in *Dīwān ʿAntarah*, ed. Mawlawī, 297.

Another poem said to be by ʿAntarah; although the poem bears his name, this attribution is false. 3.24.2

Source: al-Baṭalyawsī, in *Sharḥ al-ashʿār*, ed. al-Tūmī, 2:343.

Poem 26

On the death of Qirwāsh of ʿAbs. Some authorities say the poem is by ʿAntarah's father, Shaddād ibn Muʿāwiyah, though Ibn al-Aʿrābī says that Shaddād was not ʿAntarah's father but was his father's brother. 3.26.1

Source: al-Shantamarī, in *Dīwān ʿAntarah*, ed. Mawlawī, 309.

A poem by Shaddād ibn Muʿāwiyah, the father of ʿAntarah (or, according to Ibn al-Aʿrābī, his paternal uncle), on the killing of Qirwāsh of ʿAbs. 3.26.2

Source: al-Baṭalyawsī, in *Sharḥ al-ashʿār*, ed. al-Tūmī, 2:358.

Poem 27

A lament for Mālik ibn Zuhayr of ʿAbs slain by Badr. (Al-Shantamarī: The poem is also attributed to another poet.) 3.27.1

Source: al-Shantamarī, in *Dīwān ʿAntarah*, ed. Mawlawī, 311; al-Baṭalyawsī, in *Sharḥ al-ashʿār*, ed. al-Tūmī, 2:363.

Poem 28

3.28.1 On his raid of Ḍabbah.

Source: Ibn Maymūn, in *Muntahā*, 109.

3.28.2 The narrator: The following morning God brought the light of dawn as the sun rose over hill and vale, singing the praises of our Lord Muḥammad, comeliest and most learned of men. The troops rose, keen for combat and battle. That day ʿAntar strapped on his thirsty sword, and donned two stout coats of mail, one so heavily gilt that it was called "the golden," the other "the sparkling":[156] it had belonged to the champion of Yathrib, given to ʿAntar by King Qays to mark him as his champion. ʿAntar lined up his men and heroic warriors, and recited the following poem, as he prowled restlessly through the ranks . . . [Poem 28 is declaimed.] . . . The narrator: Lord ʿAntar the Mighty Hero declaimed this composition in his loud voice amid the troops, and issued the following challenge: "Who will face me today? This is a day of which men will vaunt, by facing danger's taunts."

Source: *Sīrat fāris fursān al-Ḥijāz*, 5:242–43.

Poem 29

See §§3.5.1–2.

Poem 30

3.30.1 [Ibn al-Sikkīt:] ʿAntarah was one of a number of brothers, all born to the same mother, and he desperately wanted his people to recognize them as equals. They had a colt that was the object of much criticism. He gave the following instructions to the brother who was the most sensible: "Give your colt milk to drink, and then later this evening bring it with you to Barīkh.[157] When I say to you, 'How is it that your colt has lost so much weight and has grown thin?' you must stab its stomach with your sword, as if you are enraged by my words." They followed his instructions. ʿAntarah asked them, "Why is your colt thin, and your bellies fat?" and declaimed his poem: "Brothers, why is your colt . . ." His brother leaped up and stabbed the horse's belly with his sword, at which the milk streamed forth. . . . [The poem and its commentary are given.] . . . Now, back to the story: When ʿAntarah's brother struck the colt's belly with his sword according to his instructions and the milk flowed out, people said, "This horse is diseased. There should not have been such a buildup of milk inside it." Thus, the source of their shame was removed.

Source: al-Baṭlayawsi, in *Sharḥ al-ashʿār*, ed. al-Tūmī, 2:251–53; *Dīwān ʿAntarah*, ed. Mawlawī, 315–17.

Poem 31

ʿAntarah of ʿAbs addressed the following poem to Shaybān and Ṣaʿṣaʿah, sons of Qushayr ibn Khālid ibn Ḥawmah, of ʿAwf ibn Jadhīmah of al-Hujaym. 3.31.1

Source: al-Baṭalyawsī, in *Sharḥ al-ashʿār*, ed. al-Tūmī, 2:253; *Dīwān ʿAntarah*, ed. Mawlawī, 317.

Poem 32

See §§3.8.1–2.

Poem 33

According to Ibn al-Naḥḥās, ʿAntarah took part in a raid on Ṭayyiʾ. His eyesight was weak, so he could not take part in the fighting. In the rout of ʿAbs,[158] ʿAntarah fell from his horse and wandered into a thick copse. Ṭayyiʾ had stationed a scout on a mountain ridge, and he saw where ʿAntarah had gone. He pointed out his location to the soldiers who captured him. The man who took ʿAntarah captive was ʿAmr ibn Salmā. When ʿAmr realized who it was who was sitting there unable to fight, he was too afraid to approach him, so he fired an arrow and put out his eye. This is ʿAntarah's poem on the event. 3.33.1

Source: al-Baṭalyawsī, in *Sharḥ al-ashʿār*, ed. al-Tūmī, 2:297; *Dīwān ʿAntarah*, ed. Mawlawī, 318.

Poem 34

3.34.1 According to Abū ʿUbaydah, this poem was composed by Ḍubayʿah ibn al-Ḥārith, as a lament for the death of his horse, killed by a thrust from a lance wielded by ʿĀmir ibn al-Ṭufayl. Upon returning to his tribe, ʿĀmir listed the knights he had killed during the battle and included Ḍubayʿah in the list. When ʿĀmir heard that Ḍubayʿah had composed his poem, "God reward my horse Blaze! He was a true comrade" his people remonstrated with him and said, "You told us that you had killed Ḍubayʿah, yet here he is, composing a lament for his horse." In response, ʿĀmir declaimed his poem:

I swear by your grandfather, Ḍubayʿah, that if you escaped me,
it was not because the talismans were put on your neck by me.[159]

Source: al-Baṭalyawsī, in *Sharḥ al-ashʿār*, ed. al-Tūmī, 2:301; *Dīwān ʿAntarah*, ed. Mawlawī, 319–20.

Poem 36

3.36.1 A poem addressed by ʿAntarah to ʿUrwah ibn al-Ward . . . [Poem 36 and its commentary are given.] . . . According to al-Baṭalyawsī, ʿUrwah ibn al-Ward ibn Zayd ibn ʿAbs was known as ʿUrwah of the Pariahs . . . [A point of syntax is explained by al-Baṭalyawsī.] . . . The point of the piece is that ʿAntarah praises ʿUrwah as a form of boasting, because both were pariahs and both belonged to the same kin group: that's why he refers to him as "best of ʿAbs." He also alludes to the time ʿUrwah abandoned his wife among her folk, Kinānah. The story is a long one. ʿUrwah's regret at his actions is mentioned in his line:

The enemies of God gave me wine to drink,
then wrapped me in a shroud of lies and deceit.[160]

Source: al-Baṭalyawsī, in *Sharḥ al-ashʿār*, ed. al-Tūmī, 2:341; *Dīwān ʿAntarah*, ed. Mawlawī, 323–24.

Poem 37

3.37.1 [Al-Baṭalyawsī:] In their pursuit of Thaʿlabah and Ṭarīf, ʿAbs, Murrah, and Fazārah stopped at pasture to refresh their horses. They were eager to get to Qalahā Pond first, so they could prevent Thaʿlabah and Ṭarīf from watering there, but Thaʿlabah and Ṭarīf got there first and they kept ʿAbs, Murrah, and Fazārah from the water. They and their horses were on the point of dying from thirst. The situation was dire. A blind shaykh from the ʿAwf ibn Ḥārithah eventually calmed both sides down and brokered a truce. ʿAntarah composed this poem on the event.[161]

Source: al-Baṭalyawsī, in *Sharḥ al-ashʿār*, ed. al-Tūmī, 2:361–62; *Dīwān ʿAntarah*, ed. Mawlawī, 324.

Poem 38

According to al-Baṭalyawsī, when ʿAbs declared war on all the clans for the assistance they had given to Badr, the clans and their confederates held a meeting at which oaths were sworn, allegiances renewed, and an army mustered. Ḥudhayfah marched on ʿAbs at the head of a vast force. ʿAbs asked Qays ibn Zuhayr if he had a plan and he told them, "Abandon your belongings and leave the womenfolk behind with the litters. Keep your camels thirsty; take them with you and hide in the mountain pass. When Ḥudhayfah's forces arrive and see the womenfolk unprotected, they will lower their guard, set about gathering booty, and break battle formation. That's when you rush out in attack, and can kill at will." When Ḥudhayfah's forces saw that ʿAbs had left their possessions and womenfolk behind they assumed that they had run away, so they took the women captive, lowered their guard, and broke battle formation. ʿAbs charged from the mountain pass and slaughtered them. They killed Ḥudhayfah and his brother Ḥamal at Dhāt al-Iṣād.[162] Abū Tammām mentions this event in his verse: 3.38.1

> In olden times, he slew Badr,
> and left them unburied at Dhāt al-Iṣād.[163]

ʿAbs took the army captive. ʿAntarah charged at them, banner in hand, and while he dispensed death, he declaimed the following poem.

Source: al-Baṭalyawsī, in *Sharḥ al-ashʿār*, ed. al-Tūmī, 2:366–67; *Dīwān ʿAntarah*, ed. Mawlawī, 325–26.

Poem 39

3.39.1 ʿAntarah charged at Ḥuṣayn ibn Ḍamḍam of Murrah and, with a thrust of his lance, knocked him from his horse. ʿAntarah's horse did not wheel and he found himself in the middle of the enemy, so Ḥuṣayn remounted and he and his comrades plucked up enough courage to charge him all at once. As ʿAntarah moved between the lines, Ḥuṣayn and his comrades attacked. Ḥuṣayn speared him in the face, thinking that he had taken his eye out, and was thus able to keep ʿAntarah from his troops. Durayd ibn Ḍamḍam charged Muʿāwiyah ibn Shaddād, ʿAntarah's uncle, and killed him. Ḥuṣayn declaimed the following poem on the event:

The riders of ʿAbs fought with their swords,
 but their leader took to flight, one eye blinded.
I saw that slave wheeling his horse among our troops
 and introduced him to my battle-hard spear;
forced his black filth to turn and run from our ranks
 at the sight of the lancers of Murrah.
He was not man enough to face them.
 Our spearheads left a mark on that slave's face
for all to see for the rest of his life.
 On the battlefield, as the knights charged,
our lances butchered his uncle.

Qays attacked the enemy cavalry and felled Durayd ibn Ḍamḍam with a stroke of his sword. ʿAntarah, wiping the blood from his face, was filled with battle rage against Ḥuṣayn. When he saw Ḥuṣayn turn tail and abandon his brother Durayd, ʿAntarah gave chase and thrust his spear at Durayd, but the spearhead lodged in the saddle. Then ʿAntarah charged Ḥuṣayn, reciting the following poem.

Source: al-Baṭalyawsī, in *Sharḥ al-ashʿār*, ed. al-Tūmī, 2:369; *Dīwān ʿAntarah*, ed. Mawlawī, 327.

Poem 40

'Antarah declaimed this piece as he attacked them. 3.40.1

Source: al-Baṭalyawsī, in *Sharḥ al-ash'ār*, ed. al-Ṭūmī, 2:370; *Dīwān 'Antarah*, ed. Mawlawī, 328.

Poem 41

'Abs and Ka'b made a pact of confederacy. On the night when 'Abs were due to camp among them, Ka'b decided to betray them. They mounted up and rode to attack them, but encountered 'Antarah on guard. "Who goes there?" he demanded. "Travelers," they replied. "Travelers do not go about at night," he said. "Go home. Come back in the morning and you will be granted passage." Ka'b realized that 'Abs were on high alert. 'Antarah informed Qays and he led the clan away to safety. 'Antarah declaimed the following poem on the event. 3.41.1

Source: al-Baṭalyawsī, in *Sharḥ al-ash'ār*, ed. al-Ṭūmī, 2:371; *Dīwān 'Antarah*, ed. Mawlawī, 328.

Poem 44

Khufāf ibn Nadbah's poem moved everyone in the army, especially 'Antar ibn Shaddād. He grew more inflamed with battle lust, and leaned back in his saddle, reciting the following poem . . . [Poem 44 is given.] The narrator: . . . The beauty of 'Antar's poem and his recitation of it filled the assembly of mighty chieftains with wonder at its themes and ideas. Everyone was moved by its verses, and the fires of pride burned fiercely in the hearts of the knights. Each warrior recollected the battles he had fought and the raids of the past. On they traveled, across desert wastes, heading for Kisrā Anūshirwān, their hearts full of war, with not a thought for food or wine,[164] or for those who had drunk of the cup of death in battle against the Persians. 3.44.1

Source: *Sīrat fāris fursān al-Ḥijāz*, 5:126–30.[165]

Poem 45

3.45.1 At this point ʿAntar returned to his senses and recovered from his wounds. He realized that his feet were manacled, in heavy chains. He found this very difficult to bear . . . [A poem is declaimed.] . . . Then he looked at his son Maysarah and his brother Māzin, and their plight moved him greatly, so he said to the Persian knights, "Wretches, where are you taking us when Kisrā has ordered we be beheaded?" "You are indeed on the way to a beheading, you curs! You will taste bitter abasement, for the Lords of the Flame have consigned you to slavery. We will capture the rest of your comrades, just as we have captured you." ʿAntar was filled with rage and lost all fear of death. He was most upset for his brother Māzin and his son Maysarah, for both were still young, though they had lived life to the full. He had learned that Maysarah's wife had given birth to a beautiful, fresh-faced baby boy. She was the slave whom al-Ḥārith the Generous had given him—we have spoken of her earlier in our narrative. She had been of great solace to Maysarah when he was getting over his love for Asmāʾ, and he had grown to love her dearly for she was as pretty as the full moon. For all his happiness at the thought of the birth, ʿAntar was mindful of his predicament. He recalled how beautiful and charming ʿAblah was. As he gazed upon his chains and fetters, he began to recite the following poem . . . [Poem 45 is given.] . . . The narrator: ʿAntar finished his sublime composition and tears welled from the eyes of the knights. All wished for death and shared in ʿAntar's lofty sentiments, as is the custom of Arab nobility. Such was the excruciating suffering of these men.

Source: *Sīrat fāris fursān al-Ḥijāz*, 5:160–61.[166]

Poem 46

3.46.1 When he was alone, ʿAntar wept, overcome with feelings of loss and longing. The fires of love burned fiercely and he bemoaned the sting of separation. Then he recited the following verses.

Source: *Sīrat fāris fursān al-Ḥijāz*, 1:635.[167]

Poem 47

King al-Nuʿmān returned to his domains and ʿAntar continued on his way to al-Sharabbah, where his loved ones were encamped. He was overjoyed at the precious gifts and wealth he had received. He was not far from al-Ḥīrah, and had entered the desert wastes, when his mind turned to ʿAblah and all that had befallen him on her account. He bewailed his withered heart and described his feelings in the following verses . . . [The poem is recounted.] . . . The narrator: ʿUrwah ibn al-Ward and his men were filled with wonder at ʿAntar's eloquence. "May God and your foes never damage your tongue!" ʿUrwah exclaimed. "And may God grant you all your wishes, Defender of ʿAbs, ʿAdnān, Fazārah, Ghaṭafān, Murrah, and Dhubyān, for you have surpassed all the heroes of the age in bravery, eloquence, generosity, and noble character!" ʿAntar thanked him and praised him. 3.47.1

Source: *Sīrat fāris fursān al-Ḥijāz*, 2:459–60.[168]

Poem 50

[The narrator:] His wife finished her poem and Mālik drew his last breath. ʿAntar wrapped him in his robes, tied his turban, and placed him on the back of his horse. He set off for the lands of ʿAbs, walking behind his corpse, broken by misfortune and giving vent to his grief with tears and sobs. He recited the following poem . . . [The poem is given.] . . . The narrator: ʿAntar made his way to the tribal lands. Only three of al-ʿUshayrah had survived, as well as two of Mālik's brothers. They were as overwhelmed as ʿAntar; in fact, they were worse: they were near to death with sorrow. As they neared the tribal lands, they were met by King Qays. 3.50.1

Source: *Sīrat fāris fursān al-Ḥijāz*, 3:153–54.[169]

Poem 51

ʿAntar scattered his foes on the desert plain. ʿUrwah looked at him, and his resolve against the enemy strengthened. He attacked the foe and they lost heart and fled. Muqrī l-Waḥsh met up with ʿAntar and asked how his wife Masīkah fared. ʿAntar told him she was safe, and informed him of what had happened when he had returned and liberated ʿAblah. Muqrī l-Waḥsh thanked him and 3.51.1

said, “Commander, you alone inspire me with confidence!” They headed back to look for their people but none had survived. ʿAntar recited the following poem.

Source: *Sīrat fāris fursān al-Ḥijāz*, 3:489–90.[170]

Notes

1 My rendering of this famous opening hemistich may seem unusual to some. The commentators focus on *mutaraddamī*, a hapax in both the corpus of ʿAntarah and the other five poets in the six poets collection. The line is then construed in terms of the meaning they ascribe to this rare and obscure epithet and in terms of the unexpressed substantive the epithet is presumed to qualify. Thus al-Shantamarī glosses it as follows: "The phrase *min mutaraddamī* has the sense of 'I patched (*radamtu*) the thing,' i.e., I fixed it and repaired its weaknesses." He then explains the hemistich as follows: "What he means is, 'Have the poets left any theme (*maʿnā*) for anyone that they have not already used?' This resembles the phrase, 'Has the first person left anything for the second person <to do>?'" The missing substantive is implicitly taken to be *shiʿr*, "poetry." This is corroborated by the variant ascribed to Abū ʿUbaydah: *mutarannimī*, i.e., "trilled, or modulated." And so we have Arberry's rendering (*The Seven Odes*, 179): "Have the poets left a single spot for a patch to be sewn?" My reading of the line seeks to give full weight to the verb *ghādara*, and harmonize it with its two other occurrences in the corpus (Poem 7, line 14; Poem 22, line 1) and with the meaning it carries in the wider corpus (see Arazi and Maslaha, *Six Early Arab Poets*, p. 798, for the twelve instances in the corpus of the six poets). The verb invariably means "to leave an opponent lying dead, and unburied, on the battlefield." If the sense of the hapax *mutaraddamī* is that of being patched up or sewn together, then in the context of the verb *ghādara*, it could mean "a piece of cloth that requires patching up as a result of the thrust of my spear and slash of my sword." The trope of a weapon spoiling an opponent's fine clothing is found in Poem 1, line 56, for example. Lane in his *Lexicon* also notes that the root *r-d-m* can be applied to the protracted nature of a conflict or illness or fever. The example he gives is *taraddamat al-khuṣūmah*, "the conflict became far-extending and long." In this case, the meaning would then be something along the lines of: "Did the poets leave <poetry>, which had persisted so long <like a conflict or hostility or fever>, dead and unburied on the battlefield?" I find the grotesquery of this reading of the line much in keeping with similar instances of the grotesque I hear in the rest of this magnificent poem.

2 Both verses begin, unusually, with a double instance of a technique (known as *tarṣīʿ* in Arabic) encountered in the opening verses of many poems, whereby the first and second

hemistich of the verses close with a repetition of the rhyme of the ode (in this case, *mutaraddamī—tawahhumī* and *yatakallamī—al-aʿjamī*, respectively). Some scholars have construed this as a sign that line 1 is a later addition to the poem, which would then have originally started with the current line 2. The *Muʿallaqah* of Zuhayr, a panegyric in honor of the chieftain who brought peace to the warring clans of ʿAbs and Dhubyān and thus brought the War of Dāḥis and al-Ghabrāʾ to an end, is a companion piece, a poem of contestation (known in Arabic as a *muʿāraḍah*) to this poem. For example, both poems share the same rhyme consonant, though they do not share the same meter, and there are resemblances between ʿAntarah line 1b and Zuhayr poem 16.4b (Ahlwardt, *The Divans*), and line 7b and Zuhayr poem 16.1b (Ahlwardt, *The Divans*). See Arberry, *Seven Odes*, 170–71.

3 A glance at Map 2 shows that the topography in line 7 and in line 12 is precise, however polysemous the names in the ode may be: see Larcher, "Fragments d'une poétique arabe."

4 That the beloved has four names in this poem—ʿAblah, Umm al-Haytham (Mother of al-Haytham), Bint Makhram (Daughter of Makhram), and Bint Mālik (Daughter of Mālik) (line 49)—is a sign of the poem's instability: see further my discussion of the poem in the Introduction.

5 The phrase rendered here as "God" is properly "the Lord of the House," possibly, though not definitively, the Kaaba. In a henotheistic system such as that of the sixth-century pre-Islamic Arabs, a dominant god could presumably have many houses. See Pavlovitch, "*Qad kunna la naʿbudu ʾllāha wa-la naʿrifuhu*"; Robin, "Matériaux pour une typologie des divinités arabiques."

6 The fawn described in this line is said not to have a twin. This is balanced by the same claim made for the hero felled by ʿAntarah in line 60.

7 Musk heralds the presence of the divine. On musk, see King, *Scent from the Garden of Paradise*.

8 I have inverted the order of lines 19 and 20 in the translation. Line 20 is found only in the version of the poem contained in MS Paris BNF 3273 on which the Arabic text of the current edition is based.

9 The question posed in this verse terminates in line 39.

10 The "Yemenis" (*ḥizaq yamāniyah*) who "rush to a stuttering stranger" are usually taken to be Yemeni camels, though cf. the use of *ḥizq* of a "troop" of raiding horsemen in Poem 32, line 10.

11 Ostriches live in groups of about fifty birds, led by an alpha female. They lay their eggs in a nest dump, tended diurnally by the female (which is dust-colored) and nocturnally by the male (which is black and white). They do this to take full advantage of the

camouflage offered by their different plumage coloration. The Arabian ostrich (*Struthio camelus syriacus*) was declared extinct in 1966.

12 The commentators explain that "Daylam" is the mountainous region of northern Iran on the southern shore of the Caspian Sea. Presumably an alternative local toponym has been masked.

13 The origins of the image may lie in the practice of conveying cheetahs by camel to the hunt. See Montgomery, "The Cat and the Camel."

14 A difficult verse. The groans made by the camel as she kneels to drink are compared with the bass notes of the *qaṣab*, properly a reed fife or pipe, and not a horn. Al-Shantamarī proposes that the poet is describing the sounds of the camel drinking from the water.

15 In the version of the ode in al-Baṭalyawsī's recension, an extra verse follows this one: "The joints wet and distended, over the short, strong neck of a stallion." For the Arabic, see the online edition.

16 Fully: "<the air from> his jugular hissing like <breath from> the lip of a harelipped camel."

17 Al-Shantamarī suggests that the rhyme constrains the poet to say "wrist" (*al-miʿṣamī*) rather than "toe," though the bottom half of the slain warrior may be clad in full-length chain mail, thus preventing unhindered access to the scavengers.

18 There are two distinct heroic virtues intoned here: excessive generosity at *maysir*, the communal game of chance, when camels were slaughtered to feed the tribe in winter and times of famine; and excessive generosity with and consumption of alcohol. On *maysir*, see Jamil, "Playing for Time."

19 The reference to soft leather boots does not mean that the poet's opponent is soft, but rather that he is rich and so has never wanted for anything or gone hungry: in other words, he is at full strength. The remark that he is an only child (lit. he does not have a twin) has the same force. The commentaries suggest that having a twin makes a person weak. See n. 6.

20 The curved Indian blade (*hindī, hunduwānī* , and, as here, *muhannad*) is distinct from the straight Yemeni blade (*yamānī*).

21 ʿAblah is both a wild animal in a sacred demesne (*ḥimā*), and so cannot be hunted, and a woman promised as bride to another.

22 In al-Baṭalyawsī's recension, three extra lines follow this one: "(71') In battle's murk I heard the bellow of Murrah, both sons of Rabīʿah / (71'') and Muḥallim under their standard. Death stood there, under the standard of Muḥallim. / (71''') Then I knew that when we met, we would exchange blows that would scare nestlings into flight." For the Arabic, see the online edition.

23 Al-Baṭalyawsī's recension records four extra verses that have no commentary, with the remark that they are found in none of the standard recensions: "(73′) "Antar!' they roared as the swords flashed like bolts of lightning in the clouds. / (73″) "Antar!' they roared, as rivers of blood burst their banks. / (73‴) "Antar!' they roared as the war-horses grimaced, shrouded in battle murk. / (73⁗) "Antar!' they roared as the lances attacked me. Such are the customs of my people from olden times!" For the Arabic, see the online edition.

24 The Arabic specifies "the two sons" of both Ḥidhyam and Ḍamḍam, in the next verse.

25 For the image of the mill of war, see Jamil, "Playing for Time."

26 According to the preface provided by al-Shantamarī (see Appendix §3.1.1), the poem celebrates the killing of Muʿāwiyah ibn Nizāl during the Battle of al-Farūq, the topic of Poem 2. However, it is Ḍamḍam whom ʿAntarah identifies as his principal victim in this line, so perhaps Muʿāwiyah was one of the other three heroes he killed in battle (lines 47–63).

27 The *ʿāliyah* (pl. *ʿawālin*) is properly the uppermost segment of the shaft of a spear or lance, two-thirds of which are enclosed with the iron head. The remaining visible third is known as the *ṣadr*, breast. The epithet *zurq*, gray-blue, indicates that the term is here used as synecdoche for the lance head: see Boudot-Lamotte, "Lexique," 38; Schwarzlöse, *Die Waffen der alten Araber*, 108, 227–28, 235.

28 "Sniffing a corpse" is fully: "sniffing at old bones." Al-Shantamarī notes that camels eat bones, which they apparently do in the desert when food is scarce.

29 The original sequence, in which the second hemistich of line 7 is followed by line 8, has been reversed.

30 "Death appeared. I said to my men, 'Who's up for a wager? Who'll face Death with me?'" is fully: "I said to the men who had placed their souls as a wager for Death to play with, 'Who's ready to help me with an issue requiring determination that has cropped up?'"

31 "Like lice-ridden hair" is fully: "their heads like the heads of women who have lost their nit combs."

32 If we read *ʿamyāʾi* in possessive construct with *mā*, as al-Shantamarī suggests, two further renderings are conceivable: "Blindly, we came up against the surprise force they had prepared for us—a mighty army, serried and drilled, big as a mountain"; or: "We brought a mighty army, serried and drilled, big as a mountain, against the surprise force they had prepared for us."

33 "Digging the trough of war" is fully: "while they repaired their watering troughs." The watering trough is a metaphor for warfare, in keeping with pre-Islamic water symbolism: see Jamil, *Ethics and Poetry*.

34 Boudot-Lamotte, *Lexique*, 27, defines *khurṣ* as a short lance, as opposed to the *rumḥ* or *qanāh*; see, however, Schwarlöze, *Waffen*, 231.

35 Al-Baṭalyawsī's recension includes an extra line: "They left Masʿūd dead on the battlefield, his chest covered in what resembled a striped Yemeni cloak." For the Arabic, see the online edition.

36 "My sparkling bride" is fully: "My sword is like a lightning bolt, my bride, my weapon."

37 "My arrowheads glint" is fully: "<arrows> like light leaves." The use of *gharb* of a bow (properly, a sharp point or edge, and commonly used of sword or spearhead) in the second hemistich is unusual.

38 The spear shafts are "straight and true" because the wood (or reeds) used for the shafts did not need to be straightened in the vise (*thiqāf*) before having the iron heads fitted.

39 A dense and difficult set of lines. I think that what the poet may possibly be saying is the following: (8) Herders soothe camels that have just weaned their eight-month-old calves, by tying their teats, or when their milk is scarce. (9) The herders care for the less-valuable she-camels till they are pregnant, and deliver the other camels as normal, in season, i.e., in their tenth month. (10) The camels pass the summer in Laṣāfi, their necks thick and large, their sides rumbling at night for their adopted foals (or: their tulchans, camel skins intended to make mothers that have lost their foals continue to milk). This reconstruction is provisional, however, as the shift from plural to singular in lines 7 and 8 is awkward, though not impossible, and the rendering of *thamānin* in line 7 as "in season" is grammatically difficult to justify. The verses are intended as an intimation of conflict: the comparison of war with a pregnant she-camel is common: see n. 61.

40 The cooing of doves in the trees often evokes tears of sadness in the poet, thereby acting as a catalyst for memories of lost bliss (as in Poem 6, line 4). It is unusual for doves to feature in that time of bliss.

41 On the departure of the litters, see Ezz ed-deen, "'No Solace for the Heart.'"

42 A dense line. Fully: "Your soul lied to you, so lie to it because it deceitfully promised you Qaṭāmi." The variant *fa-ṣdiqanhā*, "so be true to it," for *fa-kdhibanhā*, "so lie to it," is widely attested, and is the reading of Poem 29. The exhortation to lie to one's soul is proverbial. A verse by the pre-Islamic poet Labīd is explained by Lane, *Lexicon*, art. *kadhaba*, as: "Lie to the soul (i.e., to thy soul,) when thou talkest to it, i.e. say not to thy soul, Thou wilt not succeed in this enterprise; for thy doing so will divert thee, or hinder thee therefrom." ʿAntarah's soul, as we know from Poem 3, line 1, is so sick that its thirst for blood can never be quenched, except, possibly and albeit transiently, through fame and recognition (Poem 1, line 78). Thus, the poet's soul is doubly deceived in this line: it is deceived about the validity of the poet's attempts to belong to tribal society as a normal

member, and it is deceived about quenching its thirst. He will not deceive it, however, about the fame victory will bring.

43 A dense simile. Fully: "As if his flanks had been inherited in turns by the arrows shot with full force during training to test the range of the bow."

44 On the cosmic significance of water and its economy, see Jamil, *Ethics and Poetry*.

45 See further Appendix §§1.11–12 and Appendix §§2.14–16.

46 In the version of the poem given by Ibn Maymūn (*Muntahā*, 107, line 4), the line reads: "But always I respond to the shout of Murrah in war when Muḥallim herald the death of al-Akhyal's kin." But elsewhere (see, e.g., Poem 1, line 71′ in n. 22), Murrah and Muḥallim are the poet's foes. It is unclear who "al-Akhyal's kin" are.

47 The poet's sword never grows emaciated (*yanḥalī*) because it always quenches its thirst for blood and so is satiated, unlike the poet's soul, which is never cured.

48 Three types of combat are meant: *karr*, the cavalry feint, in which the horses pretend to retreat but then wheel back to the charge; *shadd*, the cavalry charge and mounted combat at close quarters; *nuzūl*, hand-to-hand combat, on foot.

49 See Ahlwardt, *The Divans*, ʿAntarah appendix 19.10, for a variant of this line, reading *maṭʿamī* as rhyme word for *maʾkalī*.

50 Fully: "When the squadron advances, with fear in their eyes, I am found to be better than any man whose family is noble on both his mother's and his father's side."

51 The *fayṣal* is specifically a "decisive" spear thrust or sword blow, i.e., one that splits the enemy lines and decides the outcome of combat.

52 "My woman" is the stock poetic figure of the *ʿādhilah*, the female carper who chides the male poet for his lifestyle.

53 Fully: "If Death were to be given a form, she would be given my form when <warriors> dismount in the press of battle." Three words for death are used: *ḥutūf*, *maniyyah*, and *mawt* (*amūtu*).

54 The cawing of a crow in the morning was a bad omen and is usually interpreted as a sign that the beloved and her tribe have departed, leaving the communal settlements behind. The crow is often referred to as *ghurāb al-bayn*, the crow of separation.

55 The "long night" (*laylī l-timāmi*) is the night when the moon is at its fullest and shines brightest.

56 "I stand my ground" is fully: "I restrain my noble self." The "self" that the poet restrains is properly his soul (*nafs*), which, as we know from other poems, is incurably sick with bloodlust.

57 For the comparison of the ruins with tattoos and writing, see Montgomery, "The Deserted Encampment in Ancient Arabic Poetry."

58 The change of vowel at the end of this line (i.e., of the *majrā*), here from a ***kasrah*** to a *ḍammah*, was classified as a defect (in this case the rhyme defect known as *iqwāʾ*) when committed by later poets, though the early poets occasionally allow themselves the license to switch between *kasrah* and *ḍammah*: see Bonebakker, "Iḳwāʾ." There is an instance of a switch from *ḍammah* to *kasrah* in Poem 35, line 3.

59 These verses contain an example of a poetic technique common in pre-Islamic poetry known as *iltifāt*, in which there is an abrupt shift of person, e.g., from first to second person or vice versa: in this instance, the verses shift from third to second person feminine and back again, but retain the same referent. Al-Shantamarī explains the reference to the staff in terms of the prefatory narrative of the beating: see Appendix §§2.5–8 and Appendix §§3.10.1–2.

60 Fully: "My possessions are yours, my slave is yours, so will your punishment be averted from me today?" It is not entirely clear whom the poet is addressing, which is why I have used the lowercase "lord".

61 "When the battle's in rut" is fully: "When the raid is inseminated." Within the imagistic matrix of the pastoral economy developed by the pre-Islamic poets, war and conflict are commonly described in terms of the insemination of camels.

62 One MS (Paris BNF 5620) contains an extra verse included by Mawlawī as line eight of his edition of the poem: "Time is fickle—of that man can be sure. Allegiances always change." For the Arabic, see the online edition.

63 The horse's name is fully: "Son of the Ostrich." The meaning of this phrase excited considerable exegetical disagreement, with explanations as various as the shadow of the ostrich (i.e., the shadow cast by the horse), the forepart of the foot next to the toes, the middle crease on the bottom of the foot, the gibbet, and the highway: see al-Shantamarī's discussion and Mawlawī, *Dīwān ʿAntarah*, ed. Mawlawī, 274, n. 6. On the womenfolk departing or being taken away in litters, see Ezz ed-deen, "'No Solace for the Heart.'"

64 The collator of MS Paris BNF 3273 deletes the reading *al-najmī*, "stars," but does not propose any emendation in the margin. From the other MSS and al-Shantamarī's commentary, the emended reading is presumably *al-fadmī*: "Burning bright like black coals."

65 Or, if Dhū l-Raḍm is a toponym: "Through the watering troughs of Dhū l-Raḍm."

66 The phrase "clap them in irons" can also be rendered: "We drag them by their snouts."

67 "Ribbons of red": The *fadm* is a piece of cloth that has been repeatedly dyed red.

68 "Scarred": The spear is *muqaṣṣad*, shattered in the thrust, with the head splintering from the haft. See Schwarzlöse, *Die Waffen der alten Araber*, 240.

69 The "cowardly bastard" is identified by al-Shantamarī as ʿUyaynah ibn Ḥiṣn. Other sources suggest that he is Ḥiṣn ibn Ḥudhayfah: see *Dīwān ʿAntarah*, ed. Mawlawī, 281, n. 7.

70 Fully: "Even if I am in a distant land, the smoke of al-ʿAlandā will reach you, as protection for my family." Al-ʿAlandā is a volcano (see Map 2) though some explanations identify it as a highly combustible type of wood. See Harrigan, "Volcanic Arabia," who notes that over the last four and a half millennia there has been on average one major volcanic eruption on the Arabian peninsula every 346 years.

71 The manuscripts oscillate between two sets of variant readings provided by the tradition (*sadīd/shadīd* and *shadīd/sadīd*), although the meaning of the phrase "cold arrow" remains basically unchanged no matter which sequence of adjectives is read. The *ʿayr* is properly the median ridge of the arrowhead, so the reading *sadīd al-ʿayr* would give an added detail to the picture: "sharp-ridged": see Schwarzlöse, *Die Waffen der alten Araber*, 306–7.

72 Al-Shantamarī takes the pronominal suffix *-hū* (in *lahū*) and the third-person verbs in lines 2 and 3 to refer to the poet's horse, though they would seem more naturally to indicate the poet's foe, Jurayyah, felled by an arrow: Hujaym rush and surround him, circumambulating him as they would an idol, thereby making it impossible for him to advance.

73 The desert hedgehog (*Paraechinus aethiopicus*) is meant.

74 "A grave for my arrows": Or, according to the variant reading, *jafīr*: "A quiver full of my arrows."

75 "Edges of trough and well": The *madlajah* is the space between the well and the trough: the ropes are so tight when drawing up the buckets full of water that they gouge the edges of the well and the trough. Another instance of how the poets developed conceptions of war within the cosmic imagery of water and water economy.

76 ʿAntarah's gifts of camel meat are dispensed to the tribe by means of the communal gamble known as *maysir*: see n. 18 above.

77 The Arabic specifies a battle that took place at al-Ḥawmān, presumably identical with Ḥawmānāt al-Darrāj, from the first verse of Zuhayr's *Muʿallaqah* (see Ahlwardt, *The Divans*, Poem 16.1), a location in the Ḥazn, on the route to al-Mutathallam: see Thilo, *Die Ortsnamen in der altarabischen Poesie*, 55.

78 "Earned as hire at the wellhead" is properly: "having the hands of ostriches, they have not been paid a wage," an obscure, if effective, lampoon.

79 Fully: "You mouth of a foul-breathed she-camel on the point of dying from thirst, speeding by night to the well of al-Kulāb." Or possibly, reading *al-kilāb*: "You mouth of a

foul-breathed she-camel on the verge of dying from rabies." On the well of al-Kulāb, see Thilo, *Die Ortsnamen in der altarabischen Poesie*, 63.

80 A horse with a "star-front" is a thoroughbred with a blaze on its front, a sign of prime stock. I have translated the third person of the verb *naḥā* as first person, i.e., as referring to ʿAntarah. Some MSS read *najā*: "He (i.e., the rider of the mare) escaped." This would require the flow of the narrative to be: The rider of the mare fled and escaped as the horses closed in on a second rider struck down amid spears. According to this reading, the rider of the mare is the addressee of the poem, while the second rider, the one struck down, is the ʿAbd Allāh referred to in line 4.

81 The battle narrative describes the addressee of the poem in the third person, i.e., his corpse.

82 The force of the tenses in this verse is significant: they imply that the victory of the poet's tribe is assured, no matter how much resistance his opponent puts up, and no matter how hard he tries to avenge the death of ʿAbd Allāh. Fully, then: "Our spears have already taken you captive once already, and, no matter how hard you tried then, you could not ensure that even the filament of a date pit was paid as sufficient recompense for the death of Maʿbad."

83 Al-Mufaḍḍal attributed this poem to Qays ibn Zuhayr: Muth, *Konkordanz*, xvii, note 41. Presumably by "war" the War of Dāḥis and al-Ghabrāʾ is meant.

84 The epithet here rendered as "I was naked in battle," *ajamm* (lit., "spearless"), is applied to a ram or a billy goat with no horns.

85 The *dhuʾābah* (here translated as "pennants," after al-Shantamarī's gloss) is properly the forelock of a horse. I suspect that the poet intends either a synecdoche (forelock for horse) or means to zoomorphize war as a horse.

86 Both variant readings (*murdin* and *mirdan*) give good sense: *murdin*, active participle of the IVth form *ardā*, would give the meaning "death-dealing" (of either an arrow or a sword, though al-Shantamarī prefers the latter), whereas *mirdan*, the preferred reading of the collator of Paris BNF 3273, is used of an arrow as hard as a rock or stone. Schwarzlöse, *Die Waffen der alten Araber*, 187, suggests that a horse's hoof is meant. The epithet *khashib* would fit either reading (the root is used of wood, and so forms a grim pun with the already grimly ironic *al-muḥtaṭib* in line 1); if a sword is intended, then *khashib* would presumably mean "unpolished" (Schwarzlöse, *Die Waffen der alten Araber*, 146–47; Boudot-Lamotte, "Lexique," 28), though al-Shantamarī asserts the opposite meaning, i.e., "polished"; if an arrow (or a hoof) is intended, then the sense is "hard, tough, or rough."

87 The preface to this poem (see Appendix §§3.23.1–2) notes that the poem was excluded from al-Aṣmaʿī's selection and attributed by him to the otherwise obscure Kuthayyir ibn ʿUrwah al-Nahshalī. *The Epic of ʿAntar* includes a twenty-line expanded version of the poem, edited and translated here as Poem 51.

88 The Arabic specifies "the two sons of Abān."

89 The attribution of this poem to ʿAntarah is rejected: see Appendix §§3.24.1–2. "Right and left": al-Shantamarī explains the term *sanīḥ* as animals that run in front of a hunter from his right-hand side, i.e., displaying their left flank, and *bāriḥ* as the opposite, though for other authorities the terms carry the opposite meaning. There is no agreement on whether these are auspicious or inauspicious auguries, and their significance presumably varied from tribe to tribe and from region to region. On the various forms of divination practiced by the pre-Islamic Arabs, see Ibn Qutaybah, *The Excellence of the Arabs*, 2:136–41 ("Augury, Cleromancy, Geomancy, and Soothsaying").

90 The poet addresses himself as a carper: see n. 52 above.

91 The poet's tribe excels at three types of warfare: *zaḥf* is a large army, the *katībah* is the mounted cavalry squadron, and by *dhaʿr al-sarḥ* ("scattering of the herd") he means the dawn raid.

92 The grinding millstone is a common image for warfare and, as part of the matrix of pastoral imagery, forms a central feature of the pre-Islamic warrior cosmos: Jamil, "Playing for Time."

93 The battle either continues all day until nightfall, as al-Shantamarī understands it, or we have an especially graphic evocation of battle murk when dust becomes as thick as night.

94 Ibn Maymūn reads an extra line at the beginning of the poem: "Where can I run to escape my death, ʿAblah, if my Lord in Heaven has decreed it?" For the Arabic, see the online edition.

95 The line is fully: "I killed <your chief who was> your backbone and I cast <him> aside, a puny <warrior>, just as hyraxes are cast aside." The rock hyrax (*Procavia capensis*) is a small herbivorous mammal.

96 The horses are Dāḥis and al-Ghabrāʾ. Fully, the first hemistich is: "I wish they had not run even half a bowshot."

97 "Hacker of limbs" is fully: "He strikes off fingers when the cavalry charges."

98 The version contained in *The Epic of ʿAntar* edited by Shalabī, *Sharḥ dīwān ʿAntarah*, 128–32, and al-Bustānī, *Dīwān ʿAntarah*, 191–94, displays a considerable number of variations, not least of which is the absence of Ibn Maymūn's lines 3, 5, 13, and 24, with the addition of a line between 26 and 27. In the developed tradition of Arabic love poetry, the blowing of the East Wind awakens in the poet thoughts and memories of his beloved.

99 The name "Dhū l-ʿUqqāl," which means "the stallion with the limp," is clearly apotropaic.

100 See *Dīwān ʿAntarah*, ed. Mawlawī, 239–45 (Poem 5) for the verses as they appear in the Cairene manuscript of Ibn Maymūn's *Muntahā* to which I did not have access.

101 I have not been able to locate Raḥā l-Adamāt.

102 The stone at the corner of the Kaaba in Mecca.

103 The Arabic specifies "the two sons of Qushayr."

104 The second hemistich is fully: "They drew for you buckets of war when they heard <your rallying cry>."

105 For the change of rhyme vowel from *ḍammah* to *kasrah* in this line, see n. 59 above.

106 For the appropriately named Pass of Woe, see Unān in Map 2.

107 I construe these obscure phrases, which are lexically unusual, as oaths referring to the female genitalia, in the style of the utterances of the pre-Islamic seers (*kuhhān*).

108 The reader is referred to the notes provided by Shalabī, *Sharḥ dīwān ʿAntarah*, 31–38 for a number of variant readings.

109 There are seven plants listed in line 13: myrtle (*ās*), saxaul (*ḍāl*), tamarisk (*ghaḍā*), the fruit of the lote tree (*nabiq*), eglantine rose or sweetbriar (*nisrīn*), rose (*ward*), and box-thorn (*ʿawsaj*).

110 A conventional description in the developed love tradition compares the slender waist of the poet's beloved to a twig, often that of a moringa tree. See Montgomery, "Convention as Cognition."

111 Fully: "I constructed such a high tent of glory that Gemini (al-Jawzāʾ), Pegasus (al-Fargh), and Virgo (al-Ghafr) prostrated themselves before it." On these names, see Kunitzsch, "Al-Manāzil"; Hartner and Kunitzsch, "Minṭaḳat al-Burūdj."

112 Fully: "I've left them and now my duty is to Him who determines right (*amr*) and wrong (*nahy*) for His Creation."

113 Al-Sharā is a mountain in southwestern Najd, between Wadi Damkh and Wadi Surrah: see Thilo, *Die Ortsnamen in der altarabischen Poesie*, 94–95.

114 The ill-omened crow, customary harbinger of the departure of the beloved (see Poem 8, line 1), here caws the death of Mālik.

115 The reader is referred to notes provided by Shalabī, *Sharḥ dīwān ʿAntarah*, 178–80, for a number of variant readings.

116 Ibn Qutaybah, *Kitāb al-Shiʿr wa-l-shuʿarāʾ*, 1:250–54.

117 See Poem 43.

118 Poem 1, line 1a.

119 Sharj is a water hole in the vicinity of Nāẓirah, a stretch of sand in Shaqīq (for which, see Map 1): Thilo, *Die Ortsnamen in der altarabischen Poesie*, 95 and 77, respectively.

120 Poem 1, lines 83–85.

121 Poem 1, lines 23–24.

122 Poem 1, lines 45–46.

123 Poem 6, lines 9 and 13. The translation has been modified to fit the context.

124 Poem 6, lines 17–20. The translation has been modified slightly to fit the context.

125 Poem 28, line 10. The translation has been modified to fit the variant *fī l-mawāṭini kullihā* for *ḥīna tashtajiru l-qanā*.

126 Poem 28, lines 8 and 9. The translation has been modified to fit the variant line 8: *innī la-tuʿrafu fī l-ḥurūbi wāṭinī // fī āli ʿabsin mashhadī wa-faʿālī.*

127 Al-Iṣbahānī, *Aghānī*, 8:237–46.

128 Poem 10. The translation has been modified to fit the context.

129 Poem 43, with an incomplete line 4 (*wa-l-shaʿarāti*) restored by the editors in accordance with the reading in the *dīwān*.

130 See Appendix §1.2 and §3.1.1.

131 See Appendix §1.3.

132 Poem 6, lines 9 and 13. The translation has been modified slightly to accommodate the commentary.

133 See Appendix §§3.6.1–2.

134 Poem 6, lines 17, 18, 19, 20, 9, 13, 14, 15, 10, 11, 21, and 12. The translation has been modified slightly to demonstrate the relation between al-Iṣbahānī's commentary and the poem.

135 At this point al-Iṣbahānī explains that the word *munṣul* ("blade") can also be vocalized as *munṣal*.

136 Translation conjectural.

137 See Appendix §3.30.1.

138 Poem 30, lines 1–2. The translation has been modified to accommodate a couple of variant readings.

139 Poem 9, line 1. As the poem survives today, it is a composition of six verses, which would not qualify it as especially "long."

140 The three verses of the poem are: "Pebbles, that's what Nabhān are worth. Their exploits can never be concealed—they are the exploits of ostriches in a barren plain" (*Dīwān ʿAntarah*, ed. Mawlawī, 332). I read *mujdib* with Mawlawī, for the *muḥr-b* of the line as printed in the text of the *Aghānī*.

141 Reading *wizr* for the *zirr* of the text. In *The Epic of ʿAntar*, ʿAntar's killer is Wizr ibn Jābir: see Lyons, *The Arabian Epic*, 3, 73 (§84).

142 Poem 33.

143 See Appendix §3.33.1.

144 See Appendix §1.6.

145 See respectively: al-Shantamarī, in *Dīwān ʿAntarah*, ed. Mawlawī, 253 and al-Baṭalyawsī, in *Sharḥ al-ashʿār*, ed. al-Tūmī, 2:326; al-Shantamarī, in *Dīwān ʿAntarah*, ed. Mawlawī, 292 and al-Baṭalyawsī, in *Sharḥ al-ashʿār*, ed. al-Tūmī, 2:307; al-Shantamarī, in *Dīwān ʿAntarah*, ed. Mawlawī, 303 and al-Baṭalyawsī, in *Sharḥ al-ashʿār*, ed. al-Tūmī, 2:351; al-Baṭalyawsī, in *Sharḥ al-ashʿār*, ed. al-Tūmī, 2:313 and *Dīwān ʿAntarah*, ed. Mawlawī, 322; al-Baṭalyawsī, in *Sharḥ al-ashʿār*, ed. al-Tūmī, 2:372 and *Dīwān ʿAntarah*, ed. Mawlawī, 329; al-Baṭalyawsī, in *Sharḥ al-ashʿār*, ed. al-Tūmī, 2:372 and *Dīwān ʿAntarah*, ed. Mawlawī, 329.

146 Al-Tūmī, in his edition of al-Baṭalyawsī, *Sharḥ al-ashʿār*, 2:191, n. 7, notes that the order of these *kunyah*s (teknonyms) seems to have been reversed. This depends on the assumption that ʿAblah is a real person, rather than being (as I suspect) an avatar of Death.

147 Reading "Ibn" for "Abū" Ḥabīb.

148 Yumn (or al-Yaman) is a water hole north of Khaybar: see Thilo, *Die Ortsnamen in der altarabischen Poesie*, 115. In view of the animosity between Ḥanīfah and ʿAbs, I suspect that in fact al-Yamāmah, the tribal heartlands of the Ḥanīfah, should be read.

149 Reading *yudhdhakiruhu l-ayyām* for the *yudhdhakiruhā l-ayyām* of the text.

150 Al-Habāʾah is a stream south of Raḥraḥān (see Map 2): Thilo, *Die Ortsnamen in der altarabischen Poesie*, 51.

151 Reading *ghināhu* (after MS Istanbul Beyazit 5385, folio 68b) for *ʿanāhu* read by al-Tūmī, in his edition of al-Baṭalyawsī, *Sharḥ al-ashʿār*, 2:272.

152 See Appendix §§2.4–8.

153 According to al-Bakrī, *Mustaʿjam mā staʿjama*, 180, Aqrun was located in ʿAbs territory.

154 Jarīr, *Dīwān*, 2:917 (Poem 27, line 97), where *taʿrifūna* is read for *tadhkurūna*, and *shukka* for *yahwī*.

155 The slave uses Qirwāsh's teknonym (*kunyah*), Abū Shurayḥ.

156 Reading *al-ajījī* for the *al-ajīḥī* of the text. My thanks to Tahera Qutbuddin for this suggestion.

157 Barīkh is an otherwise unattested place name.

158 Reading ʿAbs, with al-Iṣbahānī, *Aghānī*, 8:245, for the Ṭayyiʾ of the MSS. See Appendix §2.28.

159 See ʿĀmir ibn al-Ṭufayl, *Dīwān*, 136 (Poem 21, line 1). The entire poem is translated by Lyall on pages 111–12 of the English section.

160 ʿUrwah ibn al-Ward, *Dīwān*, 58, where *al-nasʾa* ("forgetfulness, oblivion") is read for *al-khamra* ("wine").

161 According to al-Bakrī, *Mustaʿjam mā staʿjama*, 2:1093, Qalahā is in the vicinity of Mecca and is where the War of Dāḥis and al-Ghabrāʾ came to an end. The version of the event given by Yāqūt is as follows: When ʿAbs and Fazārah agreed to a truce, they traveled to a pond called Qalahā to set up camp there. Qalahā was under the control of Thaʿlabah ibn Saʿd ibn Dhubyān, and they sought payment from ʿAbs of the blood money due for ʿAbd al-ʿUzzā ibn Jidād and Mālik ibn Subayʿ. They kept ʿAbs from the water until they had paid the blood money. Maʿqil ibn ʿAwf ibn Subayʿ of Thaʿlabah composed the following poem:

What a tribe Thaʿlabah ibn Saʿd is,
 when iron bites the flesh of men!
They drove back the odious tribes of Baghīḍ
 when War's fires burned hot.
Their blood remains unavenged.
 Qalahā Pond belongs to us. Our wish is our decree.

See al-Tūmī, 2:362, n. 2.

162 According to al-Bakrī, *Mustaʿjam mā staʿjama*, 1:161, Dhāt al-Iṣād was in the territory of Fazārah.

163 Abū Tammām, *Dīwān*, 1:382 (Poem 35, line 40).

164 Reading *al-sharb* for the *al-ḍarb* of the text.

165 See *Sharḥ dīwān ʿAntarah*, ed. Shalabī, 31: "He declaimed this poem as he left to do battle with the Persians."

166 See *Sharḥ dīwān ʿAntarah*, ed. Shalabī, 64: "ʿAntarah was taken prisoner in a battle between the Arabs and the Persians, and ʿAblah was one of the women captured. In chains and fetters, choking back his grief, and in great despair, he recalled the days he had spent in her company."

167 See *Sharḥ dīwān ʿAntarah*, ed. Shalabī, 74: "Mālik ibn Qurād settled among Shaybān with his daughter ʿAblah to keep her away from ʿAntarah, who missed her terribly and was greatly distressed at losing her. In this poem, he talks of the strength of his feelings for her and how he suffered over her absence."

168 See *Sharḥ dīwān ʿAntarah*, ed. Shalabī, 84: "A poem from his old age."

169 See *Sharḥ dīwān ʿAntarah*, ed. Shalabī, 176: "He lamented the death of his comrade Mālik ibn Zuhayr of ʿAbs."

170 See *Sharḥ dīwān ʿAntarah*, ed. Shalabī, 178: "On the Battle of Jabalah Ravine at which Laqīṭ ibn Zurārah, the father of Dukhtanūs, was killed. Dukhtanūs composed a threnody for him."

Glossary

The glossary does not include place names. The reader is referred instead to the list of place names and to the maps, in particular Map 2. Proper names are given as they appear in the poems, which is often in the form of a single word. Thus, both the individual Qays ibn Zuhayr and the lineage group Qays ʿAylān, are glossed simply as Qays. Dates of death are provided when known.

Abān Abān ibn ʿAbd Allāh, a kin group within Dārim, a subgroup of Ḥanẓalah of Tamīm, the major lineage group that inhabited the Yamāmah (see Map 1). Two sons of Abān, Jaʿd being one of them, were slaughtered by ʿAntarah's people.

ʿAbd Allāh ʿAbd Allāh ibn al-Ṣimmah, the brother of the warrior poet and chieftain Durayd ibn al-Ṣimmah, leader of Jushām ibn Muʿāwiyah, an important subset of the Hawāzin lineage group (see Map 1). ʿAbd Allāh was killed by ʿAbs in the conflict that erupted between the lineages of Hawāzin and Ghaṭafān, both of whom shared descent from Qays ʿAylān.

ʿAblah ʿAblah bint Mālik, ʿAntarah's muse and the love of his life. In *The Epic of ʿAntar*, she is his cousin, and he is denied her hand in marriage because of his lowly birth and the color of his skin. She is also referred to in the translations as "Daughter of Mālik," and once as "Bint Makhram" (or, in some MSS, "Makhzam)," and "Umm al-Haytham."

ʿAbs a powerful kin group within Ghaṭafān, which claimed descent from Baghīḍ ibn Rayth ibn Ghaṭafān. In the middle of the sixth century it became the most dominant group within Ghaṭafān, though they lost both hegemony and their traditional pasture grounds in the War of Dāḥis and al-Ghabrāʾ that raged between the ʿAbs and Fazārah of the kin group Dhubyān ibn Baghīḍ ibn Rayth ibn Ghaṭafān. The immediate cause of the conflict was a race between the stallions Dāḥis and al-Ghabrāʾ, to which ʿAntarah alludes in Poems 27 and 50.

Abū Khalīfah al-Faḍl ibn al-Ḥubāb al-Jumaḥī (d. 305/917–18), a qadi, expert on Hadith, poet, and man of letters, active in his native Basra.

Abū Nawfal the teknonym of Naḍlah of Asad.

Abū Tammām Ḥabīb ibn Aws (d. ca. 231/845), one of the most important Arabic poets of the Abbasid era. His anthology of pre-Islamic verse, *Valor* (*al-Ḥamāsah*), was enormously influential in the Abbasid reception of pre-Islamic poetry and culture.

Abū ʿUbaydah Maʿmar ibn al-Muthannā (d. 209/824–25), a philologist and expert on the history and culture of the Arabs.

Abū l-ʿUbays Abū l-ʿUbays ibn Ibrāhīm ibn Ḥamdūn (fl. second half of the third/ninth century), a musician at the court of the Abbasid caliph al-Mutawakkil (r. 232–47/847–61), a contemporary of ʿArīb, and the compiler of a collection of songs used by al-Iṣbahānī in *The Book of Songs*. See also ʿArīb.

ʿAdī a kin group within Ṭayyiʾ, attacked by Jarm, a subgroup of Quḍāʿah under the hegemony of Kilāb and Kaʿb, groups within ʿĀmir ibn Ṣaʿṣaʿah.

ʿAdnān the ancestor from whom all the Northern Arab lineages claimed descent.

Aḥmad ibn ʿAbd al-ʿAzīz see al-Jawharī.

al-Aḥnaf al-Aḥnaf ibn Qays (d. after 67/686–87), a prominent member of Tamīm, instrumental in engineering the lineage group's conversion to Islam and in the establishment of Basra as a garrison town.

al-Akhfash Abū l-Ḥasan ʿAlī ibn Sulaymān (d. 315/927), a grammarian, and the teacher of Ibn al-Naḥḥās.

ʿAkk a group that lived in Tihāmah (see Map 1) on the Red Sea coast of South Arabia.

ʿAllawayh Abū l-Ḥasan ʿAlī ibn ʿAbd Allāh ibn Sayf (d. after 235/850), known as ʿAllawayh al-Aʿsar, a court musician whose songbook was used as a source by al-Iṣbahānī in compiling his *Book of Songs*.

ʿĀmir ʿĀmir ibn Ṣaʿṣaʿah, a powerful lineage group, which sheltered ʿAbs when they had been expelled from their traditional grazing lands during the War of Dāḥis and al-Ghabrāʾ. See Map 1.

ʿĀmir ibn al-Ṭufayl renowned warrior poet and chieftain of ʿĀmir ibn Ṣaʿṣaʿah.

ʿAmīrah (sometimes vocalized as ʿUmayrah) a kin group within Sulaym, part of the Qays ʿAylān lineage. Both al-Shantamarī and al-Baṭalyawsī identify them specifically as a kin group within Fazārah.

ʿAmr the name of several enemies addressed by ʿAntarah, principal among whom are: ʿAmr ibn ʿAmr ibn ʿUdus ibn Zayd ibn ʿAbd Allāh of the Dārim grouping within Tamīm (Poem 13); ʿAmr ibn Jābir, a member of al-ʿUsharāʾ, a family that belonged either to the Fazārah group within Ghaṭafān, or to Māzin within the lineage of Murrah (Poem 14); ʿAmr ibn Aswad, brother to the Saʿd ibn ʿAwf ibn Mālik grouping within the Zayd Manāt of Tamīm (Poem 17; Appendix §3.17.1); ʿAmr of the Ḍabbah (Poem 24). The ʿAmr whose nose ʿAntarah cuts off (Poem 35) is unidentified; the ʿAmr of Poem 1, who does not thank ʿAntarah for his "gift" (an ironic allusion to killing or maiming), could be anyone of the abovenamed ʿAmrs. In Poem 48, ʿAmr and Zayd are a familiar collocation, names conventionally used in grammar, logic, and law, for example, to represent typical persons.

ʿAmr ibn Ghālib kin group within ʿAbs. See Ghālib and al-Rabīʿ ibn Ziyād.

ʿAmr ibn al-Hujaym see al-Hujaym.

ʿAmr ibn Maʿdī Karib famous warrior and poet who converted to Islam. He died in battle ca. 21/641.

Anas al-Fawāris ʿAbs warrior who claimed to have killed ʿAmr ibn ʿAmr ibn ʿUdus at the Battle of the Pass of Aqrun.

ʿandam a red tree resin or plant dye used by women to color their hands.

Anūshirwān Kisrā Anūshirwān (AD 531–79), the Persian ruler against whom ʿAntar does battle in *The Epic of ʿAntar*.

ʿArīb (d. 277/890) a slave who became the most famous female musician of the century. She was owned by two Abbasid caliphs, al-Amīn (r. 193–98/809–13) and al-Maʾmūn (r. 198–218/813–33), and was manumitted by a third, al-Muʿtaṣim (r. 218–227/833–42).

Asmāʾ a woman denied to ʿAntar's son, Maysarah, in *The Epic of ʿAntar*.

al-Aṣmaʿī ʿAbd al-Malik ibn Qurayb al-Aṣmaʿī (d. 213/828), one of the most influential scholars on early Arabic poetry, culture, and lexicography.

al-Aʿwaj a famous Arabian stud descended from a Yemeni stallion given by King Solomon as a gift to an Arab delegation.

ʿAwf ibn Ḥārithah a kin group within Khazraj to which the peacemaker at the truce of Qalahā Pond belonged.

ʿAwf ibn Jadhīmah a kin group within al-Hujaym, to which Qushayr ibn Khālid belonged.

Badr a family group within Fazārah, to which both Ḥudhayfah and Ḥamal belonged.

Baghīḍ an ancestor of ʿAbs and Fazārah, foes in the War of Dāḥis and al-Ghabrāʾ.

Bajīlah along with Khath'am, a subgroup of Anmār. It was in a state of dispersion during 'Antarah's lifetime.

Bajlah a group within Qays 'Aylān.

al-Bajlī a member of Bajlah.

al-Bakkā' a kin group within 'Āmir ibn Ṣa'ṣa'ah.

Bakr Bakr ibn Wā'il, an ancient confederation of tribes settled in eastern Arabia, in the process of relocation and migration north during 'Antarah's lifetime. See Map 1.

Bint Makhram see 'Ablah.

Bishr an unidentified individual mentioned in an anonymous verse quoted by al-Aṣma'ī.

Blaze a common equine epithet, *agharr*, which indicates the white star-shaped mark on the forehead of a thoroughbred, here construed as the name of the horse whose death is lamented by the poet of Poem 34. (According to Abū 'Ubaydah, the poem is by Ḍubay'ah ibn al-Ḥārith.) The horse was speared by 'Āmir ibn al-Ṭufayl, the chief of 'Āmir ibn Ṣa'ṣa'ah.

Ḍabāb a kin group, to which Ḍamḍam belonged, within Kilāb ibn Rabī'ah, part of the larger lineage group of 'Āmir ibn Ṣa'ṣa'ah. The group was related to Ja'far.

Ḍabbah a powerful group within the confederation of al-Ribāb, in a strong alliance with the Sa'd ibn Zayd Manāt of Tamīm. Toward the end of the sixth century they defeated an alliance of Kilāb and 'Abs at the Battle of al-Qurnatayn.

Dāḥis and al-Ghabrā' the two horses involved in the race between Qays ibn Zuhayr and Ḥudhayfah ibn Badr that became the cause of the eponymous war between 'Abs and Fazārah.

Ḍamḍam Ḍamḍam ibn Ḍabāb, a member of Dhubyān, father of Ḥuṣayn, Harim, and Durayd. Ḥuṣayn killed a member of 'Abs during the first truce in the War of Dāḥis and al-Ghabrā', and Harim died during the truce at the hands of Ward ibn Ḥābis of the Ghālib, a kinsman of 'Antarah.

Dārim a kin group within Ḥanẓalah, part of Tamīm.

Daughter of Mālik see 'Ablah.

Dhū l-'Uqqāl the purebred sire of the stallion Dāḥis, though Dāḥis was not a thoroughbred.

Dhubyān Dhubyān ibn Baghīḍ ibn Rayth, a major kin group within Ghaṭafān.

Ḍirār Ḍirār ibn 'Amr of Ḍabbah, killed by 'Abs in a raid.

Ḍubayʿah ibn al-Ḥārith warrior thought to have been the composer of a poem attributed to ʿAntarah.

Durayd a son of Ḍamḍam killed by Qays ibn Zuhayr.

Fazārah a kin group within Dhubyān, and part of Ghaṭafān, to which Ḥudhayfah ibn Badr belonged. One of the chief instigators, with Qays ibn Zuhayr, of the War of Dāḥis and al-Ghabrāʾ.

Ghālib a kin group to which ʿAntarah belonged, through Baghīḍ.

Ghaṭafān a major lineage group that traced its line back to Qays ʿAylān. It comprised various subgroups, including Murrah, ʿAbs, and Fazārah, itself a subgroup of Dhubyān. See Map 1.

Ḥabīb ibn Naṣr Ḥabīb ibn Naṣr al-Muhallabī (d. 307/919), an authority relied on by al-Iṣbahānī in *The Book of Songs*.

Ḥājib Ḥājib ibn Zurārah, captured during the famous victory by ʿĀmir ibn Ṣaʿṣaʿah (and their allies ʿAbs) over Tamīm in the Battle of Jabalah Ravine, where Laqīṭ ibn Zurārah and Muʿāwiyah ibn Ḥujr were killed.

Ham (Ar. Ḥām) a son of Noah and, according to Muslim genealogists, the ancestor of the black races.

Ḥamal ibn Badr the brother of Ḥudhayfah ibn Badr, part of the hit squad that was sent to assassinate Mālik ibn Zuhayr.

Ḥanbal one of ʿAntarah's half brothers.

Ḥanīfah an important kin group within Bakr ibn Wāʾil.

Ḥanẓalah a lineage group within Tamīm, descended from Zayd Manāt, which included Dārim, of which ʿAmr ibn ʿAmr ibn ʿUdus was a member.

Harim a son of Ḍamḍam killed by Ward ibn Ḥābis, kinsman of ʿAntarah.

al-Ḥarīsh a kin group within Kaʿb, part of Rabīʿah, within ʿĀmir ibn Ṣaʿṣaʿah.

al-Ḥārith Aretas, the Jafnid lord of the Syrian marches in *The Epic of ʿAntar*.

al-Haytham ibn ʿAdī Abū ʿAbd al-Raḥmān al-Haytham ibn ʿAdī (d. before 209/824), an important expert on many genres of history: ancient history, cities, biography, and genealogy.

Ḥidhyam Ḥidhyam ibn Jadhīmah, a member of ʿAbs and the father of two foes of ʿAntarah.

Ḥimyar an important South Arabian kingdom that flourished from about the first century BC until most of South Arabia was overrun and occupied by the Ethiopian armies of Axum in the early sixth century AD.

Hind a woman's name, here an eponym of a clan possibly cognate with the lineage line of ʿAmr ibn Hind, i.e., the son of a woman of Kindah named Hind and al-Mundhir, the Lakhmid ruler of al-Ḥīrah (see Map 1).

al-Hishāmī Abū ʿAbd Allāh al-Hishāmī (fl. mid-third/ninth century), an expert on the history of Arabic music, and a key source for al-Iṣbahānī in *The Book of Songs*.

Ḥudhayfah Ḥudhayfah ibn Badr, the chief of Fazārah whose dispute with Qays ibn Zuhayr, commander of ʿAbs, led to the War of Dāḥis and al-Ghabrāʾ.

al-Hujaym ʿAmr ibn al-Hujaym, a kin group of the Tamīm raided by ʿAbs.

Ḥuṣayn a son of Ḍamḍam of Murrah, a subgroup of Ghaṭafān.

al-Ḥuṭayʾah Jarwal ibn Aws (d. after 41/661), a poet born in the pre-Islamic era who converted to Islam. He often claimed descent from ʿAbs. He was especially feared (and admired) for the potency of his abuse poetry.

Ibn ʿĀʾishah Abū Jaʿfar Muḥammad ibn ʿĀʾishah, a singer from Medina who died during the caliphate of Hishām ibn ʿAbd al-Malik (r. 105–25/724–43).

Ibn al-Aʿrābī Muḥammad ibn Ziyād (d. ca. 231/846), an authority on pre-Islamic poetry, born in Kufa.

Ibn Durayd Abū Bakr Muḥammad ibn Durayd (d. 321/933), a lexicographer and philologist, author of an influential dictionary and many major works on language.

Ibn Ḥabīb Muḥammad ibn Ḥabīb (d. 245/860), an expert on genealogy, poetry, and history who studied with Abū ʿUbaydah and Ibn al-Aʿrābī.

Ibn Ḥujr Muʿāwiyah ibn Ḥujr, sent as an ally to Laqīṭ ibn Zurārah by his father al-Jawn, king of Ḥajr in Yamāmah (see Map 1), a scion of the powerful southern lineage group of Kindah. He died at the Battle of Jabalah Ravine. See also Ḥājib and Laqīṭ.

Ibn al-Kalbī Hishām ibn al-Kalbī (d. 204/819), an expert on pre-Islamic Arabia who composed many works on topics such as genealogy, poetry, and pre-Islamic pagan idolatry.

Ibn al-Makkī Aḥmad ibn Yaḥyā l-Makkī, third in line in a family of court musicians whose collection of musical lore was a key source for al-Iṣbahānī in *The Book of Songs*.

Ibn al-Muʿtazz Abū l-ʿAbbās ʿAbd Allāh (247–96/861–908), Abbasid prince and brilliant poet, killed on the very day he became Caliph al-Muntaṣif bi-llāh. He compiled a collection of songs used by al-Iṣbahānī in *The Book of Songs*.

Ibn al-Naḥḥās Aḥmad ibn Muḥammad ibn Ismāʿīl, an Egyptian grammarian and expert on the Qurʾan and early poetry who died in 338/950.

Ibn Qutaybah Abū Muḥammad ibn Muslim al-Dīnawarī (213–76/828–88), a theologian, qadi, and expert on Arabic language. He was one of the central figures in the development of Arabic learning, and wrote many books on the Qurʾan, Arabic poetry, and pre-Islamic Arab culture.

Ibn Sallām Abū ʿAbd Allāh Muḥammad ibn Sallām al-Jumaḥī (d. 231 or 232/845 or 846), a philologist, expert on Hadith and early poetry.

Ibn Salmā ʿAmr ibn Salmā (or Wizr ibn Jābir of Nabhān), an archer of Ṭayyiʾ who blinded ʿAntarah.

Ibn al-Sikkīt Abū Yūsuf Yaʿqūb ibn Isḥāq (d. ca. 244/858), a Baghdadi lexicographer and expert on Arabic poetry who studied with Ibn al-Aʿrābī, al-Shaybānī, Abū ʿUbaydah, and al-Aṣmaʿī.

Ibn Surayḥ ʿAbd Allāh Abū Yūsuf ibn Surayḥ, a singer at the court of Hārūn al-Rashīd (r. 170–93/786–809).

Ibrāhīm ibn Ayyūb (fl. late third/ninth to early fourth/tenth century) authority for some of the information al-Iṣbahānī relays in *The Book of Songs*. He transmitted Ibn Qutaybah's *Book of Poetry and Poets*.

Ibrāhīm al-Mawṣilī Abū Isḥāq Ibrāhīm al-Mawṣilī (d. 742/804), a talented singer, musician, and composer, and a key figure in the development of early Arabic music.

ʿIlāj an unidentified individual mentioned in an anonymous verse quoted by al-Aṣmaʿī.

ʿIqāl ancestor of a kin group said in a verse of poetry to have been surrendered by Bakr ibn Wāʾil to ʿAbs at the Battle of al-Shibāk (see Map 2).

Jabalah site of the Battle of Jabalah Ravine, fought between Tamīm and ʿĀmir. ʿĀmir emerged victorious thanks to Qays ibn Zuhayr's strategy of letting loose on the enemy a herd of camels on the point of dying of thirst before launching a cavalry charge on the foe.

Jaʿd a member of the Tamīm, son of Abān, to whom ʿAntarah addresses a poem (20) in which he claims that Jaʿd "borrowed" his spear from him, a grimly ironical description of his killing of Jaʿd.

Jadīlah a kin group within Ṭayyiʾ.

Jaʿfar Jaʿfar ibn Kilāb ibn Rabīʿah, a ruling house (within the lineage group of Kilāb) prominent among ʿĀmir ibn Ṣaʿṣaʿah.

Jāhiliyyah term used to characterize the time before the advent of Islam, variously understood to mean the “time of ignorance (i.e., of Islam),” or the “time of barbarism.”

Jarīr Jarīr ibn ʿAṭiyyah (d. 110/728–29), a major Umayyad poet and a member of Tamīm.

Jarm a kin group under the hegemony of Kilāb and Kaʿb, groups within ʿĀmir ibn Ṣaʿṣaʿah.

Jarwal a kin group that belonged to Ṭayyiʾ.

al-Jawharī Aḥmad ibn ʿAbd al-ʿAzīz al-Jawharī (fl. first quarter of fourth/tenth century), who transmitted information on the authority of ʿUmar ibn Shabbah.

Jirwah name of the warhorse belonging to Shaddād, ʿAntarah’s father (or his paternal uncle, according to some sources).

jiryāl a red plant dye.

Jubaylah ibn Abī ʿAdī a victim of ʿAntarah killed in a raid on ʿAbs by Sulaym, a subgroup of Bajlah, and therefore of Qays ʿAylān.

Jurayyah a member of the kin group of ʿAmr ibn al-Hujaym, which belonged to the lineage group of Tamīm.

Kaʿb a kin group within ʿĀmir ibn Ṣaʿṣaʿah.

Kalb the most powerful kin group within the Quḍāʿah confederation.

kāmil one of the sixteen meters of classical Arabic poetry.

Khathʿam a subgroup of Anmār that enjoyed a notable victory in the Battle of Fayf al-Rīḥ against ʿĀmir ibn Ṣaʿṣaʿah during ʿAntarah’s lifetime.

khimkhim a non-stinging nettle (*Forsskaolea tenacissima*), dried and used as camel fodder. The name is variously given: it is also written as *khumkhum*, *ḥimḥim*, and *ḥumḥum*.

Khufāf ibn Nadbah warrior poet of Sulaym (d. between 13/634 and 23/644). One of the three “Arab ravens,” black warriors whose lineage was traced back through their maternal and not paternal line.

Khulaydah a slave belonging to the wife of Qirwāsh ibn Hunayy.

Kinānah a lineage group related to Asad, with connections to Quraysh, resident on the coast southwest of Mecca (see Map 1).

Kisrā Arabic for Khusro, the name of two Sasanid rulers, used in Arabic as a title.

al-Kurānī Muḥammad ibn Saʿd al-Kurānī (fl. mid-fourth/tenth century), an informant used by al-Iṣbahānī in his *Book of Songs*.

Kuthayyir ibn ʿUrwah al-Nahshalī a pre- or early Islamic warrior considered by al-Aṣmaʿī to have composed a poem attributed to ʿAntarah; next to nothing is known about him.

Laqīṭ Laqīṭ ibn Zurārah, the leader of a major military force of Tamīm that included reinforcements from Kindah, under the command of Ibn Ḥujr, as well as from the Lakhmids of al-Ḥīrah. This army was defeated at the Battle of Jabalah Ravine in the mid-sixth century by ʿĀmir ibn Ṣaʿṣaʿah and ʿAbs. Laqīṭ died in the battle.

Laʾm a subgroup of Ṭayyiʾ.

Maʿbad an unavenged victim of ʿAbs. The reference may be to Maʿbad ibn Zurārah, brother of Laqīṭ, killed by ʿĀmir ibn Ṣaʿṣaʿah at the Battle of Raḥrahān (see Map 2). Laqīṭ's quest for vengeance led to his own death at the Battle of Jabalah Ravine. Al-Baṭalyawsī, however, explains Maʿbad as one of the names of ʿAbd Allāh ibn al-Ṣimmah.

mahrī a prized breed of camel from Mahrah, a region in Yemen. See Map 2.

Mālik (1) Mālik ibn Qurād, the father of ʿAblah, and ʿAntarah's paternal uncle. (2) Mālik ibn Zuhayr, who was killed by Badr (see Ḥudhayfah). His death marks the start of the War of Dāḥis and al-Ghabrāʾ. Mālik was the brother of Qays ibn Zuhayr, and the son of Zuhayr ibn Jadhīmah, the warlord of ʿAbs who in the mid-sixth century gained control over both Ghaṭafān and Hawāzin.

Masīkah the wife of Muqrī l-Waḥsh.

Masʿūd ibn Muṣād the chief of Kalb, killed by ʿAbs at the Battle of ʿUrāʿir (see Map 2).

Maysarah one of ʿAntar's sons in *The Epic of ʿAntar*.

Māzin (1) a kin group within Fazārah, to which al-ʿUsharāʾ belonged; (2) the half-brother of ʿAntar in *The Epic of ʿAntar*.

Muʿāwiyah ibn al-Nizāl a victim of ʿAntarah killed at the Battle of al-Farūq (see Map 2).

Muʿāwiyah ibn Shaddād paternal uncle (or father, according to some authorities) of ʿAntarah.

al-Mufaḍḍal al-Mufaḍḍal ibn Muḥammad ibn Yaʿlā l-Ḍabbī (d. ca. 170/786–87), a philologist and an expert on early Arabic poetry, highly respected for the reliability of the material he transmitted.

Muḥammad ibn al-Ḥasan see Ibn Durayd.

Mujāshiʿ ibn Hilāl an unidentified victim of ʿAbs.

al-Muqaṭṭaʿ an unidentified victim of ʿAbs.

Muqrī l-Waḥsh Syrian champion who in *The Epic of ʿAntar* fights initially on behalf of al-Nuʿmān but is subsequently reconciled with ʿAntar.

Murrah a subgroup of Ghaṭafān and thus of Qays ʿAylān. Murrah fought alongside Fazārah against ʿAbs in the War of Dāḥis and al-Ghabrāʾ. See also al-ʿUsharāʾ.

Nabhān a subgroup within the Ṭayyiʾ lineage.

Nadbah the mother of the black warrior-poet Khufāf.

Naḍlah a member of the lineage group of Asad (see Map 1) killed by Ward ibn Ḥābis.

al-Naṣr ibn Aḥmad Abū l-Qāsim Naṣr ibn Aḥmad ibn al-Maʾmūn (d. ca. 327/939), known as al-Khubzaruzzī, a popular poet, thought to be illiterate, who earned his living making rice bread (*khubz arruz*) in Basra.

al-Nuʿmān the Nasrid ruler of al-Ḥīrah in *The Epic of ʿAntar*.

Qaṭāmi a woman whom ʿAntarah refers to as his beloved.

Qays Qays ʿAylān, a major lineage from which various subgroups traced their descent, among them Hawāzin and Ghaṭafān.

Qays Qays ibn Zuhayr, brother of Mālik, the son of the warlord of ʿAbs who controlled Ghaṭafān in the middle of the sixth century. Qays was renowned for his military stratagems, such as that deployed at the Battle of Jabalah Ravine.

Qirwāsh ibn Hunayy a prominent member of ʿAbs, who killed Ḥudhayfah ibn Badr.

Quḍāʿah a federation based on shared lineage that included Kalb, against whom ʿAbs fought at the Battle of ʿUrāʿir. See Maps 1 and 2.

Qushayr Qushayr ibn Khālid ibn Ḥawmah, of ʿAwf ibn Jadhīmah of al-Hujaym, a kin group within ʿĀmir ibn Ṣaʿṣaʿah.

al-Rabīʿ ibn Ziyād Chieftain of ʿAbs who paid the blood price of one hundred camels in compensation for the killing of ʿAwf, the brother of Ḥudhayfah, by Qays ibn Zuhayr.

ramal one of the sixteen meters of classical poetry and one of the eight classes of rhythm in early Arabic music.

Raqāshi a woman ʿAntarah refers to as his beloved.

Ṣabāḥ a kin group that originated in Najd, today the ruling clan of Kuwait.

Saʿd Saʿd ibn ʿAwf ibn Mālik ibn Zayd Manāt, a kin group within the Tamīm.

sarḥah a large tree. This meaning seems to be a poetic usage, as the word *sarḥah* generally designates the plant *meru* (*Maerua crassifolia*) or the shrub *Cadaba farinosa*.

Ṣaʿṣaʿah the son of Qushayr ibn Khālid, member of the kin group ʿAwf ibn Jadhīmah within al-Hujaym.

Sawdah the mother of Ḥudhayfah ibn Badr.

shadanī a breed of camel from Shadan in Tihāmah (see Map 2).

Shaddād the father, or paternal uncle, of ʿAntarah.

Shakal a unit within the kin group of al-Ḥarīsh, within Rabīʿah, within ʿĀmir ibn Ṣaʿṣaʿah.

Shaʾs son of Zuhayr, brother to Mālik and Qays. In *The Epic of ʿAntar*, Mālik, ʿAblah's father, is advised to entrust ʿAblah to Shaʾs and to empower him as her guardian to marry her to whom he pleases. ʿAntar thus addresses Shaʾs as ʿAblah's guardian in Poem 49.

Shaybān a major kin group within the Bakr ibn Wāʾil lineage group. See Map 1.

Shaybān son of Qushayr ibn Khālid, member of the kin group of ʿAwf ibn Jadhīmah within al-Hujaym.

al-Shaybānī Abū ʿAmr al-Shaybānī (d. 213/828), a lexicographer and scholar of early Arabic poetry, who taught Ibn al-Sikkīt, among others.

Sūd an unidentified victim of ʿAbs.

Suhayyah a woman ʿAntarah refers to as his beloved in three poems. According to al-Baṭalyawsī, she was the wife of ʿAntarah's father, Shaddād. Her name is also given in some manuscripts as Sumayyah.

al-Sukkarī Abū Saʿīd al-Ḥasan al-Sukkarī (d. 275/888), a Baghdadi philologist and expert in early poetry, and a pupil of Ibn Ḥabīb.

Sulakah the mother of Sulayk.

Sulām explained as a member of a kin group that belonged to Ṭayyiʾ, though possibly al-Salāmī, a member of Salamān, a group within Dhubyān, is meant.

al-Sulayk ibn ʿUmayr al-Saʿdī one of the three "Arab ravens," black warriors whose lineage was traced back through their maternal rather than paternal line.

Sulaym a kin group within Qays ʿAylān.

Sumayyah see Suhayyah.

Taghlib an important kin group within the Rabīʿa ibn Nizār lineage.

Tamīm a large and important lineage group (see Map 1) that included Saʿd ibn Zayd Manāt.

Ṭarīf a kin group within Baghīḍ.

Ṭayyiʾ a powerful lineage group, which controlled a mountain range in Najd.

Thaʿlabah a kin group within Shaybān.

thaqīl one of the sixteen meters of classical poetry and one of the eight classes of rhythm in early Arabic music.

Thuʿal ibn ʿAmr a kin group that belonged to Ṭayyiʾ.

ʿUdhrah a kin group within the Quḍāʿah federation.

ʿUmar ibn al-Khaṭṭāb second caliph, r. 13–23/634–44.

ʿUmar ibn Shabbah (d. 262/878) an expert on poetry, poets, and history, author of several works (now lost) on the major urban centers of Mecca, Medina, Basra, and Kufa.

ʿUmārah ʿUmārah ibn Ziyād, a member of ʿAbs renowned for his generosity, and hostile to ʿAntarah.

Umm al-Haytham one of ʿAblah's names.

ʿUrwah ibn al-Ward a member of ʿAbs and a famous pre-Islamic poet, renowned for his life of brigandage and generosity to the poor and needy.

al-ʿUsharāʾ a family group within Fazārah of Dhubyān.

al-ʿUshayrah a kin group in *The Epic of ʿAntar*.

ʿUtaybah ibn al-Ḥārith a warrior and commander of the Tamīm lineage group.

al-Waḥīd eponym of a kin group within Kilāb, part of ʿĀmir ibn Ṣaʿṣaʿah.

Ward Ward ibn Ḥābis ibn Jābir, kinsman of ʿAntarah, who was responsible for the death of one of the sons of Ḍamḍam, and of Naḍlah of Asad.

Wizr ibn Jābir archer of Nabhān of Ṭayyiʾ said to have killed ʿAntarah.

Zabībah a black slave from Ethiopia, and the mother of ʿAntarah. Her name means "black raisin."

Zayd an unidentified victim of ʿAbs. See also ʿAmr.

List of Place Names in the Poetry of ʿAntarah

These place names occur in the Arabic text in the poems given. Most of them are also found in the English translation, although in a few cases the toponym was not included.

Adhriʿāt (Poem 1)
al-ʿAlandā (Poem 14)
Asquf (Poem 3)
al-Daylam (Poem 1)
Dhāt al-Ḥarmal (Poem 6)
Dhāt al-Rimth (Poem 28)
Dhū Akhtāl (Poem 28)
Dhū l-Raḍm (Poem 12)
Dhū l-ʿUshayrah (Poem 1)
al-Duḥruḍān (Poems 1, 44)
al-Farūq (Poem 2)
al-Ghaylam (Poem 1)
al-Ḥawmān (Poem 17)
al-Ḥazn (Poem 1)
Ḥimyar (Poem 49)
al-Jifār (Poem 24)
al-Jiwāʾ (Poem 1)
al-Kathīb (Poem 34)
al-Khaṭṭ (Poems 23, 51)
al-Kulāb (Poem 17)
al-Lakīk (Poem 6)
Laṣāfi (Poem 4)
al-Mutathallam (Poem 1)
al-Nujayrah (Poem 21)
Qārah (Poem 13)
Qaww (Poems 13, 29)
Raḥā l-Adamāt (Poem 29)
Raḥraḥān (Poem 3)
al-Ridāʿ (Poem 1)
al-Ṣammān (Poem 1)
Shamāmi (Poems 5, 29)
al-Sharā (Poem 49)
al-Sharabbah (Poem 47)
al-Shibāk (Poem 28)
Shuwāḥiṭ (Poems 5, 29)
Sīf (Poem 34)
al-Ṭawī (Poem 9)
Thuʿaylibāt (Poem 29)
al-Unān (Poem 38)
ʿUnayzatān (Poem 1)
ʿUrāʿir (Poem 3)
Uraynibāt (Poem 5)
ʿUsfān (Poem 10)
Uthāl (Poem 28)

Concordance of Principal Editions

In order to facilitate comparison across the various available editions of the poetry of ʿAntarah, this inventory presents the numeration of the poems in the current volume (JEM), al-Shantamarī's recension of al-Aṣmaʿī's redaction in al-Sijistānī's version (A), Ibn Maymūn's selection (IM), al-Baṭalyawsī's recension (B), Ahlwardt's edition (Ahlw), Mawlawī's edition (Mawl), and Shalabī's edition (Sh). I have also taken the opportunity to note relevant variations in the sequence of lines in the versions of the poems in the recensions of al-Shantamarī, al-Baṭalyawsī, and Ibn Maymūn.

JEM1	A1/B1/IM1/Ahlw21/Mawl1
JEM2	A2/B6/Ahlw26/Mawl2
JEM3	A3/B7/Ahlw15/Mawl3
JEM4	A4/B2/Ahlw9/Mawl4
JEM5	A5/B8/Ahlw23/Mawl5 [See also JEM29]
JEM6	A6/B25/Ahlw19/Mawl6
JEM7	A7/B26/Ahlw20/Mawl7
JEM8	A8/B5/Ahlw13/Mawl8 [See also JEM32]
JEM9	A9/B9/Ahlw27/Mawl9
JEM10	A10/B10/Ahlw16/Mawl10
JEM11	A11/B12/Ahlw5/Mawl11
JEM12	A12/B11/Ahlw22/Mawl12
JEM13	A13/B13/Ahlw4/Mawl13
JEM14	A14/B14/Ahlw9/Mawl14
JEM15	A15/B16/Ahlw10/Mawl15
JEM16	A16/B24/Ahlw14/Mawl16
JEM17	A17/B22/Ahlw17/Mawl17
JEM18	A18/B18/Ahlw8/Mawl18
JEM19	A19/B20/Ahlw1/Mawl19
JEM20	A20/B21/Ahlw6/Mawl20
JEM21	A21/B19/Ahlw18/Mawl21

JEM22	A22/B29/Ahlw3/Mawl22
JEM23	A23/B27/Ahlw25/Mawl23 [See also JEM51]
JEM24	A24/B30/Ahlw7/Mawl24
JEM25	A25/B31/IM5/Ahlw2/Mawl25
JEM26	A26/B32/Ahlw12/Mawl26
JEM27	A27/B34/Ahlw24/Mawl27 [See also JEM50]
JEM28	IM4
JEM29	IM3, an extended version of A5
JEM30	B3/Ahlw appendix 10/Mawl28
JEM31	B4/Mawl29
JEM32	[See also JEM8]
vv.1–8:	A8/B5/Ahlw13/Mawl8
vv. 9–17:	B5/Mawl, pp. 265–67
JEM33	B15/Ahlw appendix 18/Mawl30, an extended version of JEM5
JEM34	B17/Mawl31
JEM35	B23/Mawl32
JEM36	B28/Mawl33
JEM37	B33/Mawl34
JEM38	B35/Mawl35
JEM39	B36/Mawl36
JEM40	B37/Mawl37
JEM41	B38/Mawl38
JEM42	B39/Mawl39
JEM43	B40/Ahlw appendix 12/Mawl40
JEM44	Sh, pp. 31–38
JEM45	Sh, pp. 64–65
JEM46	Sh, p. 74
JEM47	Sh, pp. 84–85
JEM48	Sh, pp. 88–89
JEM49	Sh, pp. 91–92
JEM50	Sh, pp. 176–78, an extended version of JEM27
JEM51	Sh, pp. 178–80, an extended version of JEM23

The order of poems in al-Baṭalyawsī's recension is quite different from the order of the poems preserved by al-Shantamarī. The following inventory will facilitate a comparison.

B1	JEM1	B21	JEM20
B2	JEM4	B22	JEM17
B3	JEM30	B23	JEM35
B4	JEM31	B24	JEM16
B5	JEM32 [See also JEM8]	B25	JEM6
B6	JEM2	B26	JEM7
B7	JEM3	B27	JEM23
B8	JEM5	B28	JEM36
B9	JEM9	B29	JEM22
B10	JEM10	B30	JEM24
B11	JEM12	B31	JEM25
B12	JEM11	B32	JEM26
B13	JEM13	B33	JEM37
B14	JEM14	B34	JEM27
B15	JEM33	B35	JEM38
B16	JEM15	B36	JEM39
B17	JEM34	B37	JEM40
B18	JEM18	B38	JEM41
B19	JEM21	B39	JEM42
B20	JEM19	B40	JEM43

The sequence of verses in six poems in al-Baṭalyawsī's recension and four poems in Ibn Maymūn's anthology is quite different from the sequence found in al-Aṣmaʿī's redaction.

JEM 1 — B1 has the following verse order: 1, 5, 4, 6–19, 21–35, 37–38, 38', 36, 39–59, 61–63, 60, 64–71, 71', 71'', 71''', 72–73, 73', 73'', 73''', 73'''', 74, 78, 75–77, 79–85.

IM1 has the following verse order: 1, 4, 6–16, 18, 19, 21–35, 37–53, 61, 54, 56, 58–59, 62, 57, 63, 60, 64–73, 75, 76, 74, 78, 77, 79, 83–85.

JEM 2 — B6 has the following verse order: 1–7, 9–10, 8, 12, 11.

JEM 3 B7 has the following verse order: 1, 3, 2, 6, 4–5, 8–10, 7, 10'.

JEM 5 B8 has the same verse order as in al-Shantamarī's recension.

IM3 has the following verse order: 1–5, 5', 6–8, 8', 8'', 8''', 8'''', 8''''', 8'''''', 8''''''', 9, 9', 10–12, 12', 12'', 12''', 12'''' (edited and translated as Poem 29).

JEM 6 B25 has the following verse order: 1–8, 12, 9, 13, 21, 14–15, 10–11, 16–20, 22.

IM2 has the following verse order: 1, 2, 4, 6–9, 13–15, 10–12, 17–20, 22.

JEM 7 B26 has the same verse order as in al-Shantamarī's recension, but does not include verse 31 of al-Shantamarī's recension.

JEM 9 B9 has the same verse order as in al-Shantamarī's recension but without its verse 5.

JEM 25 B31 has the same verse order as in al-Shantamarī's recension.

IM5 has the following verse order: 0, 1–4, 8–19, 21. (0 denotes a verse found only in IM's anthology.)

Bibliography

Abū Tammām. *Dīwān*. Edited by Muḥammad ʿAbduh ʿAzzām. 5 vols. Cairo: Dār al-Maʿārif, 1951–65.

Abū ʿUbaydah. *Naqāʾiḍ Jarīr wa-l-Farazdaq*. Edited by A. A. Bevan. 3 vols. Leiden: E. J. Brill, 1905–12.

Ahlwardt, Wilhelm. *The Divans of the Six Ancient Arabic Poets*. London: Trübner & Co., 1870.

ʿĀmir ibn al-Ṭufayl. *Dīwān*. Edited by C. J. Lyall. Leiden: E. J. Brill and London: Luzac & Co., 1913.

ʿAntarah ibn Shaddād. *Dīwān*. Edited by Muḥammad Saʿīd Mawlawī. Cairo: al-Maktab al-Islāmī, 1964.

———. *Dīwān*. Edited by Karam al-Bustānī. Beirut: Dār Ṣādir, n.d. (1966?).

———. *Dīwān*. Edited by Fawzī ʿAṭawī. Beirut: al-Sharikah al-Lubnāniyyah li-l-Kitāb, 1968.

———. *Dīwān*. Edited by ʿUmar Fārūq al-Ṭabbāʿ. Beirut: Dār al-Qalam, 1995 (?).

———. *Dīwān*. Edited by Muḥammad Ḥammūd. Beirut: Dār al-Fikr al-Lubnānī, 1996.

Arazi, Albert, and Salman Masalha, eds. *Six Early Arab Poets: New Edition and Concordance*. Jerusalem: The Max Schloessinger Memorial Series, 1999.

Arberry, Arthur J. *The Seven Odes: The First Chapter in Arabic Literature*. London: Allen and Unwin, 1957.

Al-Bakrī. *Mustaʿjam mā staʿjama min asmāʾ al-bilād wa-l-mawāḍiʿ*. Edited by Muṣṭafā l-Saqqā. 4 vols. Cairo: Maṭbaʿat Lajnat al-Taʾlīf, 1945–51.

Al-Baṭalyawsī. *Sharḥ al-ashʿār al-sittah al-jāhiliyyah*. Vol. 1. Edited by Nāṣīf Sulaymān ʿAwwād, revised by Luṭfī l-Tūmī. Vol. 2. Edited by Luṭfī l-Tūmī. Beirut and Berlin: Klaus Schwarz Verlag, 2008.

Bellamy, J. A. "Dāḥis." In *Encyclopaedia of Islam*. 2nd ed. Brill Online.

Blachère, Régis. *Histoire de la littérature arabe des origines à la fin du XVe siècle de J.-C.* 3 vols. Paris: Adrien Maisonneuve, 1952–66.

Blackburn, Paul. "Translation (Replies to a *New York Quarterly* Questionnaire)." *New York Quarterly* 2 (1970). http://epc.buffalo.edu/authors/blackburn/blackburn_writngs_translation.html

Bonebakker, S. A. "Iḳwāʾ." In *Encyclopaedia of Islam*. 2nd ed. Brill Online.

Boudot-Lamotte, Antoine. "Lexique de la poésie guerrière dans le dīwān de ʿAntara b. Šaddād al-ʿAbsī." *Arabica* 11 (1964): 19–56.

Carson, Anne. *If Not, Winter: Fragments of Sappho*. London: Virago, 2003.

Cherkaoui, Driss. "ʿAntarah (ʿAntar ibn Shaddad al-ʿAbsi)." In *Arabic Literary Culture: 500–925*, edited by Michael Cooperson and Shawkat M. Toorawa, 77–84. Detroit: Thomson Gale, 2005.

Currie, Bruno. *Pindar and the Cult of Heroes*. Oxford: Oxford University Press, 2010.

Donner, Fred M. "The Bakr b. Wāʾil Tribes and Politics in Northeastern Arabia on the Eve of Islam." *Studia Islamica* 51 (1980): 5–38.

———. *The Early Islamic Conquests*. Princeton: Princeton University Press, 1981.

———. "The Role of Nomads in the Near East of Late Antiquity (400–800 CE)." In *The Arabs and Arabia*, edited by F. E. Peters. Aldershot: Ashgate, 1999.

Dostal, Walter. "The Evolution of Bedouin Life." In *L'antica societá beduina* (*Studi Semitici* 2), edited by Francesco Gabrieli, 11–34. Rome: Istituto di Studi Semitici, 1959.

———. "The Development of Bedouin Life in Arabia Seen from Archaeological Material." In *Studies in the History of Arabia* (*Dirāsāt tārīkh al-jazīrah al-ʿarabiyyah*), 1:125–44. Riyadh: Riyadh University Press, 1979.

Ezz ed-deen, Hassan el-Banna. "'No Solace for the Heart': The Motif of the Departing Women in the Pre-Islamic Battle Ode." In *Reorientations/Arabic and Persian Poetry*, edited by Suzanne Pinckney Stetkevych, 165–79. Bloomington and Indianapolis, IN: Indiana University Press, 1994.

Fück, J. W. "Ghaṭafān." In *Encyclopaedia of Islam*. 2nd ed. Brill Online.

Al-Ḥaḍramī. *Mushkil iʿrāb al-ashʿār al-sittah al-jāhiliyyah*. Edited by ʿAlī Khalaf al-Hurūṭ. Karak, Jordan: Muʾtah University, 1995.

Harrigan, Peter. "Volcanic Arabia." *Saudi Aramco World* 57, no. 2 (2006). https://www.saudiaramcoworld.com/issue/200602/volcanic.arabia.htm.

Hartner, W., and Paul Kunitzsch. "Minṭaḳat al-Burūdj." In *Encyclopaedia of Islam*. 2nd ed. Brill Online.

Heath, Peter. "Sīrat ʿAntar." *Encyclopaedia of Islam*. 3rd ed. Brill Online.

Heller, Bernhard. "Sīrat ʿAntar." In *Encyclopaedia of Islam*. 2nd ed. Brill Online.

Hodgson, Marshall. *The Venture of Islam: Conscience and History in a World Civilization*. Vol. 1, *The Classical Age of Islam*. Chicago: University of Chicago Press, 1975.

Ibn al-Kalbī. *Ǧamharat an-Nasab des Ibn al-Kalbī*. Edited by Werner Caskel and G. Strenzick. Leiden: E. J. Brill, 1966.

Ibn Maymūn. *The Utmost in the Search for Arab Poetry. Muntahā l-ṭalab min ashʿār al-ʿArab*. 3 vols. Frankfurt am Main: Institute for the History of Arabic-Islamic Science at the Johann Wolfgang Goethe University, 1986–93.

Ibn Qutaybah. *Kitāb al-Maʿānī al-kabīr fī abyāt al-maʿānī*. Hyderabad: Maṭbaʿat Majlis Dāʾirat al-Maʿārif al-ʿUthmāniyyah, 1949–50.

———. *Kitāb al-Shiʿr wa-l-shuʿarāʾ*. Edited by Aḥmad Muḥammad Shākir. 2 vols. Cairo: Dār al-Maʿārif, 1966.

———. *The Excellence of the Arabs*. Edited by James E. Montgomery and Peter Webb, translated by Sarah Bowen Savant and Peter Webb. New York, NY: NYU Press, 2017.

Al-Iṣbahānī, Abū l-Faraj. *Kitāb al-Aghānī*. Edited by Aḥmad Zakī Ṣafwat, ʿAbd al-Salām Muḥammad Hārūn, and Muṣṭafā l-Saqqā. 11 vols. Cairo: Dār al-Kutub al-Miṣriyyah, 1927–38.

Jacobi, Renate. "Ṭayf al-khayāl." In *Encyclopaedia of Islam*. 2nd ed. Brill Online.

Al-Jāḥiẓ. *Kitāb al-Bayān wa-l-tabyīn*. Edited by ʿAbd al-Salām Muḥammad Hārūn. 4 vols. in 2. Cairo: Maktabat al-Khānjī, 1985.

Jamil, Nadia. "Playing for Time: Maysir-Gambling in Early Arabic Poetry." In *Islamic Reflections, Arabic Musings. Studies in Honour of Alan Jones*, edited by Robert G. Hoyland and Philip F. Kennedy, 48–90. Oxford: Gibb Memorial Trust, 2004.

———. *Ethics and Poetry in Sixth Century Arabia*. Oxford: Gibb Memorial Trust, 2017.

Jarīr. *Dīwān*. Edited by Nuʿmān Muḥammad Amīn Ṭāhā. 2 vols. Cairo: Dār al-Maʿārif, 1969–71.

Jenssen, Herbjørn. "Arabic Language." In *Encyclopaedia of the Qurʾān*. Brill Online.

Al-Khaṭīb al-Tibrīzī. *Sharḥ dīwān ʿAntarah*. Edited by Majīd Ṭarād. Beirut: Dār al-Kitāb al-ʿArabī, 1992.

Kilpatrick, Hilary. *Making the Great Book of Songs: Compilation and the Author's Craft in Abū l-Faraj al-Iṣbahānī's Kitāb al-Aghānī*. London and New York, NY: Routledge, 2003.

King, Anya H. *Scent from the Garden of Paradise: Musk and the Medieval Islamic World*. Leiden: Brill, 2017.

Kunitzsch, Paul. "Al-Manāzil." In *Encyclopaedia of Islam*. 2nd ed. Brill Online.

Lane, Edward W. *Arabic-English Lexicon*. 2 vols. Cambridge: Islamic Texts Society, 1984.

Larcher, Pierre. "Fragments d'une poétique arabe." *Bulletin d'Études Orientales* 46 (1994): 111–63.

Lecomte, G. "Al-Muʿallaḳāt." *Encyclopaedia of Islam*. 2nd ed. Brill Online.

Lyons, Malcolm C. *The Arabian Epic: Heroic and Oral Story-Telling*. 3 vols. Cambridge: Cambridge University Press, 1995.

Macdonald, Michael C. "Was the Nabataean Kingdom a 'Bedouin State'?" *Zeitschrift des Deutschen Palästina-Vereins* 107 (1991): 102–19.

Melman, Billie. "The Middle East/Arabia: 'The Cradle of Islam'." In *The Cambridge Companion to Travel Writing*, edited by Peter Hulme and Tim Youngs, 105–21. Cambridge: Cambridge University Press, 2006.

Millar, Fergus. *The Roman Near East, 31 BC–AD 337*. Cambridge, MA: Harvard University Press, 1993.

Miller, Nathaniel. "Tribal Poetics in Early Arabic Culture: The Case of Ashʿār al-Hudhaliyyīn." PhD diss., University of Chicago, 2016.

———. "Warrior Elites on the Verge of Islam: Between Court and Tribe in Early Arabic Poetry." In *Cross-cultural Studies in Near Eastern History and Literature*, edited by Saana Svärd and Robert Rollinger, 139–73. Münster: Ugarit Verlag, 2016.

———. "Seasonal Poetics: The Dry Season and Autumn Rains among pre-Islamic Najdi and Hijazi Tribes." *Arabica* 64, no. 1 (2017): 1–27.

Montgomery, James E. "Dichotomy in Jāhilī Poetry." *Journal of Arabic Literature* 17 (1986): 1–20.

———. "The Cat and the Camel: A Literary Motif." In *Literary Heritage of Classical Islam*, edited by Mustansir Mir and Jarl Fossum. 137–45. Princeton, NJ: Darwin Press, 1993.

———. "The Deserted Encampment in Ancient Arabic Poetry: A Nexus of Topical Comparisons." *Journal of Semitic Studies* 40, no. 2 (1995): 283–316.

———. *Dīwān ʿAntarah ibn Shaddād: A Literary-Historical Study*. New York, NY: NYU Press, 2018.

———. "The Empty Ḥijāz." In *From the Many to the One: Arabic Theology, Arabic Philosophy*, edited by James E. Montgomery, 39–97. Leuven: Peeters, 2006.

———. "Convention as Cognition: On the Cultivation of Emotion." In *Takhyīl: The Imaginary in Arabic Poetics*, edited by Marlé Hammond and Geert Jan van Gelder, 147–78. Oxford: Gibb Memorial Trust, 2008.

———. "Listening for the Poem: Homage to Pierre Larcher." *Quaderni di Studi Arabi*, 8 (2013): 11–40.

Müller, W. W. "Mārib." In *Encyclopaedia of Islam*. 2nd ed. Brill Online.

Muth, Franz-Christoph. *Eine Konkordanz zur Ahlwardtschen Ausgabe der Gedichte von ʿAntara Ibn Šaddād al-ʿAbsī*. Wiesbaden: Harrassowitz, 2001.

Pavlovitch, Pavel. "*Qad kunna lā naʿbudu ʾllāha wa-lā naʿrifuhu*. On the Problem of the Pre-Islamic Lord of the Kaʿba." *Journal of Arabic and Islamic Studies* 2 (1998–99): 49–74.

Retsö, Jan. *The Arabs in Antiquity: Their History from the Assyrians to the Umayyads*. London and New York, NY: Routledge, 2003.

Robin, Christian Julien. "Marib." In *Late Antiquity: A Guide to the Postclassical World*, edited by G. W. Bowersock, Peter Brown, and Oleg Grabar, 562. Cambridge, MA: Belknap Press, 1999.

———. "Matériaux pour une typologie des divinités arabiques et de leurs représentations." In *Dieux et déesses d'Arabie. Images et représentations*, edited by Isabelle Sachet with Christian Julien Robin, 7–118. Paris: de Boccard, 2012.

Ṣafwat, Aḥmad Zakī, ed. *Jamharat khuṭab al-ʿArab fī l-ʿuṣūr al-ʿarabiyyah al-zāhirah*. 3 vols. Cairo: Muṣṭafā l-Bābī l-Ḥalabī, 1933.

Schwarzlöse, Friedrich. *Die Waffen der alten Araber*. Leipzig: J. C. Hinrich'sche Buchhandlung, 1886.

Sezgin, F. *Geschichte des arabischen Schrifttums*. Vol. 2. Leiden: Brill, 1996.

Al-Shantamarī. *Sharḥ dawāwīn al-shuʿarāʾ al-sittah al-jāhiliyyīn*. Edited by Muḥammad ʿAbd al-Munʿim Khafājī. Cairo: ʿAbd al-Ḥamīd Aḥmad Ḥanafī, 1963.

Sharḥ dīwān ʿAntarah ibn Shaddād, edited by ʿAbd al-Munʿim ʿAbd al-Raʾūf Shalabī. Beirut: Dār al-Kutub al-ʿIlmiyyah, 1980.

Sharḥ dīwān ʿAntarah ibn Shaddād. Edited by Sayf al-Dīn al-Kātib and Aḥmad ʿIṣām al-Kātib. Beirut: Dār Maktabat al-Ḥayāh, n.d. (1981?).

Sharḥ dīwān ʿAntarah ibn Shaddād ibn Muʿāwiyah ibn Qurād al-ʿAbsī. Edited by Amīn Saʿīd. Cairo: al-Maktabah al-Tijāriyyah al-Kubrā, n.d.

Sīrat fāris fursān al-Ḥijāz Abī al-Fawāris ʿAntarah ibn Shaddād. Beirut: al-Maktabah al-Thaqafiyyah, 1979.

Thilo, Ulrich. *Die Ortsnamen in der altarabischen Poesie*. Wiesbaden: Harrassowitz, 1958.

Toral-Niehoff, Isabel. "Talking about Arab Origins: The Transmission of the *ayyām al-ʿarab* in Kūfa, Baṣra and Baghdād." In *The Place to Go: Contexts of Learning in Baghdad from the 8th to the 10th Centuries. Proceedings of the International Conference in Göttingen 12–14 September 2011*, edited by Jens Scheiner and Damien Janos, 44–69. Princeton, NJ: Darwin Press, 2014.

ʿUrwah ibn al-Ward. *Dīwān*. Edited by ʿAbd al-Muʿīn al-Mallūḥī. Damascus: Wizārat al-Thaqāfah wa-l-Irshād al-Qawmī, 1966.

Webb, Peter. *Imagining the Arabs: Arab Identity and the Rise of Islam*. Edinburgh: Edinburgh University Press, 2016.

Whittow, Mark. "Rome and the Jafnids: Writing the History of a 6th-c. Tribal Dynasty." In *The Roman and Byzantine Near East: Some Recent Archaeological Research* (*Journal of Roman Archaeology* Supplement Series 31 (1999)), edited by John H. Humphrey, 207–24. Portsmouth, RI, 1999.

Zwettler, Michael. "*Maʿadd* in Late-Ancient Arabian Epigraphy and Other Pre-Islamic Sources." *Wiener Zeitschrift für die Kunde des Morgenlandes* (2000): 223–309.

Further Reading

Late Antiquity

Bowersock, G. W., Peter Brown, and Oleg Grabar, eds. *Late Antiquity. A Guide to the Postclassical World.* Cambridge, MA: Belknap Press, 1999.

———. *The Throne of Adulis: Red Sea Wars on the Eve of Islam.* Oxford and New York, NY: Oxford University Press, 2013.

———. *The Crucible of Islam.* Cambridge, MA, and London: Harvard University Press, 2017.

Daryaee, Touraj. *Sasanian Persia: The Rise and Fall of an Empire.* London and New York, NY: I. B. Tauris, 2013.

Daryaee, Touraj, and Khodad Rezakhani. *From Oxus to Euphrates: The World of Late Antique Iran.* Jordan Center for Persian Studies: H&S Media, 2016.

Fisher, Greg. *Between Empires: Arabs, Romans and Sasanians in Late Antiquity.* Oxford: Oxford University Press, 2011.

———. *Rome and the Arabs before the Rise of Islam.* CreateSpace Independent Publishing Platform, 2013.

Fisher, Greg, ed. *Arabs and Empires before Islam.* Oxford: Oxford University Press, 2015.

Robin, Christian Julien. "Arabia and Ethiopia." In *The Oxford Handbook of Late Antiquity,* edited by Scott Fitzgerald Johnson, 247–334. Oxford: Oxford University Press, 2012.

Munro-Hay, Stuart. *Aksum: An African Civilization in Late Antiquity.* Edinburgh: Edinburgh University Press, 1991.

Schippmann, Klaus. *Ancient South Arabia from the Queen of Sheba to the Advent of Islam,* translated by Allison Brown. Princeton: Markus Wiener, 2001.

Silverstein, Adam and Teresa Bernheim, eds. *Late Antiquity: Eastern Perspectives.* Oxford: Gibb Memorial Trust, 2012.

Pre-Islamic Arabia and the Arabs

ʿAlī, Jawād. *Al-Mufaṣṣal fī tārīkh al-ʿArab qabla l-Islām.* Beirut: Dār al-ʿIlm li-l-Malāyīn, 1968–73.

Hoyland, Robert G. *Arabia and the Arabs from the Bronze Age to the Coming of Islam.* London and New York, NY: Routledge, 2001.

———. "Early Islam as a Late Antique Religion." In *The Oxford Handbook of Late Antiquity*, edited by Scott Fitzgerald Johnson, 1053–77. Oxford: Oxford University Press, 2012.

Montgomery, James E. "The Empty Ḥijāz." In *From the Many to the One: Arabic Theology, Arabic Philosophy*, edited by James E. Montgomery, 39–97. Leuven: Peeters, 2006.

Munt, Harry. "Pilgrimage in Pre-Islamic Arabia." In *The Hajj: Pilgrimage in Islam*, edited by Eric Tagliacozzo and Shawkat M. Toorawa, 13–30. Cambridge and New York, NY: Cambridge University Press, 2016.

Neuwirth, Angelika. *Der Koran als Text der Spätantike. Eine europäischer Zugang.* Berlin: Verlag der Weltreligionen, 2010.

Peters, F. E., ed. *The Arabs and Arabia.* Aldershot: Ashgate, 1999.

Webb, Peter. *Imagining the Arabs: Arab Identity and the Rise of Islam.* Edinburgh: Edinburgh University Press, 2016.

Slavery

Ali, Kecia. *Marriage and Slavery in Early Islam.* Cambridge, MA: Harvard University Press, 2010.

Gilli-Elewy, Hend. "Soziale Aspekte frühislamischer Sklaverei." *Der Islam* 77 (2000): 116–68.

Gordon, Matthew S. and Kathryn A. Hain, eds. *Concubines and Courtesans: Women and Slavery in Islamic History.* Oxford: Oxford University Press, 2017.

Lewis, Bernard M. *Race and Slavery in the Middle East: An Historical Inquiry.* Oxford: Oxford University Press, 1990.

Race

Khannous, Touria. "Race in Pre-Islamic Poetry: The Work of Antara Ibn Shaddad." *African and Black Diaspora: An International Journal* 6, no. 1 (2013): 66–80.

Lewis, Bernard M. "The Crows of the Arabs." *Critical Inquiry* 12, no. 1 (1985): 88–97.

Rotter, Gernot. *Die Stellung des Negers in der Islamisch-Arabischen Gesellschaft bis zum XVI Jahrhundert.* Bonn: Rheinische Friedrich-Wilhelms-Universität, 1967.

Ullmann, Manfred. *Der Neger in der Bildersprache der arabischen Dichter.* Wiesbaden: Harrassowitz, 1998.

Camel Burials

Beech, Mark, Marjan Mashkour, Matthias Huels, and Antoine Zazzo. "Prehistoric Camels in South-Eastern Arabia: The Discovery of a New Site in Abu Dhabi's Western Region, United Arab Emirates." *Proceedings of the Seminar for Arabian Studies* 39 (2009): 17–30.

King, Geoffrey. "Camels and Arabian Balîya and Other Forms of Sacrifice: A Review of Archaeological and Literary Evidence." *Arabian Archaeology and Epigraphy* 20, no. 1 (2009): 81–93.

Vogt, Burkhard. "Death, Resurrection, and the Camel." In *Arabia Felix: Beiträge zur Sprache und Kultur des vorislamischen Arabien. Festschrift Walter W. Müller*, edited by Rosemarie Richter, Ingo Kottsieper, and Mohammed Marqaten, 279–90. Wiesbaden: Harrassowitz, 1994.

Pre-Islamic Poetry

Arberry, Arthur J. *The Seven Odes. The First Chapter in Arabic Literature*. London: Allen and Unwin, 1957.

Jamil, Nadia. *Ethics and Poetry in Sixth Century Arabia*. Oxford: Gibb Memorial Trust, 2017.

Montgomery, James E. *The Vagaries of the* Qaṣīdah. *On the Tradition and Practice of Early Arabic Poetry*. Warminster: Gibb Memorial Trust, 1997.

Stetkevych, Suzanne P. *The Mute Immortals Speak: Pre-Islamic Poetry and the Poetics of Ritual*. Ithaca, NY: Cornell University Press, 1993.

Stetkevych, Suzanne P., ed. *Early Islamic Poetry and Poetics*. Surrey: Ashgate, 2009.

ʿAntarah ibn Shaddād

Cherkaoui, Driss. "ʿAntarah (ʿAntar ibn Shaddad al-ʿAbsi)." In *Arabic Literary Culture: 500–925*, edited by Michael Cooperson and Shawkat M. Toorawa, 77–84. Detroit: Thomson Gale, 2005.

Jones, Alan. "ʿAntara." *Encyclopaedia of Islam*. 3rd ed. Brill Online.

Qurashī, Ḥasan ʿAbd Allāh. *Fāris Banī ʿAbs*. Cairo: Dār al-Maʿārif, 1957.

The *Muʿallaqah* of ʿAntarah

Arberry, Arthur J. *The Seven Odes. The First Chapter in Arabic Literature*, 148–84. London: Allen and Unwin, 1957. Introduction and translation.

Hammond, Marlé, ed. *Arabic Poems: A Bilingual Edition*, 46–59. London and New York, NY: Alfred A. Knopf, 2014. A reprint of the spirited translation from 1903 by Lady Anne Blunt (d. 1917), baroness, violinist, artist, translator, horse breeder, author of *Pilgrimage to Nejd* (1881), and wife of Wilfred Scawen Blunt.

Larcher, Pierre. "Fragments d'une poétique arabe." *Bulletin d'Études Orientales* 46 (1994): 111–63. A detailed analysis of the proper names in the first twelve lines of the poem, with a French translation of the complete ode.

Montgomery, James E. *The Vagaries of the* Qaṣīdah. *On the Tradition and Practice of Early Arabic Poetry*, 63–69. Warminster: Gibb Memorial Trust, 1997. A reading of the poem.

———. "Listening for the Poem: Homage to Pierre Larcher." *Quaderni di Studi Arabi*, 8 (2013): 11–40. Contains on pages 36–40 a discussion and translation of lines 1–26.

Nöldeke, Theodor. "Fünf Moʿallaqāt übersetzt und erklärt. II. Die Moʿallaqāt ʿAntara's und Labīd's." *Sitzungsberichte der Philosophisch-historischen Classe der Kaiserlichen Akademie der Wissenschaften* 144, no. 5 (1902). A classic of philology in the old style.

O'Grady, Desmond. *The Seven Arab Odes*. London and Dublin: Agenda Editions and Raven Arts Press, 1990. Reprinted as *The Golden Odes of Love: Al-Muʿallaqat. A Verse Rendering from the Arabic*. Cairo: The American University in Cairo Press, 1997. Version by the renowned Irish poet (d. 2014).

Sells, Michael A. *Desert Tracings. Six Classic Arabian Odes*, 45–57. Middletown, CN: Wesleyan University Press, 1989. Translation with analysis.

The Battle Lore of the Arabs

Jones, Alan. "Ayyām al-ʿArab." *Encyclopaedia of Islam*. 3rd ed. Brill Online.

Meyer, E. *Der historische Gehalt der Aiyām al-ʿArab*. Wiesbaden: Harrassowitz, 1970.

Toral-Niehoff, Isabel. "Talking about Arab Origins: The Transmission of the *ayyām al-ʿarab* in Kūfa, Baṣra and Baghdād." In *The Place to Go: Contexts of Learning in Baghdad from the 8th to the 10th Centuries. Proceedings of the International Conference in Göttingen 12–14 September 2011*, edited by Jens Scheiner and Damien Janos, 44–69. Princeton, NJ: Darwin Press, 2014.

The Discovery of the *Jāhiliyyah*

Drory, Rina. "The Abbasid Construction of the Jahiliyya: Cultural Authority in the Making." *Studia Islamica* 83 (1996): 33–49.

Webb, Peter. *Imagining the Arabs: Arab Identity and the Rise of Islam*. Edinburgh: Edinburgh University Press, 2016. Especially relevant are chapters 5 and 6.

The Epic of ʿAntar

Heath, Peter. *The Thirsty Sword: Sīrat ʿAntar and the Arabic Popular Epic.* Salt Lake City, UT: University of Utah Press, 1996.

———. "Sīrat ʿAntar." *Encyclopaedia of Islam.* 3rd ed. Brill Online.

Lyons, Malcolm, C. *The Arabian Epic: Heroic and Oral Story-Telling.* 3 vols. Cambridge: Cambridge University Press, 1995.

Index

About the NYU Abu Dhabi Institute

The Library of Arabic Literature is supported by a grant from the NYU Abu Dhabi Institute, a major hub of intellectual and creative activity and advanced research. The Institute hosts academic conferences, workshops, lectures, film series, performances, and other public programs directed both to audiences within the UAE and to the worldwide academic and research community. It is a center of the scholarly community for Abu Dhabi, bringing together faculty and researchers from institutions of higher learning throughout the region.

NYU Abu Dhabi, through the NYU Abu Dhabi Institute, is a world-class center of cutting-edge research, scholarship, and cultural activity. The Institute creates singular opportunities for leading researchers from across the arts, humanities, social sciences, sciences, engineering, and the professions to carry out creative scholarship and conduct research on issues of major disciplinary, multidisciplinary, and global significance.

About the Typefaces

The Arabic body text is set in DecoType Naskh, designed by Thomas Milo and Mirjam Somers, based on an analysis of five centuries of Ottoman manuscript practice. The exceptionally legible result is the first and only typeface in a style that fully implements the principles of script grammar (*qawāʿid al-khaṭṭ*).

The Arabic footnote text is set in DecoType Emiri, drawn by Mirjam Somers, based on the metal typeface in the naskh style that was cut for the 1924 Cairo edition of the Qur'an.

Both Arabic typefaces in this series are controlled by a dedicated font layout engine. ACE, the Arabic Calligraphic Engine, invented by Peter Somers, Thomas Milo, and Mirjam Somers of DecoType, first operational in 1985, pioneered the principle followed by later smart font layout technologies such as OpenType, which is used for all other typefaces in this series.

The Arabic text was set with WinSoft Tasmeem, a sophisticated user interface for DecoType ACE inside Adobe InDesign. Tasmeem was conceived and created by Thomas Milo (DecoType) and Pascal Rubini (WinSoft) in 2005.

The English text is set in Adobe Text, a new and versatile text typeface family designed by Robert Slimbach for Western (Latin, Greek, Cyrillic) typesetting. Its workhorse qualities make it perfect for a wide variety of applications, especially for longer passages of text where legibility and economy are important. Adobe Text bridges the gap between calligraphic Renaissance types of the 15th and 16th centuries and high-contrast Modern styles of the 18th century, taking many of its design cues from early post-Renaissance Baroque transitional types cut by designers such as Christoffel van Dijck, Nicolaus Kis, and William Caslon. While grounded in classical form, Adobe Text is also a statement of contemporary utilitarian design, well suited to a wide variety of print and on-screen applications.

Titles Published by the Library of Arabic Literature

For more details on individual titles, visit www.libraryofarabicliterature.org

Classical Arabic Literature: A Library of Arabic Literature Anthology
Selected and translated by Geert Jan van Gelder (2012)

A Treasury of Virtues: Sayings, Sermons, and Teachings of ʿAlī, by al-Qāḍī al-Quḍāʿī, with the **One Hundred Proverbs** attributed to al-Jāḥiẓ
Edited and translated by Tahera Qutbuddin (2013)

The Epistle on Legal Theory, by al-Shāfiʿī
Edited and translated by Joseph E. Lowry (2013)

Leg over Leg, by Aḥmad Fāris al-Shidyāq
Edited and translated by Humphrey Davies (4 volumes; 2013–14)

Virtues of the Imām Aḥmad ibn Ḥanbal, by Ibn al-Jawzī
Edited and translated by Michael Cooperson (2 volumes; 2013–15)

The Epistle of Forgiveness, by Abū l-ʿAlāʾ al-Maʿarrī
Edited and translated by Geert Jan van Gelder and Gregor Schoeler (2 volumes; 2013–14)

The Principles of Sufism, by ʿĀʾishah al-Bāʿūniyyah
Edited and translated by Th. Emil Homerin (2014)

The Expeditions: An Early Biography of Muḥammad, by Maʿmar ibn Rāshid
Edited and translated by Sean W. Anthony (2014)

Two Arabic Travel Books
Accounts of China and India, by Abū Zayd al-Sīrāfī
Edited and translated by Tim Mackintosh-Smith (2014)
Mission to the Volga, by Aḥmad ibn Faḍlān
Edited and translated by James Montgomery (2014)

Disagreements of the Jurists: A Manual of Islamic Legal Theory, by al-Qāḍī al-Nuʿmān
Edited and translated by Devin J. Stewart (2015)

Consorts of the Caliphs: Women and the Court of Baghdad, by Ibn al-Sāʿī
Edited by Shawkat M. Toorawa and translated by the Editors of the Library of Arabic Literature (2015)

What ʿĪsā ibn Hishām Told Us, by Muḥammad al-Muwayliḥī
Edited and translated by Roger Allen (2 volumes; 2015)

The Life and Times of Abū Tammām, by Abū Bakr Muḥammad ibn Yaḥyā al-Ṣūlī
Edited and translated by Beatrice Gruendler (2015)

The Sword of Ambition: Bureaucratic Rivalry in Medieval Egypt, by ʿUthmān ibn Ibrāhīm al-Nābulusī
Edited and translated by Luke Yarbrough (2016)

Brains Confounded by the Ode of Abū Shādūf Expounded, by Yūsuf al-Shirbīnī
Edited and translated by Humphrey Davies (2 volumes; 2016)

Light in the Heavens: Sayings of the Prophet Muḥammad, by al-Qāḍī al-Quḍāʿī
Edited and translated by Tahera Qutbuddin (2016)

Risible Rhymes, by Muḥammad ibn Maḥfūẓ al-Sanhūrī
Edited and translated by Humphrey Davies (2016)

A Hundred and One Nights
Edited and translated by Bruce Fudge (2016)

The Excellence of the Arabs, by Ibn Qutaybah
Edited by James E. Montgomery and Peter Webb
Translated by Sarah Bowen Savant and Peter Webb (2017)

Scents and Flavors: A Syrian Cookbook
Edited and translated by Charles Perry (2017)

Arabian Satire: Poetry from 18th-Century Najd, by Ḥmēdān al-Shwēʿir
Edited and translated by Marcel Kurpershoek (2017)

In Darfur: An Account of the Sultanate and its People, by Muḥammad ibn ʿUmar al-Tūnisī
Edited and translated by Humphrey Davies **(2 volumes; 2018)**

War Songs, by ʿAntarah ibn Shaddād
Edited by James E. Montgomery
Translated by James E. Montgomery with Richard Sieburth **(2018)**

Arabian Romantic: Poems on Bedouin Life and Love, by ʿAbdallah ibn Sbayyil
Edited and translated by Marcel Kurpershoek **(2018)**

Dīwān ʿAntarah ibn Shaddād: A Literary-Historical Study
By James E. Montgomery **(2018)**

English-only Paperbacks

Leg over Leg, by Aḥmad Fāris al-Shidyāq **(2 volumes; 2015)**
The Expeditions: An Early Biography of Muḥammad, by Maʿmar ibn Rāshid **(2015)**
The Epistle on Legal Theory: A Translation of al-Shāfiʿī's *Risālah*, by al-Shāfiʿī **(2015)**
The Epistle of Forgiveness, by Abū l-ʿAlāʾ al-Maʿarrī **(2016)**
The Principles of Sufism, by ʿĀʾishah al-Bāʿūniyyah **(2016)**
A Treasury of Virtues: Sayings, Sermons, and Teachings of ʿAlī, by al-Qāḍī al-Quḍāʿī with the **One Hundred Proverbs**, attributed to al-Jāḥiẓ **(2016)**
The Life of Ibn Ḥanbal, by Ibn al-Jawzī **(2016)**
Mission to the Volga, by Ibn Faḍlān **(2017)**
Accounts of China and India, by Abū Zayd al-Sīrāfī **(2017)**
A Hundred and One Nights (2017)
Disagreements of the Jurists: A Manual of Islamic Legal Theory, by al-Qāḍī al-Nuʿmān **(2017)**
What ʿĪsā ibn Hishām Told Us, by Muḥammad al-Muwayliḥī **(2018)**
War Songs, by ʿAntarah ibn Shaddād **(2018)**
The Life and Times of Abū Tammām, by Abū Bakr Muḥammad ibn Yaḥyā al-Ṣūlī **(2018)**

About the Editor–Translators

James E. Montgomery is Sir Thomas Adams's Professor of Arabic, Fellow of Trinity Hall at the University of Cambridge, and an Executive Editor of the Library of Arabic Literature. Currently, he enjoys reading the poetry of Gerard Manley Hopkins and Seamus Heaney, the novels of Javier Marías and Vladimir Nabokov, and listening to the music of The Band and Johnny Cash. He counts himself lucky to have a wonderful wife, three amazing children, and two brilliant dogs. He has deadlifted 180 kg, played Rugby Union for Norway, and likes to get out of Cambridge and go to Scotland as often as possible. His latest publications are *Loss Sings*, a collaboration with the celebrated Scottish artist Alison Watt, and *Dīwān ʿAntarah ibn Shaddād: A Literary-Historical Study*. He is preparing a translation of poems by al-Mutanabbī for Archipelago Books.

Richard Sieburth teaches French and Comparative Literature at NYU. In addition to his various editions of Pound for the Library of America and New Directions, he has published translations of works by Hölderlin (*Hymns and Fragments*), Büchner (*Lenz*), Benjamin (*Moscow Diary*), Scholem (*Greetings from Angelus: Poems*), Nostradamus (*The Prophecies*), Scève (*Emblems of Desire*), Labé (*Love Sonnets & Elegies*), Nerval (*Selected Writings* [PEN/Book-of-the-Month Club Translation Prize]; *The Salt Smugglers*); Michaux (*Emergences-Resurgences*; *Stroke by Stroke*; *A Certain Plume*), Leiris (*Nights as Day, Days as Night*), and Guillevic (*Geometries*). He is currently finishing up a translation/edition of *Late Baudelaire*, for which he was awarded a Guggenheim Fellowship. He is a Fellow of the American Academy of Arts and Sciences and a Chevalier de l'ordre des palmes académiques.